James VI and I and the History of Homosexuality

Michael B. Young

First published 2000 by
MACMILLAN PRESS LTD
Houndmills, Basingstoke, Hampshire RG21 6XS
and London
Companies and representatives
throughout the world

ISBN 0–333–63378–4

A catalogue record for this book is available
from the British Library.

This book is printed on paper suitable for recycling and
made from fully managed and sustained forest sources.

10   9   8   7   6   5   4   3   2   1
09   08   07   06   05   04   03   02   01   00

Printed and bound in Great Britain by
Antony Rowe Ltd, Chippenham, Wiltshire

To three outstanding professors

Hwa Yol Jung
Frederick W. McConnell, Jr
and the late J. Richard Jones

all of Moravian College

Contents

Acknowledgements

I am profoundly grateful to four people who gave this project critical endorsement at an early stage: Alan Bray, Winfried Schleiner, Niko Pfund, of New York University Press, and Giovanna Davitti, then of Macmillan Press. These four people saw the potential in my first faltering effort and gave me the support to expand and improve it into the present book. It was particularly magnanimous of Alan Bray to encourage my work since I question key aspects of his own viewpoint. I should note that he had many criticisms of my original draft, and I am afraid that our area of disagreement has widened as my thinking has progressed. This makes me all the more conscious of the debt I owe him.

When I began work on this book, I was not personally acquainted with anyone working on the history of homosexuality. Several scholars have generously responded to my inquiries and shared their ideas with me, including Rictor Norton and Joseph Cady. Most notable by far in this respect is Randolph Trumbach, who read an entire draft of the manuscript and gave me very constructive criticism. I am sure that Trumbach, like Bray, would not want to be thought of as endorsing all my views. I will have to take responsibility for these while remaining deeply grateful for their help.

In my footnotes I hope I have acknowledged all the other historians who have shared their knowledge with me. Four who come to mind here as deserving special thanks are Susan D. Amussen, Sabrina A. Baron, Alistair Bellany and Linda Levy Peck.

Several of my colleagues at Illinois Wesleyan University have also helped me in one way or another along the way. At the risk of forgetting someone, I must list here: Mary Ann Bushman, Paul Bushnell, James D. McGowan, Robert L. Mowery, Carole Myscofski, Carolyn A. Nadeau, Charles Springwood, Daniel P. Terkla and W. Michael Weis. A small grant from my university helped me to make a research trip to Yale University, where, as always, I benefited from the expertise of Maija Jansson at the Yale Center for Parliamentary History. A reduction of one course in my teaching load for the spring 1998 semester gave me valuable time to finish the manuscript. A series of students have assisted me over the years, most importantly Ann Goliak, Walter S. Wadiak, Mark DeMonte and Jonathan Musch.

This book could not have been written without the microfilm collection of early English books, a marvellous research tool that was readily accessible to me at Illinois State University. I was also fortunate to be located near the University of Illinois, where the rare book room and library contain a superb collection in British history. I am grateful to all the people who helped me at these places and at my own university, where Connie Wheeler and Kristin Vogel were especially helpful with interlibrary loan requests.

Finally, I wish to thank Ruth Willats, whose judicious editing improved my prose but allowed me to speak in my own voice.

Introduction

James Stewart was the sixth King of Scotland and the first King of England named James. He is known to history, therefore, as James VI and I. He was a king nearly all his life. He was a mere baby in 1567 when rebels overthrew his mother and placed him on the throne of Scotland. He was a seasoned ruler by the time he succeeded to the throne of England in 1603 upon the death of Queen Elizabeth. From that point forward he ruled the whole British Isles until his death in 1625. James was also the most prominent man in early modern Britain who had (or was suspected of having) sexual relations with other men, yet few historians have treated this subject well, and no one has studied it in depth.[1]

Even the best scholars have stumbled when dealing with James's sexuality. In 1956 David H. Willson published what is still the standard, though now outdated, biography of James. Willson viewed James's sexual relations with other men as a moral failing. He told his readers that this 'vice was common to many rulers and we need not be too shocked', but still 'the completeness of the King's surrender to it indicates a loosening of his moral fibre'.[2] Maurice Lee Jr, a more recent author of several impressive books about James, avoided the sanctimonious tone and Victorian moralizing that coloured the work of earlier writers like Willson. He scolded previous scholars for 'their obvious distaste for James's lifestyle and their prudish revulsion at the sexual implications involved'. Yet Lee had his own way of avoiding implications. Although he said that 'the question of James's sexual nature must be faced', he did not face it very squarely. Instead, he claimed that James was an asexual man whose 'predilection for handsome young men' did not involve sex, because 'James was one of those people...who are simply not much interested in physical sex at all'.[3]

1

Even Jenny Wormald, the most respected contemporary authority on James, seems uncomfortable with the issue of his homosexuality. While she rightly attributes criticism of James on this score to 'nineteenth-century distaste for his sexual morals', she does not spell out what those sexual morals were, let alone consider whether they deserve reproach. Wormald's work has been consistently devoted to rehabilitating James's reputation. One of her strongest arguments is that there was a great deal of unfair prejudice against James in England simply because he was a Scot. He was the victim of xenophobia. It does not occur to her to ask whether he was also the victim of homophobia.[4]

Political historians have thus made great progress in overcoming the prejudice that used to colour accounts of James, but they have not appreciably advanced our understanding of his sexual relations or the public perception of those relations. At the same time, however, other scholars in newer forms of cultural history have been pushing back the frontiers of our knowledge with respect to the general history of homosexuality in England – particularly male homosexuality, which is our only concern in the present book.[5] We now have a much improved understanding of the larger historical context, though no one so far has made an extensive effort to situate King James's particular case within this larger context. The best opportunity occurred in Alan Bray's pathbreaking book *Homosexuality in Renaissance England* (1982). But Bray barely mentioned James except for one well-known passage in the king's writings that condemned sodomy. There is no hint (except in a footnote) that James himself was suspected of practising sodomy.[6]

The case of James practically cries out for attention. It offers a unique opportunity to combine older political history with newer cultural history in a way that is mutually illuminating. This is both a worthy and a timely undertaking because in the decades since Willson published his biography of James, the history of sex has come of age. It no longer seems sensible to treat the subject with prudish disdain, naive denial or deft evasion; and it no longer is necessary to treat it in isolation from society and the longer history of sexuality. We have reached the point where at last we can and should do justice to the subject.

Of course, the very fact that the history of homosexuality is a relatively new and controversial field of study raises problems of its own. There has been a tendency to accept the work of pioneering scholars as gospel, to interpret facts in light of pre-established theoretical frameworks and to shape history into 'a usable past'. We will have to be alert to these problems, not simply to avoid them, but also to consider how the particular example of James relates to them. One special problem involves the word 'homosexuality' itself. The word was not coined until the late nineteenth century, and many scholars would maintain that it is an anachronism to use it when speaking about an earlier period when the word did not yet exist. Strictly speaking, in early modern Britain, no one was *a* homosexual because the word, and arguably the connotations that went with it, did not exist either. Thus, nowhere in the present book is James labelled 'a homosexual'.

On the other hand, as the writings of major scholars such as Alan Bray and Michael Rocke illustrate, it is impossible to avoid using the words 'homosexuality' and 'homosexual' altogether. Both authors featured homosexuality in the titles of their books: *Homosexuality in Renaissance England* and *Forbidden Friendships: Homosexuality and Male Culture in Renaissance Florence*. Bray used the word 'homosexuality' throughout his book, although he explained that he was using it 'in as directly physical – and hence culturally neutral – a sense as possible'.[7] Rocke was more cautious about using the noun, but he used the adjective liberally, referring to homosexual acts, homosexual activities, homosexual relations and homosexual experience; and sometimes he too found that the best word for the general phenomenon was simply homosexuality, as, for example, when he described his subject as 'the story of homosexuality in Florence' or the 'panorama of homosexuality in Florence'.[8] Thus, 'homosexuality' and 'homosexual' cannot be avoided in a book about sex between males addressed to a modern audience, but at the same time one must be acutely aware that this is late nineteenth- and twentieth-century terminology being applied to previous centuries. As much as possible, we must confine these words to their 'neutral' meanings, as Bray phrased it, and not import other modern connotations. Certainly, we must not put these words into the mouths of people in a previous century who spoke in different terms.

Some scholars believe that the whole mental construct of homosexuality, like the word itself, is of relatively recent origin. One school of thought locates the 'invention of homosexuality' at the very end of the seventeenth century. Others postpone it till the eighteenth or nineteenth century.[9] In either case, when we go back to Scotland and England at the beginning of the seventeenth century, we should find ourselves in an entirely different world. Bray's pioneering work has been especially influential in establishing this viewpoint. Bray emphasized the 'immense distance' between Renaissance England and our own day. He described the transition from pre-modern to modern ways of thinking about homosexuality as a 'momentous', 'revolutionary', 'striking change in mentality', and he located this transition at the very end of the seventeenth century. Only then, he contended, did 'conceptions of homosexuality in a recognisably modern form first appear'.[10] Although Randolph Trumbach does not agree with Bray in every respect, his recent *Sex and the Gender Revolution* (1998) is similarly predicated on the assumption that there was a key change around 1700 among males who had sex with other males, and in the way people viewed these all-male relationships. The effects of this change are supposed to have spread throughout society and escalated into an even more thoroughgoing 'revolution in gender relations'.[11]

The evidence surrounding James, however, suggests two alternative possibilities. The more radical is that there was no change. The word is uniquely modern, but the phenomenon is not. Despite minor variations in the cultural construction of homosexuality throughout the ages, at heart it has remained substantially the same. This view emphasizes continuity rather than discontinuity in the history of homosexuality. It is sometimes referred to as the 'essentialist' position, and if it is correct, then there was no 'new invention' of homosexuality in the seventeenth, eighteenth, nineteenth, or any other century.[12] The other possibility is that there was a change from pre-modern to modern constructions of homosexuality, perhaps sufficient enough change that we are justified in speaking of the invention of modern homosexuality, but that change was already well underway in Jacobean England. If there was a change of this sort, then it was not as sudden or revolutionary as it is usually made to seem; it was more gradual or evolutionary. Pre-modern ways of thinking may still have predominated in James's reign, but they existed alongside other ways that would eventually come to be thought of as modern. Perhaps James was so prominent a figure that he elicited the expression of these inchoate ideas, bringing to the surface what otherwise would be hidden from historians. Viewed this way, rather than a sharp break at the end of the seventeenth century, our study tends to confirm the suspicion of another historian, James M. Saslow, that, where homosexuality is concerned, 'we should "push back" the temporal frontier of an emerging modern consciousness, at least in embryonic form, well into the early modern period'.[13]

To put this in more concrete terms, the closest formal analogue to homosexuality that existed in the Renaissance was sodomy, and scholars tend to emphasize the differences rather than the similarities between this pre-modern sodomy and modern homosexuality. Bray alleged that there were 'great differences between the "sodomite" of

Elizabethan England and the "homosexual" of our own'.[14] However, the case of James makes sodomy look much more familiar than it is supposed to have been. Furthermore, although sodomy was the closest equivalent to modern homosexuality in the formal language of the Church and the law, it was certainly not the only analogue for homosexuality in the Renaissance. There were other, less formal ways of denoting and discoursing about James's love of other males, and these other ways also have familiar features.

One especially familiar feature is effeminacy. There has been a tendency to minimize effeminacy in the history of male homosexuality.[15] It is frequently asserted that pre-modern constructions of homosexuality were not yet linked to effeminacy, except perhaps in relationships between adults and adolescents where only the youthful 'passive' partner might have been considered effeminate.[16] In this view, effeminacy was not associated with the adult male in a homosexual relationship until the eighteenth century. One author even maintains that effeminacy was not fully established as a sign of male homosexuality until the trials of Oscar Wilde in 1895.[17] As we shall see, homosexuality and effeminacy were already linked in the public perception of James's court. Far from being irrelevant, effeminacy, it turns out, was an integral part of Jacobean discourse about sexual relations between males.

The stigma of effeminacy was attached most obviously to the king's youthful favourites, but it was also attached to the king. It is sometimes alleged that James was referred to during his lifetime as *Queen James*.[18] This appellation cannot be found in any contemporary document, but it is strongly implied in many of the tracts we will examine. In the late sixteenth and early seventeenth centuries, the English experienced what David Cressy has described as 'the reigns of a manly queen and a queenish king'.[19] The problem for Queen Elizabeth had been to prove that she was enough of a man to command respect and lead the nation in wartime. As the Spanish Armada sailed towards England, she is reputed to have said, 'I may have the body of a weak and feeble woman, but I have the heart and stomach of a king.'[20] When James succeeded Elizabeth, he immediately terminated the war against Spain, pursued a peaceful foreign policy and allowed effeminate favourites to dominate his court. It soon became a commonplace comparison that Elizabeth had been more of a man than he was.[21] Effeminization of the court contributed to a growing concern that Englishmen in general were becoming effeminized and the nation was becoming soft. This, in turn, contributed to a cultural backlash – a reassertion of manliness and militarism that culminated in England's resumption of war against Spain. War became an imperative, not simply for the conventional reasons of state and religion, but also as an arena for Englishmen to prove their manhood.

While this book focuses on James's sexuality, this is not meant to imply that his sexuality was his chief or defining characteristic. It was, however, an important characteristic that needs to be included if we are to get the full picture. James was an intelligent and complex man. In his early years when he ruled Scotland as James VI, he exercised considerable political skill. Later, when he ascended to the English throne as James I, his quality of leadership was more debatable but clearly superior to that of his son Charles, who precipitated a civil war. Moreover, James was a poet, a patron of the arts and the author of learned treatises on an impressive array of subjects, including politics, religion, tobacco and witchcraft. He was, not least, the sponsor of the Authorized Version of the Bible that bears his name, a rich irony when one considers how often the King James version of the Bible is invoked to condemn homosexuality. There are many solid reasons why James's reputation has steadily risen in recent years, but this rehabilitation has been achieved by emphasizing his talents and accomplishments to the exclusion of controversial topics such as his sex life and the generally scandalous nature of his court.[22] Only recently have historians begun to show an interest again in 'the widespread and growing distaste for James's court', 'the aura of sleaze' that surrounded it, the popular perception that it was a site of decadence and inversion, and the growth of a dissident anti-court sentiment in the nation which contributed to the erosion of the monarch's majesty and helped make the civil war possible.[23] Now that historians have decided that the popular image of James's court is worthy of serious study again, so too should his sexuality, which was so large a part of that image, be taken seriously.

Any historian wishing to tackle the subject of King James's homosexuality faces a peculiar obstacle. Many of the more scandalous accounts of the subject were printed after James's reign in the heated partisan atmosphere surrounding the civil war, which makes them especially untrustworthy regarding matters of fact and of dubious value even with respect to the perception of James's court during his own lifetime. To make matters worse, several of these polemics (including Sir Anthony Weldon's notorious *Court and Character of King James*) were collected and reprinted in 1811 by Sir Walter Scott under the title of the *Secret History of the Court of James the First*. Although Scott's editorial project made these sources more readily available, it also further discredited them as reliable sources. Anyone using these sources today runs the risk of being accused of naively accepting Scott's character assassination of James and continuing his scandalmongering. It needs to be emphasized, therefore, that the present book is not dependent on the controversial works collected in Scott's *Secret History*. There are only a few references to these works until the end of the book where a separate chapter is devoted to determining what can and cannot be learned from them.

I have tried to make this book readable, thought-provoking and accessible to a wide audience. For readers not already well acquainted with James, there is an opening chapter that establishes the major people and events in his life and explains how scholarly opinion on these subjects has fluctuated over time. Chapter 2 examines the evidence for believing that James had sex with his favourites, what James might have thought about this and what his subjects might have thought about it in relation to the contemporary understanding of sodomy. Chapter 3 explores the various terms, codes and historical analogies available to James's subjects by which they could discourse about sex between males and express their disapproval of it. The remaining chapters proceed in roughly chronological order to illuminate the ways in which everyday events in the political arena were increasingly influenced by the impression that sodomy and effeminacy were prevalent at court. Chapter 4 describes how James's peaceful foreign policy and effeminate favourites contributed to the fear that England was becoming soft. Chapter 5 describes the growing demand for James to behave in a more manly manner and give Englishmen a chance to prove their manhood by engaging in the Thirty Years War. Chapter 6 explains how the repercussions of James's homosexuality continued into the reign of his son Charles, who was fiercely determined to be different from his father. And Chapter 7 analyses how the polemical tracts written in the wake of the civil war dealt with the issue of James's sexuality. The concluding chapter sums up all of this material and considers its relevance to the larger history of homosexuality.

Richard Cust has drawn attention to the 'need for political historians to integrate issues relating to sexual behaviour into their account of early modern political culture'.[24] No one better illustrates the truth of that statement than King James. How people perceived his love of other males, how they described it, how they reacted against it – all this had important implications for the politics of his own day and continues to have important implications for the writing of history in our own day.

Chapter 1

Life and Loves

James Stewart was the only child of Mary Queen of Scots and Lord Darnley. It was a dysfunctional family from the outset. Mary quickly discovered that Darnley's attractions were purely superficial: he proved a cold and treacherous husband. For a while she took comfort in the warmer company of her Italian secretary, David Riccio, but Darnley soon put an end to that by conspiring in the secretary's murder. Riccio was literally dragged away from Mary and murdered within earshot, a shocking experience for the queen who was pregnant with James at the time. Although Riccio was dead, the rumour survived that he was the father of Mary's child. Born three months later, on 19 June 1566, James would always be sensitive about this false and painful rumour concerning his legitimacy. After the murder of her secretary, Mary turned for support to certain members of the Scottish nobility and became especially enamoured of the Earl of Bothwell. Although hard evidence is lacking, Mary and Bothwell have always been the prime suspects in Darnley's murder, which occurred the following year. The house he was staying in was blown up and he was found outside the building: he had been strangled.

Thus James was deprived of his murderous father, perhaps through the plotting of his murderous mother, at the tender age of eight months, though we should hasten to add that there is no reason to expect that if Darnley had lived, he would have made much of a father. Next James was deprived of his mother, for Mary was no sooner rid of Darnley than she married Bothwell, a precipitous act which enflamed a faction of the Scottish lords into open rebellion. They drove Bothwell out of Scotland, imprisoned Mary and forced her to abdicate in favour of James, who was then a mere thirteen months old. In 1568 Mary escaped and tried to regain the throne, but she was defeated and fled to England, where Queen Elizabeth kept her under house arrest for nearly twenty years until executing her in 1587.

As a result of these bloody events, James spent his childhood without a father or mother in the hands of custodians who had little interest in his emotional needs. Ostensibly he was King James VI of Scotland, but in reality he was a powerless pawn surrounded by factious noblemen who fought to control his person and rule through him. A series of regents tried to restore order, but the period was marked by recurring feuds, murders and executions. Raised in this unstable environment, it is not surprising that James developed a deep-seated aversion to violence. All his life he abhorred war and took great personal satisfaction in playing the role of an arbitrator or peacemaker. On an even deeper personal level, it appears that this perilous childhood devoid of parental love also left James starved for affection.

Yet it would be a mistake to exaggerate the hardships of James's early years.[1] His guardians, chiefly the Earl and Countess of Mar, were not the soft-hearted surrogate parents that modern readers might wish for him, but they did treat him well by the standards of their own day. There was adequate provision for his physical needs. He had playmates; he learned to ride and hunt, the latter becoming a lifelong passion; but chiefly he studied. James had two tutors, the more famous of whom was George Buchanan, a formidable scholar and stern taskmaster. Although Buchanan failed to indoctrinate James with his own strong opinions on the subject of politics (he hated James's mother and was not particularly keen on monarchy in general), he nevertheless had a profound and lasting influence on the shaping of the young king's character.

James became an impressively learned man, a true scholar skilled in Latin, Greek, French and a little Italian, well grounded in theology and conversant with a wide range of ancient and contemporary works. Over time he became an author in his own right, publishing poetry, treatises on political theory, theological tracts and a number of occasional pieces on subjects as diverse as witchcraft and tobacco. James always took great pride in his learning, and justifiably so: he 'was one of the most learned and intellectually curious men ever to sit on any throne'.[2] All his life James lived off the legacy of the knowledge that Buchanan had crammed into him by the age of thirteen. On the other hand, James did not reach Plato's ideal of the philosopher-king. His learning was not as deep or infallible as he himself believed. He liked to parade his knowledge, pontificate, lecture people on why they were wrong. But these qualities would become more evident in later life when those around him dared not question or correct him (let alone strike him, as Buchanan did).

Summing up James's early education under the domineering figure of Buchanan, one of his biographers wrote that 'rarely has more information been pumped prematurely into a youthful mind'.[3] The analogy that comes to mind is the famous Victorian intellect John Stuart Mill, whose gruelling education drove him into a mental crisis from which he recovered by reading romantic poetry, cultivating his emotional side and striking up a relationship with a woman whom he eventually married. The young James was neither as precocious as John Stuart Mill nor as emotionally unstable, but he too went through a transforming experience when he discovered love.

James's first love was one of his cousins, Esmé Stuart, otherwise known as Lord d'Aubigny because he was the sixth Seigneur of Aubigny in France. Esmé Stuart was a middle-aged man, already married and the father of five children when he arrived from France in 1579, shortly after James's thirteenth birthday. He was a fascinating individual whose continental sophistication and *joie de vivre* must have been a welcome relief to the dourness of James's tutors and guardians. James learned how to have fun – drinking, joking and writing poetry late into the night. In a pattern he would repeat on a more lavish scale with his later favourites, James gave money and titles to his cousin, eventually creating him Duke of Lennox. He also appointed Lennox to the offices of Lord Great Chamberlain and First Gentleman of the Chamber. These offices had the effect of formally installing Lennox in the King's Bedchamber, overseeing such tasks as dressing the king and sleeping in the same room with him. The men associated with the Bedchamber had always enjoyed unusual physical proximity to the king, but this did not normally translate into political power. It was Lennox who enhanced the political importance of the Bedchamber, a practice that James would continue throughout his life.[4] This reorganization of the Bedchamber was probably influenced by Lennox's personal experience of the French court under Henry III – a court that was notorious for the alleged sexual relations between the king and his minions.[5] It did not take much imagination to suspect that Lennox was becoming James's minion. As one horrified onlooker remarked, 'we should repent that ever the French court came in Scotland'.[6] James fed the active imagination of observers like this by embracing and kissing Lennox, as he would later favourites, in public.[7]

James and Lennox meanwhile tried to consolidate the king's power. In 1581 the Earl of Morton, the last regent, was executed. Powerful counterforces were developing against Lennox's influence, however. The Presbyterian clergy hated him because they suspected he was an agent of France and the Roman Catholic Church, and the nobility resented him because he was displacing them at court. Spurred on by the fiery preaching of the clergy, a faction of the nobility decided to take matters into their own hands. In 1582, in what is known as the Ruthven Raid, they captured James and kept him in custody for ten months. James would emerge from this captivity and regain control of his own destiny, but Lennox was not so fortunate. Banished from Scotland, he fled back to France, where he died in 1583, leaving instructions that his heart should be embalmed and sent to James.[8]

James was grief-stricken by the banishment and death of Lennox. One way he compensated for this loss was by taking care of Lennox's children, especially the oldest son, Ludovic Stuart, second Duke of Lennox, who became a lifelong associate. On a more personal level, James gave expression to his feelings in a poem entitled the 'Metaphoricall Invention of a Tragedie Called Phœnix'. In this poem, James is both a passive character and the narrator who tells the sad tale of the persecution and death of a phoenix, the mythological bird from the ancient world that was distinguished by its capacity to regenerate itself from its own ashes. Here the imaginary bird is used, metaphorically, as James says, to represent Lennox. According to tradition, the phoenix reproduced asexually and its gender was ambiguous. It is interesting that James made the phoenix in his poem female even though it stood for a male person. 'I lament my Phoenix,' wrote James. She was a gorgeous bird, 'so strange and rare a sight'. Paradoxically, the very love that James bore for the phoenix caused her destruction, for when she perched in his chamber, others became envious. They attacked her and she took refuge 'betwixt my legs'. Nevertheless, the assailants continued their onslaught, so violently that they made James's legs bleed. Since the king proved powerless to protect her, the phoenix fled to another land and there died. James wrote this poem as a therapeutic exercise – as he himself said, to 'live in lesser grief'. He lamented the loss of someone he loved dearly, wished for Lennox's miraculous resurrection (as in the ancient fable) and assuaged his sense of guilt for having failed to protect the person he loved.[9]

Lennox had entered James's life at a particularly opportune moment when he was highly impressionable and eager to take control of his kingdom. The experience with Lennox was both personally and politically liberating. On the other hand, Lennox was able to capitalize on his personal ascendancy over James to gain political ascendancy for himself. The Duke, it was said, 'guides all as if he were King'.[10] A similar exchange of sexual favours for political influence would occur again decades later in James's relationships with his two greatest favourites in England, the Earl of Somerset and the Duke of Buckingham. By that time, of course, the roles would be reversed in one respect. Lennox had been a mature man in his late thirties who gained the confidence of the adolescent James. In England, James would be the older man who took the younger protégés under his wing.

James was a virtual prisoner for ten months after the overthrow of Lennox, but he was still the king and his captors gradually relaxed their grip until he was able to escape altogether with the aid of another faction of the nobility. From this point in the summer of 1583, James set about the difficult and gradual process of turning the tables on his former captors and establishing his authority in Scotland. Just one year into that process, in August 1584, an agent sent to Scotland by Mary Queen of Scots, Monsieur de Fontenay, wrote a discerning, well-known report that captures many of the qualities in James's complex character which were already apparent at the age of eighteen.[11] In general, Fontenay formed a very high opinion of James, esteeming him 'for his age the premier Prince who has ever lived'. What most impressed Fontenay were James's 'lively and perceptive' intellect, his judiciousness, his memory, his knowledge – in short, his 'marvellous mind'. Fontenay was unimpressed by James's manners, and it is true that James lacked polish. Of course, he could, when he wished, communicate in the idiom of an intellectual or a theologian, but his everyday speech and behaviour were cruder. His profuse swearing horrified the dour ministers of Scotland. One of them 'privately admonished the king to forbear his often swearing, and taking the name of God in vain', but James seems only to have been amused by the poor man's discomfiture.[12] James's physical condition was as contradictory as his mental condition. He was a vigorous hunter who would stay in the saddle for hours, and yet he also had 'a feeble body', especially a weakness in the legs which made his carriage 'ungainly'. (Modern writers have speculated that James suffered from rickets, porphyria or cerebral palsy.) Fontenay summed up the contradictions in the king's condition by calling him 'an old young man'.

These blemishes aside, Fontenay found only three serious defects. One was a tendency in the king to overlook his poverty and other liabilities, which led him to overrate himself and underestimate other rulers. Another was that he spent too much time in frivolous activities, especially the chase, to the exclusion of hard work. On this point

James himself tried to set Fontenay straight, and it is true that James worked a lot harder at governing than may have immediately met the eye. The third defect that worried Fontenay was that James 'loves indiscreetly and obstinately despite the disapprobation of his subjects'.[13] There is no hint from any source that James experienced any involvement with women by this date; the indiscreet love Fontenay referred to must have involved men.

James's indiscreet relationships with other men, and the resultant disapproval, did not end with the Duke of Lennox. However, the consensus among historians is that the other men James loved at this stage in his life did not enjoy the political influence that Lennox had earlier or that his major English favourites would later.[14] One author calls them 'apolitical playthings'.[15] Alexander Lindsey, whom James nicknamed Sandie, was one of these less consequential favourites. On the other hand, George Gordon, the Earl of Huntly, whom James appointed captain of the guard, should not be dismissed so casually. Huntly was a Catholic who generated the same sort of suspicion and hostility Lennox had. Indeed, James arranged for Huntly to marry Lennox's oldest daughter. There were good reasons to ally with Huntly. It gave James a strong arm in the north of Scotland and a friendship with Catholics that could serve as leverage in his diplomatic dealings abroad and with the Scottish clergy at home. But Huntly was an impulsive and violent man who kept bringing Scotland to the brink of rebellion. To restore order, James repeatedly moved against Huntly, then just as often relented. One particularly critical juncture occurred in early 1589, shortly after the defeat of the Spanish Armada, when Huntly was accused of entering into treasonous dealings with Spain. James arrested Huntly, released him, dined with him, allowed him in his chamber over night, raised an army against him, arrested him again, set him at liberty again – all to the bewilderment of onlookers who feared that the king's affection for Huntly would lead to civil war.[16] James survived this crisis, though it is debatable whether the credit should go to his skill at playing one faction off against another or to the wiser judgement of his Lord Chancellor, John Maitland. After the events of 1589, Huntly was removed from the centre of events, though even from his stronghold in the north he continued to foment trouble throughout the 1590s. Twice, in fact, James had to raise an army to subdue him.[17] As one historian observed, 'James overlooked Huntly's long career of conspiracy, rebellion, and murder as far as he decently could'.[18] How much James did this for political reasons and how much for personal reasons, we can never know.

Meanwhile the pressures were mounting for James to marry. Up to this point he had shown no interest in women. As one observer reported, he 'never regardes the company of any woman, not so muche as in any dalliance'.[19] James himself wrote, 'God is my witness I could have abstained longer.' There were practical considerations, however, that drove James into marriage, and he explained these in a revealing letter addressed to his Scottish subjects. As king of Scotland and heir-apparent to the throne of England, James needed heirs of his own to strengthen his position. His lack of heirs had 'bred disdain', James noted, and 'I was generally found fault with by all men for the delaying so long of my marriage'. People had even begun to suspect 'my inability, as if I were a barren stock'.[20] Consequently, James sought a suitable mate and eventually settled on Anne, Princess of Denmark. During the course of the marriage negotiations, one observer described James as 'a cold wooer' who was 'not hasty of marriage'. This impression may have arisen solely from the fact that James was driving a hard bargain, trying to extract a large dowry from the Danes, rather than from any underlying concern about his emotional suitability for marriage. Another observer expressed a deeper concern, however, when he remarked that Anne had already 'made good proof divers ways of her affection, which his majesty is apt in no way to requite'.[21]

Arrangements for the marriage were completed in August 1589. Anne set sail for Scotland almost immediately, but bad weather forced her to stop in Oslo. Then something quite remarkable happened. When James heard that Anne was prevented from reaching him, he set sail on a romantic adventure to join her. The same winds that held back Anne carried James swiftly to her side. They were married in late November and spent several happy months in Norway and Denmark before reaching Scotland in May 1590. James was twenty-three years old; Anne was fifteen. It was a story-book beginning for a marriage that lasted nearly three decades until Anne's death in 1619.[22]

The marriage lasted, but the romance did not. Too often the fault has been attributed to Anne. A.L. Rowse described her as 'a featherheaded woman';[23] Maurice Lee Jr described her as 'young, silly, and meddlesome';[24] Maurice Ashley actually called her a 'dumb blond';[25] and David Willson ended his chapter on Anne with these words: 'Alas! The King had married a stupid wife.'[26]

It would be more correct to say that Anne had married a difficult man. Anne was not the dull or frivolous woman she has often been made to seem at the hands of male historians.[27] She was actually, as the Venetian ambassador described her, 'intelligent and prudent'.[28]

Precisely because she did have a mind of her own, it was inevitable that she would engage in an occasional contest of wills with James. James expected unquestioning obedience, not only because he was king but also because of his overall view of marriage, which was typical for his day. He believed it was the husband's 'office to command', the wife's 'to obey'. A husband, in James's own words, should behave towards a wife as follows: 'Treat her as your own flesh, command her as her Lord, cherish her as your helper, rule her as your pupill, and please her in all things reasonable; but teach her not to be curious in things that belong her not.'[29]

One thing Anne certainly thought belonged to her was the care and raising of her own children, but James was adamantly opposed to her on this subject. He insisted that the children be removed from the royal household and entrusted to guardians, thereby repeating the pattern to which he himself had been subjected. Apparently James did not feel that he had suffered any great deprivation in being raised without parents. Anne had been raised in a closer family and consequently viewed the situation quite differently.[30] She resented being separated from her children, and she carried on a bitter and prolonged feud with James over this issue.[31] Another issue dividing Anne and James was religion. It is usually argued that Anne placed a strain on her marriage when she converted to Roman Catholicism in the later 1590s, but one wonders if it was not the other way round. The strains in her marriage may have been one factor that induced Anne to convert to Catholicism, a small act of defiance against her domineering husband.[32]

Of course, the chief source of tension between James and Anne cannot possibly be attributed to the queen. This was James's affection for other males. As we shall see, Lennox and Huntly were only the beginning of a lifetime pattern. Much later, after James's death and after the civil war, when people were able to write more freely about this subject, they made an issue of James's relationship with his wife. In a well-known phrase, Sir Anthony Weldon charged that James 'was not very uxorious', which prompted Godfrey Goodman to retort that 'there was little in the Queen to make him uxorious'. As this exchange illustrates, James's detractors insinuated that his persistent involvement with other males was damaging to his marriage. Goodman's feeble rebuttal was typical of the king's defenders, who were hard-pressed to find a better explanation.[33]

It is not just that James loved men; he actively disliked women. This is one prejudice that Buchanan, an old bachelor, probably helped inculcate in his young pupil, but more generally James was raised in a very male world without the presence of a mother or sister as moderating influences. James's early love poems are sometimes cited as evidence of his genuine affection for Anne, but other poems betrayed his low opinion of women. As one modern commentator noted, James's later poems are 'exceptionally antifeminine, and... often turn into bitter invective'.[34] In one such poem, James observed that animals possess certain characteristics that are inescapably ingrained in their natures: hens cackle when they lay eggs, hounds follow the scent of rabbits, goats climb, birds fly, fish swim and salmon spawn. By the same token, James wrote, it is inescapably ingrained in women's nature to be vain, prejudiced, gossipy, ambitious and foolish.[35] Granted that this negative view of women was commonplace in James's day, still the French ambassador thought that James's attitude was so hostile as to merit comment. The ambassador wrote that James 'piques himself on great contempt for women... he exhorts them openly to virtue, and scoffs with great levity at all men who pay them honour'.[36] If Anne had been a deeply learned woman and a brilliant conversationalist, it is still doubtful that James would have had any respect for her mind.

Ironically, despite James's contempt for women, much of the credit for the success of his marriage belongs to his wife. As we shall see, Anne proved to be a resourceful and resilient woman who found ways of expressing her displeasure over her husband's behaviour and worked out accommodations with him. Most of the time their marriage was at least amicable, and in one important respect, it was a great success. While they still lived in Scotland, Anne gave birth to five children, three of whom survived infancy – Prince Henry, Princess Elizabeth and Prince Charles (as many children as King Henry VIII and all six of his wives had managed to produce). Looking across the border from England, the unmarried and childless Elizabeth I could only be envious that her apparent successor was producing heirs of his own. The son and grandchildren of Mary Queen of Scots looked more than ever likely to establish themselves firmly on the English throne. When James later succeeded to the English throne in 1603, Anne stayed behind briefly during another pregnancy which ended in a miscarriage. After the move to England, she gave birth to two more ill-fated children: Sophia, who died shortly after her birth in 1606, and Mary, who died at the age of two in 1607. After this date the king and queen increasingly lived apart. Several historians agree that it was probably the loss of these two children so close together that ended any physical intimacy between Anne and James. Whatever other motives there were, Anne, broken in health and spirit, surely had reason to avoid further pregnancies.[37] She had, after all, more than discharged her principal duty as queen: the production of 'an heir and a spare', as they say.

Anne's frequent pregnancies are noteworthy. On average, she became pregnant every two years during the first sixteen years of her marriage. She and James obviously engaged in fairly regular sexual intercourse. These are the very same years when favourites, though they still existed, played a far less significant role in James's life. That hardly seems a coincidence.

In many ways, the best years of James's marriage were the best years of his life in general. After the misfortunes and missteps of his youth, he gradually made himself King of Scotland in fact as well as name. Considering the conditions he inherited, this was a remarkable feat.[38] In Scotland, as elsewhere in early modern Europe, the monarchy faced two powerful opponents – the nobility and the Church (or Kirk) – and James managed to subdue both these rivals. As James rightly described them, the nobility suffered from 'a fectlesse arrogant conceit of their greatnes and power'.[39] Feuding was still commonplace, and civil war threatened to break out at any time. On the other hand, James and the nobility needed each other. By skilfully rewarding some and punishing others, even to the point of exile, he succeeded in curbing their lawlessness and gaining their loyalty. James also recruited men from a lower social status into his regime who formed a new aristocracy to complement the traditional lords.

All these people had the same vested interest in preserving the monarchy as the pinnacle of the whole privileged hierarchy to which they belonged. In this respect, the Kirk was a far more dangerous competitor because it had adopted the levelling ideology of Jean Calvin and John Knox, which showed little respect for worldly magistrates. 'I was oftentimes calumniated in their popular sermons', James explained, 'not for any evil or vice in me, but because I was a King, which they thought the highest evil.' James's relations with the Kirk were indeed stormy and several times he had to retreat in his efforts to bring it under control. Eventually, however, he managed to isolate the extremists and gain direction over the Kirk's governing body, the General Assembly. Nevertheless, it remained an awkward and potentially explosive situation. In particular, James insisted on maintaining a token episcopacy in a church that was otherwise Presbyterian; and these bishops would remain a serious bone of contention. Meanwhile, through his experience with the fiery and rebellious clergy of the Kirk,

James had developed a strong personal antipathy to the Puritans, whom he described as 'pests...breathing nothing but sedition and calumnies'.[40]

During these same years when James was strengthening his grip over Scotland he was also establishing his reputation as a scholar. He began by publishing his poems: *Essayes of a Prentise in the Divine Art of Poesie*, published in 1584, which included the 'Phoenix', and *His Majesties Poeticall Exercises at Vacant Houres*, published in 1591.[41] James continued to write poetry throughout his life.[42] These poems are rather mechanical and undistinguished, but they remind us of the contradictions in James's character. Behind his rough exterior he was an aesthete who appreciated the music of words and turned to the writing of poetry not only for pleasure, but also to express his deepest emotions, as, for example, during the absence or loss of a loved one.[43] Fortunately, however, James's reputation as a scholar does not rest on his poetical works. In 1598 he published *The Trew Law of Free Monarchies* and in 1599 *Basilikon Doron*. These works on the theory and practice of kingship do much greater justice to his talents as a thinker and writer.[44]

The political theory expressed in *The Trew Law* used to be characterized as 'absolutist', but today that term is considered unfair. Recent commentators emphasize, instead, that James, like most of his contemporaries, believed that kings should not act arbitrarily, that they have a duty to promote the welfare of their subjects and that they are ultimately accountable to God.[45] As the subtitle of *The Trew Law* stated, there are reciprocal and mutual duties between a king and his subjects.[46] A king should be a 'loving Father, and careful watchman'. Yet the predominant message of *The Trew Law* was that kings must be allowed to rule as they themselves think fit, while subjects must obey and leave the judging to God. James saw himself as the 'great Schoolemaster of the whole land'. He wrote *The Trew Law* to instruct his unruly subjects 'in the right knowledge of their alleageance' or, as he said in another place, 'to teach you the right-way'. James claimed that he had found the root of his kingdom's 'endlesse calamities, miseries, and confusions' in its disposition to rebellion. Consequently, he said, 'my onely purpose and intention in this treatise is to perswade...good Christian readers...to keepe their hearts and hands free from such monstrous and unnaturall rebellions'. James's main concern in *The Trew Law* was to refute contractual views of kingship and resistance theories that limited the freedom of the monarch and encouraged unrest – theories of the sort he had encountered in the Scottish clergy.

The Trew Law was a theoretical work, which James intended to complement and support his practical efforts to tame the nobility and the Kirk. Given the circumstances from which it arose, it was not outrageous. Its divine right view of monarchy was commonplace at the time, especially on the European continent, from which James got many of his ideas. But it is not altogether surprising that James's views proved provocative in England, where the traditions of the English common law and the concept of the 'fundamental constitution' were often invoked as counterbalances to the monarch's freedom of action. Particularly alarming were James's assertions that 'the King is above the law'. True, a good king will rule within the law, 'yet is hee not bound thereto but of his good will'. James's predecessors, including Queen Elizabeth, viewed their power in substantially the same way, but they did not write books on the subject which had the effect of making those views seem more extreme and inflexible. Ironically, then, while James distinguished himself as a thinker and author, he also inadvertently raised concerns about how high-handed a ruler he would be in England.

It has been suggested that the English would have been less alarmed by James's political theories if they had read more carefully his *Basilikon Doron*, which is a gentler, more 'fatherly' advice book.[47] James wrote the *Basilikon Doron* (which, in English, means 'royal gift') to instruct his son Prince Henry. It is a practical manual for successful kingship that reflects the way James viewed himself and, equally important, wished others to view him. It admonishes the prince to fear and love God, study the scriptures, respect the law, promote justice, reward goodness, employ competent servants, choose his companions carefully, and so forth. It even advises the prince with regard to his clothing, speech and deportment, because 'a King is as one set on a stage, whose smallest actions and gestures, all the people gazingly doe behold'.[48] James was keenly aware that he was being watched, although, as we shall see, he did not follow all the rules he laid down here, to the detriment of his public image. *Basilikon Doron* is not just more pragmatic than *The Trew Law*; it is a more humane, engaging, even wise book (though modern readers would be appalled by its views on marriage cited earlier). On the other hand, both books pontificate. In his writing, as in his public speeches, James adopted a know-it-all attitude, condescending to his audience, assuming the superior role of teacher or instructor to the ignorant who simply needed to have the right way spelled out for them.

James's concern to instruct his subjects was evident in two other works published about this time. In 1597 he published his

Daemonologie to warn his subjects about witchcraft. This tract is written in the form of a dialogue in which James names the character representing his own viewpoint Epistemon, from the Greek, which we might translate as Mr Knowledge. That, of course, is how James viewed himself and wished others to view him. The *Daemonologie* was based on a real witch-scare that had occurred in Scotland in 1590–1, at a time when James had been less secure on the throne and only recently married. It is revealing that he was still sufficiently concerned about witches to keep sounding the alarm against them in 1597. It was said that James became convinced about the reality of witches when one of them revealed the very words that had passed between him and Anne on their wedding night.[49] James was persuaded that these witches were responsible for causing a storm that sank one of the ships in his wedding fleet and that they were trying to kill him through black magic. He therefore took an active role in the trials. At one point he berated a jury because they had acquitted an alleged witch, telling them, 'I have been occupied these three quarters of this year for the sifting out of them that are guilty herein.'[50]

In his *Daemonologie*, James revealed how much he was a man of his time. He argued, for example, that people's refusal to confess until they were tortured amounted to further proof of their guilt. He explained that most witches were women because 'that sex is frailer than man is'. And he declared that magistrates who spared the lives of convicted witches were committing 'treason against God'.[51] Of course, it does not enhance James's reputation that he helped to foster this form of persecution, even though his actions are made more understandable, if not excusable, because he believed that he was personally in danger. James's active role in Scotland fits the general pattern in Europe that the witch-hunts were driven not by the ignorant masses but by the over-zealous intelligentsia.

In contrast to James's views on witchcraft, which seem horribly backward today, his views on tobacco seem enlightened and ahead of his time. He published his *Counterblaste to Tobacco* in 1604.[52] James objected to the 'vile use (or rather abuse)' of tobacco on several grounds. He considered it 'a custom loathsome to the eye, hateful to the nose, harmful to the brain, [and] dangerous to the lungs'. He knew that tobacco was habit-forming. He deplored the money wasted on it. He even objected to the fact that non-smokers were exposed to tobacco smoke at meals. James wrote against tobacco, he said, because 'it is the King's part (as the proper physician of his politic-body) to purge it' of disease. In this, as in his other writings, James took his responsibilities as head of the body-politic seriously and tried to educate his subjects.

James's many accomplishments during his final years in Scotland were blighted by one awful episode: in August of 1600 he was nearly killed in a hand-to-hand struggle with a young man named Alexander Ruthven.[53] It is a great and insoluble mystery how James came to be alone (or nearly alone) with the nineteen-year-old Ruthven in a small upstairs room fighting for his life.[54] James managed to shout for help through a window, the battle spread into the stairway and, when it was over, Alexander and his brother John, the Earl of Gowrie, were both dead. The episode became known as the Gowrie Conspiracy.

The official version of the story, which James forced the ministers of Scotland to preach, was that the younger Ruthven had lured him to the scene by asking him to inspect a mysterious pot of gold coins that had been discovered. The Ruthven brothers allegedly concocted this strange tale to draw James into their trap, intending to kidnap or kill him. They certainly did have a grudge against James because he had executed their father for his role in the Ruthven Raid eighteen years earlier. The official story about a pot of gold was ludicrous, however, and James had difficulty making people accept it, not only in Scotland but also in England and France, where it was mocked so mercilessly that it had to be withdrawn from circulation.[55] Nearly sixty years later, the story was still being used as political propaganda against James. Francis Osborne wrote: 'For no Scotch man you could meet beyond Sea but did laugh at it, and the Peripatetick Polititians said the [official] Relation in Print did murder all possibility of Credit.'[56] The date of the king's escape from the Gowrie Conspiracy became an annual day of thanksgiving, and 'to endorse the official account of the deliverance by celebrating it with as much verve as possible was an important way to display one's loyalty to James'.[57]

The king's energetic effort to punish sceptics and suppress alternative rumours smacks of a cover-up, although we can never know for certain what he was concealing. Some said a quarrel had simply erupted spontaneously. Certainly the parties had much to quarrel over – James's execution of the Ruthvens' father, his refusal to honour an old debt to the Earl, who badly needed the money, or Gowrie's open opposition to a tax James wanted. The most far-fetched theory, although it has had many adherents, is that James himself deviously orchestrated the whole affair to eliminate the Ruthvens. Granted that James had good reason to want the brothers out of the way, surely he could have found a way to accomplish that end without exposing himself to such personal danger.

None of the foregoing explanations provides a wholly satisfactory answer to the central question: why did James go to Gowrie House and allow himself to be led by the younger Ruthven to a small, secluded, upstairs room? James had started the day hunting. According to his own version of events, he originally had no intention of visiting Gowrie House, but the younger Ruthven spoke to him twice during the day and persuaded him to make the trip. What inducement did Ruthven use to bring James to his home and lead him to that upstairs room if it was not the pot of gold? Why was the true inducement so embarrassing to James that he invented the absurd pot of gold story? Some have suggested that the lure Ruthven used was not gold, but sex.[58]

Queen Anne's behaviour in the aftermath of the Gowrie Conspiracy adds to the mystery. She was pregnant at the time and her husband had narrowly escaped being murdered. Yet Anne, instead of sympathizing with James, spoke sharply to him and was so angry that for a while she refused to dress or leave her room. It was even said that she had threatened to 'remain in some part by herself' after the birth of her child. Anne had rational reasons to be angry. She liked the Ruthvens. In fact, one of her ladies-in-waiting was a sister of the Ruthvens and James promptly banished her from the court. Perhaps it was simply because Anne sympathized with the Ruthvens that she doubted the official version of events, but it is at least possible that she was upset with her husband because his susceptibility to attractive young men had got him into trouble again.[59]

The real pot of gold awaited James in England, where Queen Elizabeth finally died in March 1603. James made a triumphant progress to his new kingdom and stayed there until his death, except for one trip back to Scotland in 1617. James came to the English throne with many advantages. The mere fact that he was a man with several children (and legitimate children at that) was an advantage in a country that had suffered from disputed successions and grown tired of the old Virgin Queen. Far more important, however, was his experience. James was already a seasoned ruler, having spent some two decades learning how to manoeuvre in the far more treacherous political waters of Scotland. He knew how to manipulate people and wield power – forcefully, shrewdly, realistically. He had made the government of Scotland work, and there was every reason to expect that he would have an easier time in England.

It used to be thought that, despite these high expectations, James's reign in England proved to be a failure paving the way for the later civil war and execution of his son, Charles. James's reputation suffered because historians were reading history backwards, assuming the inevitability of the civil war and looking for its causes in the early 1600s. Today, however, this teleological or Whig approach has been discredited, and James is no longer assumed to have started the monarchy down the 'high road to civil war' that ended in regicide. In fact, some historians have gone so far as to exonerate James of any blame whatsoever. For them, whatever caused the civil war, it must have happened after James's death. In this view, James was a consummate ruler who did just about everything right until his son succeeded to the throne and wrecked his father's work.[60] Somewhere between these two extremes the truth lies.

The recent re-evaluation of James has been most convincing with respect to his enlightened religious policy.[61] In an age marked by religious dogmatism, James was a pragmatist who described himself as 'free from persecution, or thralling of my Subjects in matters of Conscience'.[62] Of course, James had to insist upon conformity to the established Church of England, but within that Church he continued the Elizabethan policy of allowing a reasonable degree of comprehensiveness or inclusiveness. In his choice of bishops, for example, he was careful to improve their overall quality while allowing them to represent a range of viewpoints. He also has been praised for his 'remarkable patronage of preaching at court'.[63] James wasted no time in asserting his control over the Church. In 1604 he convened the Hampton Court Conference to preside over a debate, as he loved to do, about the direction of the Church. The more extreme Puritans were disappointed by the conference. James tended to equate English Puritans with the Scots Presbyterians, who attacked the hierarchical underpinnings of Church and State. At Hampton Court he expressed his hostility towards Presbyterianism in the famous expression: 'No bishop, no king.' But overall the conference must be judged a success, and in general the whole phenomenon of Puritanism subsided in James's reign except towards the very end when renewed religious warfare on the continent stirred up domestic zealots again. Of course, the greatest achievement to result from the Hampton Court Conference was the Authorized or King James Version of the Bible, which appeared in 1611.

James was equally statesmanlike in his approach to Roman Catholicism. Circumstances forced him to persecute Catholics more than he would have liked to, especially after the abortive Gunpowder Plot of 1605, so named because barrels of gunpowder had been placed in the cellars of Westminster Palace to annihilate the king, Lords and Commons in one grand explosion. In general, however, James was personally conciliatory towards Roman Catholics. He gave major offices to

Catholic peers such as the Howard family (including the Earls of Northampton, Suffolk and Arundel); and he was friendly towards Catholic Spain in his foreign policy. Again, it was only the burning hatred of Roman Catholicism among the English populace at large, fanned by continental religious war towards the end of the reign, that threatened to destabilize the *modus vivendi* James achieved.

In foreign policy, as in religion, James began his reign quickly and decisively. Although Elizabeth's ministers had already been thinking about extricating themselves from the debilitating war against Spain that had been dragging on since the Armada of 1588, it was James who boldly brought the Spanish to London to negotiate a treaty ending the war in 1604. James prided himself on being a peacemaker. He truly believed, as he once told Parliament, that 'it is an unchristian thing to seek that by blood which may be had by peace'.[64] He was eager to serve as a conciliator or mediator between warring parties, and indeed he was allowed to play that role several times in continental disputes, most notably in 1613 when he facilitated a peace between Denmark and Sweden.[65] What James emphatically did not want to do was fight. He had a strong aversion to war and is usually described as a pacifist. This virtue, too, has sometimes been made to seem a fault. Many of James's contemporaries – for reasons of religion, nationalism and commercial rivalry – wanted to continue the war against Spain; and until recently, historians tended to share this view that James should have been more bellicose. He has been criticized for his 'policy of unadventurous and inoffensive goodfellowship', which reduced England 'to a cipher in international affairs'.[66] But James understood that adventurousness was risky, and it was better to be a bystander than a participant in the expensive deadly contests on the continent. Today there is growing respect for James's foreign policy. He is represented as a visionary who wanted to reconcile the differences between Protestant and Catholic nations, not inflame them. Unlike the other combatants in an era of religious warfare, James dreamed of a reunited Christendom and worked consistently toward that enlightened, ecumenical and far-sighted goal.[67]

The wisdom of James's foreign policy was overtaken by events in the last years of his reign when he came under increasing pressure to join the Protestant side in the Thirty Years War that broke out in 1618. James had arranged the marriage of his daughter Elizabeth to a German ruler, Frederick V, Elector of the Palatinate. James saw this marriage as a way of strengthening his ties with continental Protestantism, but he could not have foreseen that Frederick would soon plunge himself into difficulties by accepting the Crown of Bohemia, thereby making himself the focal point in a war between Protestants and Catholics. Frederick and Elizabeth were quickly driven from their homeland by Catholic Habsburg forces, and James was expected to intervene on their behalf for reasons of family and of religion. James, however, was furious with Frederick for having foolishly created this situation, and he sought a way of mediating a solution without having to enter the war himself. Just as he had married his daughter Elizabeth to a Protestant, so did he intend to marry his son Charles to a Catholic.[68] James now came to believe that he could offer his son as a bargaining chip in the Thirty Years War. For years he pursued the idea of marrying Charles to a Spanish princess in return for Spain's assistance in restoring Frederick and Elizabeth to the Palatinate. James's desire to balance his family's ties between Protestant and Catholic countries on the continent and his friendliness towards Catholic Spain were broadminded and yet at the same time astonishingly naive. The so-called Spanish Match never had any real hope of succeeding. When the project collapsed and James was driven into the Thirty Years War after all, through a course of events we will examine in greater detail below, it looked like a total repudiation of his foreign policy.[69]

Although James's religious and foreign policies did not provoke substantial opposition until the final years of his reign, he was beset by controversy on many other fronts from the outset. For much of this controversy, he was not personally to blame. Some of it even reflects favourably on him. For example, a great deal has been written recently about James's plan for a Union of Scotland and England.[70] It is customary these days to paint James as an enlightened statesman whose hopes for an amicable union of the two kingdoms were ahead of his time. Those hopes were dashed from the start by English xenophobia against the Scots.[71] James continued to govern Scotland effectively from his new throne in England. 'Here I sit and governe it with my Pen', he boasted, 'I write and it is done...which others could not doe by the sword.'[72] This boast was fully justified because during these years Scotland enjoyed 'more peace, more order, more general prosperity, more widespread acceptance of the authority of the crown than she had ever known before'.[73] Yet James remained bitterly disappointed by the failure to effect a true union, and many English remained suspicious of James because in their eyes he remained a foreigner.

The xenophobic reaction against the Scots was intensified by the positions James gave them at court. Perhaps because of English hostility, James refrained from appointing many Scotsmen to high office. He kept one of Elizabeth's officials, Robert Cecil, as his own chief minister, elevating him to the peerage as Earl of Salisbury. James compensated for this English dominance of the main public offices, however, by giving Scotsmen a near monopoly in the more private Bedchamber. He packed the Bedchamber with Scots and made a powerful inner circle of them, thereby continuing the politicizing of the Bedchamber which the first Duke of Lennox had instituted in Scotland. Most chief officers of state were still English, but the Bedchamber officials comprised an inner circle of James's closest friends that was almost entirely Scottish.[74]

James was also the victim of rising expectations. Elizabeth's regime had become settled in its ways, and many of the English now expected reform in politics, religion and the law. Some Members of Parliament were especially eager to capitalize on the opportunity presented by the accession of a new monarch. This impatience for change was expressed in the 'Apology' that was drafted in James's first Parliament (though it was never approved by the full House of Commons). The authors of the 'Apology' said that they had delayed acting in the last years of Elizabeth's reign out of respect for her age and sex, and because they did not want to endanger a smooth succession, but now they expected 'to redress, restore, and rectify'.[75] This aggressive attitude was bound to lead to disagreements, however, when it came to questions about what should be redressed, restored and rectified, in what ways and at what cost.[76] James was all the more likely to disappoint these hopes for reform because at the same time there was an even greater pent-up demand for offices, titles and money. Elizabeth had been frugal to a fault, and now many people expected to benefit from greater liberality on the part of the Crown.

The disappointments and tensions of James's rule in England came to a head in one contentious Parliament after another. The English Parliament was a far less manageable body than the Scottish Parliament which James was accustomed to, and he often expressed exasperation over its dilatory and querulous proceedings.[77] Historians used to exaggerate the degree of lofty constitutional conflict in James's parliaments, as if James were attempting to establish absolutism and his parliaments were defending liberty. Of course, constitutional issues did arise, but the most contentious issue was simply money. Conflict over money was inevitable because the Crown's sources of revenue were insufficient without resorting to controversial measures such as increasing the customs duties. It must be admitted, however, that James made the situation worse by squandering the money he did have. Granted that a king had to be bountiful to garner support and maintain an aura of grandeur, James went far beyond these demands to the point of reckless extravagance.[78] Even he admitted in 1607 that his first three years on the English throne 'were to me as a Christmas'.[79] In 1610 an agreement was almost reached in Parliament whereby James would have relinquished several old and irksome sources of income in return for one new and steady source amounting perhaps to £200,000 per annum, but this 'Great Contract' eventually fell through because both parties feared they were giving away more than they would gain.[80] The failure of 1610 drove James to more desperate financial expedients. He resumed the sale of monopolies that Elizabeth had been forced to abandon. He sold knighthoods and titles of nobility, creating the title of 'baronet' expressly for this purpose. Nevertheless, by 1617 his debts amounted to over £700,000, with no end in sight.[81]

Meanwhile James's relations with Parliament deteriorated. The Parliament of 1614 was so rancorous and ineffectual that it was dubbed the 'Addled Parliament'. The Parliament of 1621 attacked monopolies, impeached the Lord Chancellor, Sir Francis Bacon, and sent a petition to James exhorting him to change his foreign policy – in particular, to ally with the Protestant side in the Thirty Years War, abandon the unpopular proposal for a Spanish Match, and arrange for Prince Charles to marry a Protestant. When James expressed his outrage over this intrusion into royal affairs, the Commons responded by protesting that he was the one infringing their privileges.[82] The argument escalated until James angrily dissolved Parliament and personally tore the 'Protestation' of the Commons out of their journal.

The spiral of events in 1621 was symptomatic of the growing problem between James and his Parliaments. While the penny-pinching, quarrelsome, parochial members of Parliament must bear much of the blame for this breakdown in relations, James was also partly to blame. Besides his ruinous extravagance, James raised unnecessary alarms by making long, pompous speeches on subjects such as the royal prerogative, the common law and the privileges of Parliament. Though his objective was to allay apprehensions, these bombastic lectures often succeeded in raising them to a higher level. A speech intended to express his respect for the common law, for example, was more memorable for what it implied about his view of himself, 'For Kings are not only GODS Lieutenants upon earth, and sit upon GODS throne, but even by GOD himself they are called Gods'.[83] By 1624 James could boast that 'I have broken the Neck of Three Parliaments, one after another', but it was a boast based on failure to establish a working relationship.[84]

Behind the concrete issues that upset James's Parliaments, there was a more diffuse worry about who James was and what he really represented. Life at James's court was a far cry from what it had been under Elizabeth. The oppressive regime of the straitlaced Elizabeth quickly gave way to a party atmosphere and James was deeply implicated in this deterioration of court life. His personal behaviour was often at odds with his high-minded pronouncements. He condemned swearing and drunkenness, but he swore and drank liberally. He exhorted his son to 'make your Court and companie to bee a patterne of godlinesse and all honest vertues', but his own court and company were scandalous. He singled out sodomy as one of the most horrible crimes that a ruler should never forgive, yet, as we shall see, his own actions led to the suspicion that he himself not only countenanced but committed sodomy.[85]

James's drinking provoked comment. The French ambassador once reported that James drank 'to such purpose, that he fell on the table, after having sat at it for five hours'.[86] Queen Anne was said to have complained that 'the King drinks so much, and conducts himself so ill in every respect, that I expect an early and evil result'. In 1604 she predicted that James had only a few years left before his drinking would either kill him or turn him into an imbecile.[87] In 1607 the visit of Anne's brother, who was now King of Denmark, became the occasion of a particularly notorious drinking binge. One observer, aghast at this sight, contrasted the 'good order, discretion, and sobriety' of Elizabeth's court with the 'wild riot, excess, and devastation' at James's court. It was now the fashion, he wrote, to 'wallow in beastly delights'.[88] James had a stronger constitution than his wife imagined. In 1622, three years before he died, he was still drinking so much that the French ambassador concluded: 'The end of all is ever the bottle.'[89] James failed to follow his own advice in *Basilikon Doron* to 'beware of drunkennesse, which is a beastlie vice, namely in a King: but specially beware with it, because it is one of those vices that increaseth with aage'.[90]

James's reputation also suffered from the impression that he was surrounded by a small group of greedy and dissolute cronies. As noted above, there was strong resentment against the Scots who monopolized the Bedchamber, and it is fashionable these days to discount this resentment by attributing it all to xenophobia.[91] But there were other, perfectly good reasons to resent this privileged inner circle.[92] It has been estimated that James gave £40,000 per annum to these Scots in money alone, not including any grants of land.[93] Certainly

James's appeals to Parliament for money were undercut by the impression he himself created that any money he received would be frittered away on the Scots at court. How could he reasonably expect more money from Parliament when, besides such largesse, he also used royal revenues to pay off the personal debts of Bedchamber Scots? In 1607 he paid off the debts of three of these insiders amounting to £44,000. He was rumoured to have said that 'he will this once set them free, and then let them shift for themselves'. But in 1611 he paid off another round of personal debts amounting to £34,000.[94] As one MP phrased it, what was the point of taxing the people to fill the royal cistern 'if it shall dayly runne out thence by private cocks?'[95] The pun was almost certainly intentional. Cock had the same double meaning in Jacobean England that it has today.[96]

The extravagance of James's court was linked in the public mind to wantonness. In 1610, when the Lord Treasurer pressed the king's request for money, he inadvertently acknowledged this fact, insisting that 'the demand of the Kinge was a supplie of his wants; wants, sayd he, not of wantones'. Thomas Wentworth angered James later in this Parliament by insinuating that 'the Kinge spent all upon his favorites and wanton courtiers'.[97] Similar accusations surfaced in the Parliament of 1614, where one MP charged that these courtiers were 'their masters' spaniels but their country's wolves', and another MP urged the king to send the Scots back to Scotland because 'we have nothing but ill examples of all riot and dissoluteness'. Again, these remarks hit home: after dissolving Parliament, James temporarily imprisoned both speakers.[98]

Lurking behind these charges of 'wantonness' and 'dissoluteness' were suspicions about sexual transgression at James's court. At the very beginning of James's reign in England, his favourites were relatively minor figures. There was, for example, Philip Herbert. The great royalist historian, the Earl of Clarendon, wrote that Herbert was 'the first who drew the King's eyes towards him with affection'. Herbert 'pretended to no other qualifications than to understand horses and dogs very well', but in 1605 James elevated him to the Earldom of Montgomery.[99]

Two years later, at about the time James and Anne started going their separate ways, the first major favourite appeared in England.[100] Robert Carr was a young Scotsman who had frequented the court in a series of menial positions. He got his big break, quite literally, in 1607 when he broke his leg performing in a tilting match before James. The king visited Carr while he was recovering and soon the two were close friends. James showered honours and titles on the young Scot.

'Carr hath all favours,' wrote one observer.[101] He was appointed a Groom and Gentleman of the Bedchamber, made a Knight of the Garter and created Viscount Rochester, by virtue of which he also became the first Scot to sit in the English House of Lords.[102]

Carr's story took a strange turn in 1613. He fell in love with Frances Howard, the Countess of Essex, and decided to marry her. But two obstacles stood in his way. The first was his close friend and adviser, Thomas Overbury, who disliked Lady Essex and apparently opposed the marriage because it would diminish his own influence. To prevent Overbury from thwarting the marriage, he was imprisoned in the Tower of London, where he conveniently died. Only later was it discovered that he had been poisoned. The second obstacle to the marriage was the fact that Frances Howard was already married to the Earl of Essex. To overcome this obstacle, a special commission was appointed which confirmed Lady Essex's claim that the marriage had never been consummated, owing to the Earl's alleged impotence. A panel of women who physically examined Lady Essex certified that she was a virgin, though contemporaries found this hard to believe. All obstacles having been cleared out of the way, Carr and the Countess were married at the end of 1613.

One person who was not an obstacle to Carr's marriage was James. In fact, he had done everything in his power to facilitate it. He arranged for Overbury's imprisonment, intimidated the investigating commission and packed this body with two more members when it appeared the verdict would go the wrong way.[103] He even elevated Carr to the Earldom of Somerset, thereby assuring that Lady Essex would lose no status. As the new Earl of Somerset, Carr was more powerful after his marriage than he had been before. In the spring of 1614 it was reported that 'Somerset hath so great a power of prevailing with the king as never any man had the like'.[104] Somerset's power was enhanced even further by his appointment to the office of Lord Chamberlain. According to court gossips, James declared 'no man shold marvayle that he bestowed a place so neere himself upon his frend, whom he loved above all men living'.[105]

Yet Somerset's downfall was imminent. The chief cause of his ruin was the murder of Overbury, which had cleared the way for the controversial marriage in the first place but nevertheless, like a timebomb, was ticking away in the background. The bomb exploded in 1615 when revelations about Overbury's murder became public. In 1616 Somerset and his wife were put on trial for murder. Lady Somerset confessed. The Earl maintained his innocence, but he too was found guilty.

James commuted the death sentence of the unfortunate couple, and they were imprisoned in the Tower until 1622, at which time they were allowed to withdraw to the countryside where they died in obscurity.[106] James's own relationship with Somerset, the question of the Earl of Essex's potency, the issue of Lady Essex's virginity, the poisoning of Overbury and finally the murder trial – all these sensational subjects became part of the public rumour-mill and added to the impression of decadence surrounding the Jacobean court. Lady Essex became a particularly notorious figure in the public mind. She was the daughter of the Earl of Suffolk who would soon be stripped of his office as Lord Treasurer and the Countess of Suffolk who was also convicted of bribery and extortion. She suffered, as did the other members of the Howard family, from the stigma of Roman Catholicism. Furthermore, she was thought to have used not only poison but magic to effect her divorce and remarriage; and she was a veritable sexual libertine according to contemporary gossips.[107] She became a symbol of sexual and gender inversion, aptly described by a writer later in the century as 'mounted on her *Car*'.[108] James tried to distance himself from this 'sleaze', as one historian has recently called it, but the behaviour of his favourite and, more generally, his court could not help but reflect upon him.[109]

If the revelations about Overbury's murder had not ruined Somerset, he would probably have been ruined by other means because another favourite was already in the process of displacing him at court. The last and the greatest of James's favourites was not a Scot but an Englishman named George Villiers. Unlike Somerset, Villiers did not come to the attention of the king by any accident. Quite the contrary, Villiers had been purposely chosen for his role by opponents of Somerset, who calculated that the best way to counterbalance the power of the Earl was to interest James in another young man. Perhaps they were encouraged to believe that Somerset's marriage made the king more vulnerable to the attentions of another male suitor. In any case, their plan was already succeeding when the Overbury trial conveniently removed Somerset for them. Villiers had managed to catch the king's eye in the latter half of 1614. At that time the young man was about twenty-two years old and James was forty-eight. Villiers's promoters gained an important strategic advantage when they succeeded in having him appointed cup-bearer, a position that brought him into frequent direct contact with the king.[110] Somerset had fought furiously against Villiers's advancement, but his threats and resistance only served to alienate the king. Near the beginning of 1615 James wrote a long letter to Somerset, expressing his hurt and dismay at the Earl's 'frenzy ... so powdered and mixed with strange streams of unquietness, passion, fury, and insolent pride'.[111]

Even before the Overbury trial, Villiers's status as the new favourite had been acknowledged in a ceremony that reveals the kind of accommodation Queen Anne had worked out with her husband. As George Abbot, the Archbishop of Canterbury, explained, 'James had a fashion, that he would never admit any to nearness about himself but such an one as the Queen should commend unto him.' This way, Anne at least had a voice in the selection of favourites; and 'if the Queen afterwards, being ill-treated, should complain of this dear one', James could reply that she had no grounds to complain because 'you were the party that commended him unto me'. By this time Anne was not eager to promote another 'dear one'. In Abbot's words, she 'knew her husband well; and, having been bitten with Favorites both in England and Scotland, was very shie to adventure upon this request'. But she disliked Somerset and reluctantly agreed to help Abbot and his allies. On 23 April 1615 (appropriately chosen because it was St George's Day), James, ostensibly acting at the queen's behest, knighted George Villiers. James also appointed the young man a Gentleman of the Bedchamber against the objections of Somerset, who wanted him to have the inferior position of Groom.[112] It was not long after this event that the facts of the Overbury murder began to surface and Somerset was removed from the scene, allowing Villiers to dominate the stage as no other Jacobean favourite had done before.

James bestowed innumerable offices and honours on Villiers, the highest formal office being Lord High Admiral of England. Villiers rose inexorably through the ranks of the peerage (Viscount in 1616, Earl in 1617, Marquis in 1619), achieving the exalted status of Duke of Buckingham in 1623.[113] 'He was', in the words of one royalist, 'the greatest subject that England ever had.'[114] Even Buckingham was awed by the king's generosity. He told James, 'you have filled a consuming purse, given me fair houses [and] more land than I am worthy of ... filled my coffers so full with patents of honour, that my shoulders cannot bear more.' In the letters James sent to him, Buckingham found 'expressions of more care than servants have of masters, than physicians have of their patients ... of more tenderness than fathers have to children, of more friendship than between equals, of more affection than between lovers in the best kind, man and wife.'[115]

That James loved Buckingham there can be no doubt. Contemporaries particularly commented on this fact at the outset when it was still news. In 1616 Viscount Fenton reported that 'his Majestie loves' Buckingham 'beyond measure'.[116] When Buckingham was created a Knight of the Garter, William Beecher wryly observed that the king had returned from the installation 'of the knights or rather *his* knight'.[117] 'This is now the man by whom all things do & must pass', wrote Edward Sherburn, '& he far exceeds the former [Somerset] in favor & affection.'[118] In 1617 George Gerrard wrote that 'the king was never more careful, or did more tenderly love any that he hath raised than this Ld. of Buckingham'.[119] The Venetian ambassador observed that Buckingham was able to act on behalf of the king, 'who has given him all his heart, who will not eat, sup or remain an hour without him and considers him his whole joy'.[120]

In 1620 Buckingham, like Somerset before him, married, with the encouragement and assistance of the king. James's ardour, rather than diminishing, now extended itself to Buckingham's wife Kate and the daughter who was later born to them named Mary (otherwise known as Mall).[121] Originally James had thought that Buckingham's marriage might produce 'sweet Bedchamber boys to play me with', but he showed no disappointment in the birth of this daughter.[122] It is touching to see how happily he involved himself in Buckingham's family, constantly sending gifts, visiting Kate when she was sick, making a special fuss over little Mall. At the end of his life, James behaved more solicitously towards Buckingham's family than he had previously towards his own. And having never shown much interest in the company of women, he now delighted in the company of Buckingham's mother, wife and daughter.[123]

In the wider political world, Buckingham's influence over James was at first salutary. Several corrupt officials were driven from office and a programme of financial retrenchment was implemented. A merchant named Lionel Cranfield (later Earl of Middlesex) was employed to reform one department of government after another, eventually assuming the office of Lord Treasurer himself.[124] For a while at least it appeared as if economy and efficiency might finally displace the rampant waste and malfeasance associated with James's regime. None of this could have been accomplished without crucial backing from Buckingham. Yet all this good work was ruined when the favourite turned his attention from domestic affairs to foreign affairs.

Buckingham entered the arena of foreign affairs in conjunction with James's son, Charles; and the issue that brought them together was the proposal to marry Charles to a Spanish princess. It was critically important for Buckingham to befriend Charles since he was the heir to the throne and would soon have the power to perpetuate or terminate Buckingham's career at court. James himself had urged his son and favourite to be friends, but what really cemented the relationship was the adventure the two young men undertook in 1623 in conjunction with the proposed Spanish Match. James was still hoping that this dynastic union would help bring the Thirty Years War to an end and restore his daughter and son-in-law to the Palatinate by peaceful means. By this time, however, Buckingham and Charles were tired of the waiting game the Spanish were playing. In a bold move to force the hand of the Spanish, they made a sudden, secret and highly dangerous trip to Spain to conclude the marriage in person. After six months of exasperating negotiations, they realized the hopelessness of their situation and returned to England empty-handed. Smarting from their failure in Spain, both men were now determined to embark on a war of revenge, a prospect that James viewed with trepidation.

James did not live long after Buckingham and Prince Charles returned from Spain. But he did live long enough to see the two young men drive the reforming Lord Treasurer Cranfield out of office and manoeuvre England into the Thirty Years War. In some ways it was fortunate for James that he died at the beginning of 1625 before the disastrous consequences of these changes in policy could be known. Three years later Buckingham was stabbed to death by a disgruntled sailor who was applauded by a nation groaning under the strains of a costly, inglorious war. And even worse was yet to come. After a brief interlude of peace, in the 1640s Charles stumbled into a deadly civil war with his own subjects that resulted in his execution and, indeed, the temporary abolition of the monarchy.

Today's conventional wisdom absolves James of blame for the troubles that engulfed his son. In many respects, it is true that Charles brought ruin upon himself. He had neither the intellectual gifts nor the political aptitude of his father. He was combative, insensitive, uncompromising and untrustworthy. But there are also many ways in which Charles suffered from the legacy of his father. It was James who bequeathed Buckingham to Charles, and it was he who finally allowed the two young men to embark on war, thereby setting the stage for the military defeats and power struggles that poisoned Charles's relations with his early parliaments. It was he who upset English Puritans by issuing a *Declaration of Sports*, encouraging recreational activities on the sabbath; and it was he who angered Scots Presbyterians by restoring bishops and promulgating the Articles of Perth in an effort to bring the Scottish Kirk into closer conformity with the English.[125] When Charles took up these very same provocative causes and tried to further his father's work, this (along with much else) precipitated a rebellion. On a more abstract level, despite his exalted view of kings, James diminished the reputation of the monarchy. He wrote learned treatises and made lofty speeches proclaiming the divine right of kings, but the aberrations, excesses and corruption of his court eroded that aura of divinity. Modern historians may not understand this, but Charles did. He realized that his father's legacy included a crown of tarnished majesty. He worked diligently to make his court a model of order and virtue, his family a model of conjugal love.[126] Charles was determined to be more manly than his father, too. James had been proud to be styled *Rex Pacificus*, the king of peace; Charles would become *Rex Bellicosus*, a man who provoked fights and hated to back down in the face of opposition. The tragic legacy of the peacemaker, therefore, was that he produced a warmaker.

Chapter 2

Sodomy

King James loved other males, but did he have sex with them? It must
be admitted at the outset that we cannot answer this question with
absolute certainty. There is no incontestable proof, no physical evidence, no DNA. Such evidence as does exist is more circumstantial
than direct. Much of it is hearsay. Nevertheless, there is enough evidence of sufficient credibility to leave little doubt of the fact. To put it
as baldly as possible, except for the obvious absence of offspring, there
is at least as much evidence indicating that James had sex with his
male favourites as there is evidence that he had sex with his wife.
People did not generally talk about James being physically familiar
with his wife in public; they did remark on the fact that he embraced,
hung about the necks of and kissed his favourites in public. These were
not platonic relationships; they were physical. Both James's contemporaries and subsequent historians have made the reasonable inference
that what James did in public is indicative of what he did in private,
especially since he lodged his favourites in his bedchamber. Furthermore, two letters which we will examine in greater detail below – one
written by James to the Earl of Somerset, the other written by the Duke
of Buckingham to James – apparently refer to sexual relations. Finally,
if these were not sexual relationships, then many of James's contemporaries were badly mistaken because, as we shall see in this chapter and
the three that follow, they were under the impression that the king was
having sex with his favourites.

We should not expect to find an abundance of contemporary documents referring to James's sexual relations with his favourites directly,
explicitly and unambiguously. Sexual behaviour had not yet been
clinically dissected and narrowly defined as it would be later. There
was no compulsion to categorize a person as either homosexual or

heterosexual, gay or straight, in a society where these rigid bipolar categories did not yet exist and a person's identity was not yet defined by his or her sexual practices. Furthermore, although James's contemporaries surely talked a great deal about sex, the subject was not as ubiquitous as it is today. Sex was blatant on the stage, but it was rarely mentioned in personal correspondence. Such reticence is especially understandable when the person in question was the king. It may have offended propriety to write about the king's sexual behaviour, and it certainly was dangerous. When slanderous writings came to light, they were destroyed and the authors dealt with harshly. For example, in 1600 a merchant of Edinburgh named Frances Tennent was found guilty of 'false, malicious, undutiful writing and dispersing of slanderous, calumnious, and reproachful letters, to the dishonour of the King's Majesty'. The original sentence called for Tennent's tongue to be cut out, but this part was remitted, and he was simply hanged.[1] This case is only one of several tantalizing instances, suggesting that the best evidence was destroyed.[2]

Although James's contemporaries were less quick to write about sex and did not have modern labels or constructs at their disposal, they were hardly at a loss for words. Indeed, there has been a tendency in recent works to underestimate how many terms, metaphors and analogies people had in the early seventeenth century to discourse about sex between males. In the next chapter we will see how varied the possibilities were. In the present chapter we focus on the single most prominent word or construct that was used to denote sex between males – that is, sodomy. Of course, sodomy was a highly charged term. If we judge only from the formal or official condemnations of it, sodomy was a crime, a sin, a moral outrage of gigantic proportions. It was a religious transgression associated with other forms of religious transgression – atheism, witchcraft, the devil, Sodom and Gomorrah, total moral depravity. English Protestants also tended to associate sodomy with Roman Catholicism, thereby doubly vilifying the enemy. Sodomy was, therefore, something projected onto a horrible alien 'Other' such as monks or foreigners. The satanic figure of the Spanish ambassador, Gondomar, for example, was once referred to as 'the Butte-slave' of Christendom.[3]

The more precise legal definition of sodomy reduced it to more human proportions but still preserved the idea that it was a sin against God and nature. As Sir Edward Coke, the famous jurist of the period, explained in his *Institutes*, sodomy was 'a detestable, and abominable sin, amongst Christians not to be named, committed by carnal knowledge against the ordinance of the Creator, and order of nature'. Given the severity of the crime, sodomy was classified as a felony, and the person convicted of it was to be 'hanged by the neck, untill he ... be dead'.[4]

In his pathbreaking book about *Homosexuality in Renaissance England*, Alan Bray argued that these extreme formulations from the Church and the law made sodomy so heinous, so hideous, so vile and loathsome that ordinary Englishmen who engaged in same-sex erotic behaviour were not likely to recognize themselves as sodomites. Nor were they likely to recognize this unspeakable abomination where it occurred among their neighbours. As a result, although sodomy as an abstraction was categorically condemned on an official level, actual homoerotic activity among males may have persisted undisturbed on the everyday level of ordinary people. In Bray's own words, 'there was no civilisation in the world at that time with as violent an antipathy to homosexuality as that of western Europe', and yet in the mundane world of real people there was 'tacit acceptance'. This was not toleration but, rather, 'a reluctance to recognise homosexual behaviour, a sluggishness in accepting that what was being seen was indeed the fearful sin of sodomy'. Homosexuality may even have been commonplace in certain situations – among servants, between servants and masters, between teachers and students, and in the theatre. In these situations, sex between males was sometimes a prerogative of age and power – older and more powerful men exercising their authority over the younger men in their charge. Unless violence or property rights were involved, such acts rarely led to prosecutions, perhaps not least because the penalty was death by hanging.[5]

Of course, some of the reluctance to recognize and condemn sodomy arose from the fact that Christians were not supposed even to talk about it. Sodomy's status as a sin 'amongst Christians not to be named' was unique and it had several odd consequences. To begin with, it made sodomy a peculiarly difficult sin either to confess or to preach against. It also prevented people from clarifying exactly what they meant by sodomy in their own minds or in church doctrine. There were ambiguities and contradictions inherent in the concept of sodomy dating back at least as far as the coining of the word in the eleventh century, and six intervening centuries of circumscribed speech on the subject had not contributed to greater clarity or precision.[6] (The problem was especially acute when it came to spelling out which specific sex acts constituted sodomy, as we shall see later in this chapter.) Most importantly for our purposes, since people were discouraged from writing or speaking about sodomy in a straightforward fashion, they were forced to use circumlocutions, insinuations and clusters of suggestive associations. We have to be alert to this coded speech, the clues and signs that James's contemporaries employed to imply what they were not supposed to name.

Knowing these limitations in the evidence, then, we can return to our original question: did James have sex with the males he loved? Let us consider them in the order in which they occurred. James's first love was his cousin, Esmé Stuart, Lord d'Aubigny, the Duke of Lennox. Numerous contemporary observers remarked on James's love of Lennox. The king was described as 'carried away' by Lennox, or in his 'possession'.[7] One English agent, Sir Henry Widdrington, described Lennox's influence on the king more graphically. James, he wrote, 'altogether is persuaded and led by him, for he can hardly suffer him out of his presence, and is in such love with him, as in the open sight of the people, oftentimes he will clasp him about the neck with his arms and kiss him'.[8] James's contemporaries suspected that more than kissing occurred, but they expressed these suspicions obliquely. One gets the impression that they were not sure what could occur between men in bed, and did not want to think too hard about the subject. David Moysie is a case in point. This minor Scottish government official wrote in his memoirs that James 'having conceived an inward affection to the said Lord Aubigny, entered in great familiarity and quiet purposes with him'.[9] The words 'great familiarity and quiet purposes' leave the door open to interpretation, but according to David H. Willson, they carried 'a special connotation in the Scots idiom of the time'.[10]

The people who complained most vocally about James's relationship with Lennox were the clergy. Immediately after noting the 'great familiarity and quiet purposes' between James and Lennox, Moysie added that this 'being understood to the ministers of Edinburgh, they cried out continually against atheists and papists that rounded [whispered] continually in the King's ears'.[11] The Presbyterian clergy of Scotland were especially hostile to Lennox because they saw him as an agent of France sent to advance the cause of Roman Catholicism. According to one English informant, 'the ministers of Scotland do daily preach in every borough of that realm against the said Duke'. They were even rumoured to be plotting his death.[12] The dour, straitlaced ministers were appalled by the pleasure-loving French. They accused Lennox and his associates of all kinds of immorality. One minister charged him with 'the introducing of prodigality and vanity in apparel, superfluity in banqueting and delicate cheer, deflowering of dames and virgins, and other fruits of the French court'. Worst of all, Lennox 'laboured to corrupt' the king.[13] Another minister confronted the king in person, imploring him 'to remove evil company from about you', for 'the more sharply vice be rebuked, the better for you'.[14] Similarly, a long list of complaints against Lennox and his associates referred to them as 'licentious libertines' of 'intolerable concupiscence' who used 'diabolical' and 'devilish' means to abuse the king's good nature. Lennox was described in this document as the master not only of the king's chamber but also of his 'person'.[15] David Calderwood, a contemporary who witnessed and recorded much of this history, agreed about the influence of Lennox and the French courtiers on James: 'They fostered him in his bawdy talk, provoked him to the pleasures of the flesh, and all kind of licentiousness.'[16] Meanwhile, an English agent reported that the clergy were given to believe that Lennox 'goes about to draw the King to carnal lust'.[17] An anonymous memorandum likewise reported that 'The ministers... go up and down like masterless hounds, casting into the King's teeth the example of young kings in old time ruled by wicked counsellors, and menace the punishment of Sodom and Gomorrah to be poured over the realm.'[18] The nobles who finally drove Lennox out of Scotland accused the French of working in 'a strange and unaccustomed manner' to 'corrupt the king's Majesty's tender age' by 'giving him all the provocations to dissolute life in manners that was possible'.[19]

In all of this there is no overt mention of sodomy. Indeed, carnal lust is sometimes specifically linked to heterosexuality, as for example in the deflowering of dames and virgins. But the absence of any explicit mention of sodomy should not surprise us since sodomy was a sin among Christians not to be named. Perhaps this is what one observer had in mind when he remarked that the clergy 'cry out upon the King, the Duke, and all the rest with such vehemency that I think you could not will them to speak those things which they leave unspoken'.[20] Moreover, Lennox and his French cohorts were depicted as a thoroughly depraved band, practically a witches' coven, using strange and diabolical methods to corrupt James in every imaginable way. They are the monstrous 'Others', the foreigners who imported 'French fashions and toys' and introduced the king to their alien vices.[21] Some of these vices are named, but others are merely alluded to in that vaguely inclusive phrase 'other fruits of the French court'. We should remember that the French court at this particular time was presided over by Henry III and his notorious minions.[22] The very exaggeration of this caricature is suggestive. It fits the monstrous construction of sodomy that associated the sin with Roman Catholicism, witchcraft, the devil and foreigners. Furthermore, the nature of the king's sexual transgressions is left tantalizingly vague in all these complaints. What is noteworthy, however, is that nowhere is he accused of engaging in illicit sex with women: the evil-doers are all male.[23] Finally, why did the ministers invoke the image of Sodom and Gomorrah? Of course, these cities could have been used to symbolize sinfulness in general, but by this time Sodom was already linked to one sin in particular.

When these suggestive complaints are viewed in light of what we know with greater certainty about James's later relationships, it is reasonable to believe that he had his first sexual experience with Lennox. John Hacket, who was a chaplain under James in England, believed the pattern began with Lennox. In Hacket's words, 'from the time he [James] was 14 years old and no more, that is, when the Lord *Aubigny* came into *Scotland* out of *France* to visit him, even then he began, and with that Noble Personage, to clasp some one *Gratioso* in the Embraces of his great Love'.[24] Modern historians have generally concurred with Hacket's opinion, though daring more than he did to state that James's love found physical expression. David H. Willson, whose biography of James was first published in 1956, wrote that the king's 'interest in beautiful young men ... was first awakened by Lennox', and it did contain 'a sexual element'.[25] Of course, Willson did not approve of what he called James's 'perverted love for Lennox'. He described Lennox's influence over James as 'malignant' and concluded that 'the depraved court of France had made him no fit companion'.[26] In her biography of James published in 1974, Lady Antonia Fraser joined in the opinion that it was Lennox who awakened James's sexuality, and she too found this regrettable. James has been judged too harshly, she wrote, precisely because 'the first object which came his way was a man'. Fraser speculated that 'had an equally attractive woman come his way at the same propitious moment, the homosexual inclinations of King James might never have been aroused'. As it was, however, Fraser concluded that James's love for Lennox was in fact 'consummated, thus setting James firmly in the pattern where he associated sexual love with men'.[27]

Not all historians believe that James and Lennox engaged in sex. Maurice Lee Jr characterized James's relationship with Lennox as a mere 'adolescent's crush'; and S.J. Houston agreed that 'to the unbiased observer, [it] seems like an adolescent crush'.[28] Gordon Donaldson vacillated. At one point he judged that James's relationship with Lennox had 'a physical, but not necessarily gross side to it'. At another point he alleged that although the 'attraction was partly physical', the results were not. Reversing the logic of other historians, Donaldson reasoned that 'the mere fact that the king made so much of his favourites in public suggests that nothing to be ashamed of took place in private'. Since Donaldson, by his own words, considers homosexuality gross and something to be ashamed of, it is not surprising that he preferred to believe James did not engage in it.

After Lennox, in the later 1580s Thomas Fowler reported from Scotland: 'It is thought that this King is too much carried by young men that lies [sic] in his chamber and is [sic] his minions.'[29] One of these was Alexander Lindsey. Lindsey was described by Fowler as 'the King's best beloved minion'.[30] He was described by another observer as 'the King's only minion and conceit' and 'his nightly bed-fellow'.[31] Yet another remarked that Lindsey was envied because he 'was in great favour with his Majesty, and sometimes his bedfellow'.[32] A more formidable companion was George Gordon, the Earl of Huntly. We have already seen how reluctant James was to dissociate himself from Huntly during the Earl's allegedly treasonous dealings with Spain in early 1589. At one point James arrested Huntly but then dined with him and, in Fowler's words, 'yea he kissed him at times to the amazement of many'.[33] A few days later Huntly was freed 'and lodged that night in the King's chamber'.[34] James's wavering, his obvious reluctance to take action against Huntly, was attributed to his excessive affection for the Earl. Fowler called it 'a strange, extraordinary affection', which made James want 'to have him his familiar in court'.[35] Another observer said that the world thought James was 'bewitched' by Huntly.[36] As pressure mounted to take decisive action, the king was described as being in 'a great brangle [confusion], for he had great love to Huntly'.[37]

After James's marriage in 1589 we do not have comparable testimony about the physical closeness between James and his favourites until the spectacular rise of Robert Carr, which began in 1607. The attraction between James and Carr was definitely physical. Carr was a handsome young man about twenty years old, described as 'straight-limbed, well-favourede, strong-shouldered, and smooth-faced'. He enhanced these natural attractions by wearing clothes that appealed to James, having 'changed his tailors and tiremen many times, and all to please the Prince [i.e. James]'. Lord Thomas Howard, who wrote these descriptions, was astonished at Carr's ability to 'win the Prince's affection ... wonderously in a little time'. As Howard observed, James 'leaneth on his arm, pinches his cheek, smoothes his ruffled garment'. Like Lennox, Carr had acquired a smattering of continental sophistication in France, and James tried to further his education by teaching him

Latin.[38] As we saw in the previous chapter, Carr eventually acquired the title of Earl of Somerset and office of Lord Chamberlain. He was the most powerful man in England next to the king.

In the case of Somerset, we at last have something more than circumstantial and hearsay evidence of sex between James and his favourites. It appears in an extraordinary letter written by James himself in 1615. At this point Somerset had been married to Frances Howard, and James was shifting his affection to George Villiers (soon to be Earl, Marquis, then Duke of Buckingham). James thought that his old and new favourites should peacefully coexist, but Somerset fiercely opposed his rising young competitor. James became exasperated with Somerset's insubordinate and increasingly threatening behaviour. He wrote a long letter to Somerset scolding him for his 'furious assaults of me at unseasonable hours' and 'strange frenzy...mixed with strange streams of unquietness, passion, fury, and insolent pride'. He listed his complaints against the Lord Chamberlain, and then he added: 'I leave out of this reckoning your long creeping back and withdrawing yourself from lying in my chamber, notwithstanding my many hundred times earnestly soliciting you to the contrary'.[39]

By complaining about Somerset's 'long creeping back and withdrawing yourself from lying in my chamber', James revealed a great deal. First, these words would appear to make nonsense of Maurice Lee Jr's contention that the king was 'simply not much interested in physical sex at all'.[40] What purpose did James have for 'many hundred times earnestly soliciting' Somerset to lie in his chamber if it was not for sex? What did James want from Somerset that could not have been obtained elsewhere without requiring 'lying in my chamber'? Diehard deniers of James's sexual relations with other men could argue that these words show that Somerset refused to go to bed with James. But then they would have to admit that 'many hundred times' that is what James was asking him to do. It seems more reasonable to infer that Somerset initially won favour by pleasing James sexually but later, probably after his marriage to Frances Howard, withdrew from physical relations. 'Withdrawing', in fact, was the word James used. This is precisely the way the French ambassador Tillières later recounted the story in his memoirs. According to Tillières, at the outset Somerset 'submitted entirely to the whims of his master, and he appeared to have no other passion than to second all his desires'. Later, however, Somerset became arrogant and 'rejected with rudeness the caresses of the king'.[41] Furthermore, James's attitude is worth reflecting upon. When he solicited Somerset hundreds of times to lie with him, he apparently knew what he wanted to do, and he did not think it was unreasonable. He felt no shame or embarrassment. Quite the contrary, he persisted in his overtures. By the same token, James blamed Somerset for refusing his sexual advances; he did not consider himself to blame for making those advances. At the age of forty-eight when he wrote this letter, it is unlikely that James would have unabashedly persisted in making requests of Somerset that he had not previously fulfilled, if not with Somerset, then with one of his earlier male companions. Finally, at the same time Somerset was refusing James's sexual advances, the king was looking for gratification elsewhere – in young Villiers – and there he found it less than one year after writing this letter.

The evidence for James's sexual relations with other males is most plentiful and conclusive with respect to Villiers or, as he was soon known, Buckingham. In the first place, James gave striking displays of his affection for Buckingham in public which gave rise to rumours. Sir Simonds D'Ewes recorded several of these in his diary. On one occasion James was reported to have blurted out spontaneously, 'Becote [By God] George I love thee dearly.' On another occasion, James called for Buckingham, and 'as soone as he came, hee fell upon his necke without anye moore words'. And yet another time, when Buckingham was suffering from a toothache, James implored him not to pull the tooth: '"Whye, man", quoth the king, "What doost thou meane to doe to spoile and kill thy selfe and then becott (swearing Scottishlye) I shall not ioy one good day after." And a little before, hugging him one time verye seriouslye, hee burst foorth, "Begott man, never one loved another moore then I doe thee."'[42]

The language James and Buckingham used to express their love for each other exceeded the normal bounds of male friendship.[43] While there is no overt mention of sex in these expressions, they do seem sexually charged. This was true even of the most famous incident which on the surface has seemed more ethereal than in fact it was. In 1617 the Spanish ambassador reported that James summoned members of his Privy Council and made his position clear. I am 'not God, nor an angel', explained James, 'but a man, a man like any other', though he 'confessed' those whom he loved, he loved more than other men. In particular, said James, 'he loved the Earl of Buckingham more than all other men and more than all who were there present'. This was not a 'defect', said James, and he should not be blamed for it because Jesus Christ had done the same thing. Just as 'Christ had his John', so 'he had his George'.[44] What James was looking for here was a parallel to demonstrate that even though he was a veritable God upon earth

('For Kings are not onely GODS Lieutenants upon earth…but even by GOD himselfe they are called Gods'), still he had his human side and human needs.[45] It was not at all unusual to stress Christ's humanness. Renaissance artists routinely did this by depicting the genitals of the baby Jesus. It was not therefore a great stretch for James to assert Christ's need for the love of another man. But did James have more in mind? Was he hinting at a physical relationship between Christ and St John, between himself and Buckingham? To some this idea may seem outlandish. Maurice Lee Jr even took James's use of this analogy as proof that he was not sexually involved with Buckingham. 'It is really impossible', Lee wrote, 'to suppose that if James had engaged in physical sexual relations with his George, he would have drawn this parallel.'[46] What Lee apparently did not know, however, is that this parallel was previously used expressly to denote a sexual relationship between men. The most notable recent case in James's time was Christopher Marlowe, who was reputed to have said not only that Christ and St John were 'bedfellows' but more specifically that 'he used him as the sinners of Sodoma'.[47] With this knowledge in mind, Rictor Norton even considers it 'possible that James was consciously using a queer tradition'.[48]

James's analogies, to put it mildly, were not always perfectly drawn. This is even more evident and suggestive in the letters he wrote to Buckingham treating him as a son and wife. James used such language even after the Duke's marriage, oddly incorporating himself into this expanded family. In one especially revealing letter, James addressed Buckingham as 'My only sweet and dear child'. Elsewhere in this same letter he combined the role of father with that of husband. He referred to Buckingham as 'my sweet child and wife' and himself as 'dear dad and husband'. He thought of himself as married to Buckingham and expressly wished for a 'new marriage ever to be kept hereafter'. He declared that he would 'rather live banished in any part of the earth with you than live a sorrowful widow's life without you'.[49] By thinking of himself as both father and husband to Buckingham, James made himself both parent and grandparent to the Duke's little daughter Mall, of whom he was especially fond. While these may be mere figures of speech, they suggest that James did not view Buckingham's marriage to a woman as an impediment to his own continuing spousal relations with his favourite. The modern critic Jonathan Goldberg has gone even further, alleging that such language showed that the king's 'relationship with Buckingham's family was particularly incestuous, and James seems to have indulged fantasies in which his favorite's children were his own'.[50]

James often used terms of endearment towards Buckingham, calling him 'Sweet heart', for example.[51] His most sustained expressions of love, however, occurred in a series of letters he wrote to Buckingham during the trip to Spain in 1623.[52] These can justifiably be called 'love letters'. As Goldberg explained, 'These are the letters of lovers separated, chafing at the time it takes for letters to arrive, lamenting absence, longing for reunion.'[53] James had not wanted Charles and Buckingham to leave. Just before their departure, he told Buckingham, 'I rode this afternoon a great way in the park without speaking to anybody and the tears trickling down my cheeks, as now they do that I can scarcely see to write.' To make their separation more bearable, James said he would keep reminding himself of Buckingham's faults, yet he knew this technique would not work, 'for as it proceeds from love so it cannot but end in love'. As another way of consoling himself, James asked Buckingham to provide him with a picture.[54] Buckingham may have had to take this miniature from his wife to give it to James, who subsequently wore it 'in a blue ribbon under my waistcoat next my heart'.[55] At a particularly depressing moment during the Spanish adventure, James worried that he might not live to see his son and favourite return. 'Alas', he wrote, 'I now repent me sore that ever I suffered you to go away. I care for match nor nothing, so I may once have you in my arms again. God grant it! God grant it! God grant it! Amen, amen, amen.' In a later letter, in a similar vein, James wrote, 'my extreme longing will kill me'.[56]

James had learned to deal with emotionally stressful situations by writing poetry, and he composed a poem at this time wishing for the safe return of Buckingham and Charles. The two young men are referred to in the poem as Jack and Tom (Tom Badger being a nickname the king sometimes used for Buckingham). James represented himself in this poem in the self-deprecating guise of the ancient god Pan, an ugly, bearded man with the horns, tail and hooves of a goat. The theme of the poem is that the idyllic land of Arcadia has turned gloomy and fallow. It will not flourish again until the return of Jack 'And Tom [who] was to our royal Pan / The chiefest swain and truest man'.[57] The word 'swain' was well chosen for its ambiguity. It could mean a servant, attendant, young man, rustic labourer, shepherd, or – as the *Oxford English Dictionary* explains – 'a lover, wooer, sweetheart, esp. in pastoral poetry'.[58]

Buckingham was not as disconsolate as James, but his letters from Spain did express his affection and longing to return. In these letters Buckingham routinely signed himself 'your Majesty's humble slave and dog, Steenie'. Just as James had dubbed one of his favourites in Scotland Sandie, so did he give Buckingham the name of Steenie, apparently because of his resemblance to the angelic-faced St Stephen.[59] Business dominated the letters written jointly by Buckingham and Charles, but the Duke sometimes added a few lines of his own and occasionally wrote an altogether separate letter in which he adopted a noticeably more personal tone. In one postscript he described himself as a man who 'threatens you, that when he once gets hold of your bed-post again, never to quit it'. Another time, he told James he was so excited about the prospect of returning to England, 'I cannot now think of giving thanks for friend, wife, or child; my thoughts are only bent on having my dear Dad and Master's legs soon in my arms.' And in yet another short note to the king, Buckingham confided that 'never none longed more to be in the arms of his Mistress'.[60] Thus Buckingham, too, used family metaphors to express his affection, but not quite the same that James had used. He shared the metaphor of father and son, but he refrained from describing himself as husband or wife to James, preferring instead to compare James to a 'Mistress'.

Buckingham's expressed eagerness to have the king's 'legs soon in my arms' and get 'hold of your bed-post again' is highly suggestive. Fortunately, in another letter Buckingham was much less ambiguous about which side of the bed-post he had in mind. In this undated letter Buckingham, recalling a visit James made to Farnham Castle in the summer of 1615, wrote that he had been debating with himself 'whether you loved me now...better than at the time which I shall never forget at Farnham, where the bed's head could not be found between the master and his dog'.[61] Anyone who has ever had a dog for a pet knows that a dog instinctively lies on the floor around its master's bed unless the master is kind enough to allow it to get onto bed. The unmistakable meaning of this letter is that Buckingham got into bed with James. Roger Lockyer, who has written the definitive biography of Buckingham, has no doubt that this letter shows that Buckingham 'played the trump card which ensured his victory over Somerset'. Buckingham won in this contest of favourites by 'giving in to the King's importunity' or, more precisely, 'by giving himself to James'.[62]

If James did have sex with his favourites and did, as we know, have sexual intercourse with the queen until at least 1606, then modern readers might be tempted to ask, was James bisexual rather than homosexual? Of course the question is ill put. It attempts to apply modern labels to a pre-modern situation. Furthermore, these labels imply an exclusivity, an either/or choice between sex with males or sex with females that some scholars believe did not exist before the eighteenth century. In James's day, these scholars claim, a man could have sex with both men and women because there were no straitjacket, binary constructs and labels to force him to choose exclusively between one or the other. The question is useful, however, because it does force us to recognize James's sexual preference. Unlike most kings who have extramarital affairs, James had male favourites, not female mistresses. In fact, James might never have married if it had not been for the pragmatic need to produce heirs. His lifelong preference, which he expressed in his choice of sexual partners outside marriage, was for sex with males.[63]

What did James think he was doing? Of course, if homosexuality was not distinguished from heterosexuality as it is today, if a man's sexual relations with a woman were not assumed to preclude sexual relations with other males, he had no reason to think about the matter at all. Furthermore, even if contemporary categories of thought had not given James this latitude, his position as king did. He may simply have taken it for granted that he could enter into sexual relations with younger men in his court as a prerogative of his age and power.[64] All of James's favourites were necessarily subordinate to him. He was the royal master; they were his royal servants. He exercised his power over them; he made them what they were. As he tartly reminded Somerset, 'Remember that all your being, except your breathing and soul, is from me.'[65] The court was also like a household or school in which the king again served as the ruling patriarch. James in fact likened himself to a 'great Schoole-master of the whole land'.[66] Although he rebelled against his old tutor, George Buchanan, on issues of Church and State, he never shook off the experience of his early education and continued to model his own behaviour on Buchanan's. One is reminded of how James liked to tutor his favourites, teaching Protestantism to Lennox and Latin to Somerset, for example. In the case of Buckingham, as Sir Henry Wotton explained, 'the king had taken, by certain glances... such liking of his person, that he resolved to make him a master-piece; and to mould him, as it were, Platonically to his own idea.'[67] The Earl of Clarendon wrote that James 'took much delight in indoctrinating his young unexperienced favourite, who, he knew, would be always looked upon as the workmanship of his own hands'.[68] Buckingham himself called James 'my purveyor, my good-fellow, my physician, my maker, my friend, my father, my all'.[69] Sex with subordinates was a pre-rogative of patriarchy, and James was the chief patriarch of the whole realm. Viewed this way, James may have thought nothing at all about the sexual activities he engaged in with his favourites. It was something to which he was entitled as king, simply one of the prerogatives that went with the Crown.

But how is this possible in light of the uncompromising attitude James took elsewhere towards sodomy? In his *Basilikon Doron*, the book of advice he wrote to instruct Prince Henry on how to be a good king, James listed sodomy as one of the 'horrible crimes that yee are bound in conscience never to forgive'.[70] How, then, could he forgive it in himself? As we saw earlier, Alan Bray suggests that a man who had sex with other men in James's day may simply have failed to make the connection between what he was doing and what he knew as the monstrous abomination called sodomy. There was no pressure on a seventeenth-century Englishman to define his sexual identity, and even less pressure to recognize his own practices as those of a hideous sodomite. Although Bray does not discuss James, he may be the prime example from early modern Britain of precisely this phenomenon.[71] James could have been perfectly earnest in condemning sodomy while simultaneously engaging in what we today would call homosexual behaviour. When James invited Somerset into his bed or succeeded in getting Buckingham into bed, there is no reason to believe that he recognized what he was doing as that 'detestable, and abominable sin, amongst Christians not to be named'.

Indeed, it is a good question whether James in fact committed sodomy. That depends on what he did when he went to bed with his favourites. Can we get beyond this euphemism and be more specific about what James and his favourites did in bed? There is just one possible clue, and it suggests masturbation. Buckingham and James enjoyed double meanings and wordplay in their letters. Perhaps Buckingham had a double meaning in mind when he wrote the following thanks to James for creating him a Duke: 'There is this difference betwixt that noble hand and heart, one may surfeit by the one, but not by the other, and sooner by yours than his own.'[72] Whether or not these specific words refer to masturbation, it is entirely possible that James and his favourites refrained from anal intercourse. And if they did not engage in anal intercourse, it is arguable that they did not engage in sodomy. Sir Edward Coke was among those who thought that it was necessary to prove that penetration had occurred in order to establish a case of sodomy. In his own words, there had to be ejaculation or *emissio seminis*, but also 'there must be *penetratio*, that is, *res in re*'.[73] For Coke, therefore (if we set aside bestiality), sodomy meant two men

having anal intercourse to the point of ejaculation. This legal definition was exceedingly narrow. It specified only one sex act between
men, anal intercourse, and excluded all other genital sex acts – masturbation, oral sex and intracrural or intrafemoral intercourse. Men
rubbing their bodies together or mutually masturbating were not committing sodomy. Of course, we cannot know if James made this distinction in his own mind. He was a notorious hypocrite where swearing
and drinking were concerned; he could simply have been the same
where sodomy was concerned. Or he could simply have felt that, as an
absolute monarch, the normal rules did not apply to him. But if he
refrained from anal intercourse, there is no necessary reason why the
accusation of sodomy should even have crossed his mind.

The public mind was another matter, however. Whether or not
James was technically free of sodomy, his relations with his favourites
raised suspicions in the public at large. These people had no way of
knowing precisely what James and his favourites did in bed, and in any
case there is no reason to think that they drew the fine distinctions
that lawyers such as Coke did. It is true that there were very few legal
prosecutions against sodomy in early Stuart England, and it may be
true that there was 'tacit acceptance' of sex between males in many
households and schools. But people did take notice of James and his
favourites. One of these was Sir Simonds D'Ewes, who recorded in his
diary in 1622 that a good friend came to visit, and 'things I discussed
with him that weere secrett as of the sinne of sodomye, how frequente
it was in this wicked cittye, and if God did not provide some wonder-
full blessing against it, wee could not but expect some horrible punishment for it; especially it being as wee had probable cause to feare, a
sinne in the prince [i.e. James].'[74]

Chapter **3**

Base Fellows

As we have seen, Alan Bray and other early historians of homosexuality following in his footsteps argued that sodomy was viewed as a monstrous sin in seventeenth-century England, so monstrous in fact that the English would have had difficulty equating it with anything they observed in the ordinary lives of themselves or their neighbours. It comes as a surprise, therefore, to find Sir Simonds D'Ewes using the word 'sodomy' in connection with James. D'Ewes considers sodomy a sin, and expects God to inflict 'some horrible punishment' for this form of wickedness. But he is thinking in terms of ordinary human beings, not witches, papists or atheists. Moreover, although sodomy was a sin 'amongst Christians not to be named', D'Ewes does name it and does recognize it when he sees it, even in his king (although he discreetly refers to James in the abstract or impersonally as 'the prince', as if it would be too disrespectful or dangerous to express himself more directly). Finally, what we find in D'Ewes's diary is not tacit acceptance, but explicit disapproval.[1]

The example of D'Ewes suggests, then, that there were multiple ways of thinking about sodomy in his day, multiple ways of discoursing about the subject. As Gregory Bredbeck explains, alongside the 'demonized rhetoric of sodomy' emphasized by Bray there simultaneously existed a more down-to-earth rhetoric. In Bredbeck's words, 'the monstrous buggerers in the law and the church become, in the broadsides and pamphlets, very real, fleshly people with very erect penises'.[2] Bray's description of sodomy was too monolithic and horrific. It did not take into account the diversity of opinions on the subject, ranging from the tight-lipped taboo of high culture to the bawdy parody of low culture. Sodomy was not invisible. It could be reduced to human terms, recognized and criticized. James's intimate relations with other males, far from being tacitly accepted, provoked negative, even hostile, reactions. Of course, James was a special case that tended to draw opinion out into the open because power, reputation, the nation's very concept of itself were at stake. That very exceptionality, however, brought views to the surface that might otherwise be hidden from us. The reactions to James, therefore, provide the modern historian with a unique window into the minds of his contemporaries. By examining their reactions, we discover not only that the unmentionable could be mentioned, but also that there were different ways of discoursing about sex between males in the early seventeenth century.

One had to be exceedingly careful in criticizing the king. In other countries, D'Ewes claimed, 'men talked familiarly' about James's sexuality, but in England it was a 'secrett' matter that was best discussed in private.[3] Similarly, when Thomas Howard reported on James's interest in young men at court, he could only go so far. 'I could relate and offer some other remarks on these matters', Howard explained, 'but Silence and Discretion should be linked together like dog and bitch, for of them is [en]gendred Security.'[4] We will, therefore, find James's critics adopting various codes and voices through which to express their criticism, some more or less direct than others, some more or less dangerous.

Some critics continued in the manner of D'Ewes to employ the formal discourse of sodomy. Not surprisingly, this was most typical of the clergy in England, just as it had been of the clergy in Scotland. For example, in 1622 D'Ewes remarked upon a sermon 'that Doctor White had preached at Court upon Remember Lots wife'. References to Lot and his wife fleeing from the city of Sodom while God destroyed it should not always be assumed to be references to sodomy. But given the context in which this sermon was delivered, the preacher was playing with fire. D'Ewes reported that some people thought White would be imprisoned for preaching on this subject at court 'exceeding plainelye and boldelye'.[5]

The most well-known minister in England who used the language of sodomy to attack James was Thomas Scott, whose sermons turned into such hostile polemics that he was forced to flee to the continent for safety. There was no mistaking the meaning in Scott's biblical allusions. Knowing that James liked to compare himself to Solomon for his wisdom, Scott published a pamphlet in 1622 lecturing James on the nature of true wisdom. 'To eate, drinke, daunce, and rise up to play with the Sodomites; to abuse our bodies woorse then beasts in sinnes not to be named, there needs no other wisedome then to follow the sway of our owne corrupt concupiscence; a beast can do this,' Scott wrote. The truly wise man, on the other hand, would flee from Sodom. This, said Scott, 'requires wisedome, and this is to be thus *wise*'.[6] Scott's imagery of men abusing their bodies 'woorse then beasts' is reminiscent of the complaint we saw in an earlier chapter that it had become the fashion at court to 'wallow in beastly delights'. Beastliness suggested sodomy. But Scott did not rely on subtle suggestion. He spelled out his meaning quite clearly here. If James were a truly wise king, he would 'flee from Sodom' and eschew the company of 'Sodomites' who practise 'sinnes not to be named'.

In 1623 Scott published another work containing several thinly veiled criticisms of James. Again Scott intentionally used the example of Solomon as a good judge and ruler. Good judges, wrote Scott, 'ought to beware, that not onely themselves be innocent, but that their *Favourites*...their Shadowes, their Followers I mean, be cleane-hearted, and cleane-handed too'. A good judge will 'let Vertue and Justice be onely his *Favourites*'. Justice, Scott explained, is incompatible with sin. Therefore, if justice makes '*sinne* either a wife, or a childe, or a friend, or a servant, or a favorite and companion at bed, or at board, or on the bench; this could not be done without a *Diabolicall contract, a Sodomiticall mixture*, a sinne against Nature'.[7]

Scott was unusual in referring to sodomy so explicitly. This paucity of direct references to sodomy was more a reflection of the prohibition against mentioning it, however, than a reliable measure of the level of awareness. Forbidden to name sodomy, people found other ways to discourse about James's sexual relations with his favourites, code words and allusions that communicated the meaning without employing the taboo word. One alternative word was Ganymede, a word that came not from the biblical tradition but from classical mythology. Ganymede was the name of a beautiful young Trojan boy whom Jupiter, the king of the gods, fell in love with. Jupiter abducted Ganymede and carried him off to Mount Olympus where he became Jupiter's lover and served as cup-bearer to the gods.[8] As Bruce Smith observed, 'the story of Jupiter and Ganymede was the best known myth of homoerotic desire in early modern England', and Ganymede was 'the commonest epithet in early modern English for a homosexual male'. Another recent author calls Ganymede 'the archetypal gay toyboy'.[9] In keeping with the myth, a person referred to as a Ganymede was a younger, passive male who submitted to an older, more powerful male.[10] Innumerable examples can be found of English poets and playwrights using the term.[11] In one play dating from 1610, an older male character tells his boyish page, 'I will turne *Jupiter*, hate the whole sexe of women, and onely embrace thee my *Ganimede.*'[12] Since Buckingham got his entrance at court serving as cup-bearer to James, the myth of Jupiter and Ganymede so perfectly fit his case that 'it is hard to decide where art leaves off and life begins'.[13]

Comparisons of Buckingham to Ganymede can be found in the poetry of the day, especially one anonymous underground poem dating from 1623 entitled 'The Warre of the Gods.'[14] In this poem Jupiter, representing James, is portrayed as a ruler who has fallen under the spell of his 'white fayst boy' and 'upstart love / That makes him drunke with Neckter'. The other gods are not happy with this state of affairs, and they set out to 'destroy' this overmighty boy and 'remove' Jupiter. The goddess of love, Venus, is so upset with the influence of this upstart love that she thinks someone should 'scurdge his arse'. Diana and one thousand maids will not be satisfied until Jupiter 'Be quite displaced / Or else disgraced / For lovinge so 'gainst nature'. The avenging furies threaten 'To have him burnd / That thus hath turnd / Loves pleasures arse wise'. Meanwhile Jupiter, oblivious to this rebellion, 'with Ganimede lyes playing'. The references to arses and loving against nature indicate that what the other gods are revolting against is sodomy. Perhaps they also resented Ganymede's unnatural political power, but the issue appears to be his sexual, not his political, influence. Ganymede must be destroyed, not because he wields too much power, but because under his influence Jupiter's 'marrowe so had wasted'. On the other hand, the hostility of the gods is not confined to Ganymede alone but also extends to Jupiter, where it definitely does have political implications. The gods think their ruler should be disgraced, displaced or removed. Sodomy in the ruler could thus generate political disaffection to the point of open rebellion. That is a surprisingly radical notion in Jacobean England.

People wishing to criticize James's homosexuality were not limited to the formal discourse of sodomy or the classical analogy of Ganymede. There were other ways of denoting and disparaging James's love of other males. For example, in 1608 the French ambassador reported that James was ridiculed on the English stage. Among other things, James was depicted as cursing to heaven because a bird had been stolen from him.[15] The meaning of this scene has never been explained. One recent author, who apparently thinks the bird is merely an allusion to James's passion for hunting, cites this episode as proof that James was *not* criticized for his sexual behaviour.[16] The truth is just the opposite. For anyone familiar with James's personal history, the real symbolism is not hard to decipher: the only 'bird' that was ever taken away from James was his phoenix, the Duke of Lennox. Since the playwright knew this story and expected the audience to know the story well enough to get the joke on James, this episode suggests how widely the king's love of other males was known and made the butt of humour.

After a government crackdown, critical references to James became more circumspect, but they continued in a number of arenas. The poet George Wither was imprisoned twice in James's reign for works that were considered offensive. No evidence survives to tell us which parts of his works were deemed offensive, but in one of these he complained about princes who were wronged 'by those they love'. These false friends rob his coffers, 'yea (worser farre they use *Him*)'. According to one correspondent of the time, Wither was imprisoned in the Marshalsea for this work, 'the king threatening to pare his whelp's claws'.[17] The other work that landed Wither in jail complained about 'base fellowes (whom I must confesse, I cannot find words able to expresse)'. Yet Wither did find words to express his contempt for these base fellows; he called them 'great mens *darlings*', the 'absolutest *Gallants* in this land'.[18] Here, too, the code could have been broken by contemporaries. As we shall see later, the most infamous pamphlet of James's reign referred to the king's 'darling sinne'; and D'Ewes used the same phrase, 'darling sin', when ascribing sodomy to Sir Francis Bacon.[19]

Critics of James's homosexuality had to disguise their identity or their intent sufficiently to escape prosecution. Otherwise, they might end up living in exile like Scott or imprisoned like Wither – or worse. James spent years, for example, trying to track down the author of a book entitled *Corona Regia*, which was published in 1615. This book appeared on the surface to be a lengthy praise of James written by Isaac Casaubon, an eminent scholar who had taken up residence at the English court under James's patronage. In reality, however, it was a scandalous parody written by someone else, probably a German named Kaspar Schoppe (otherwise known as Scioppius). Whoever the author was, he ridiculed James in numerous ways, not least for his sexual attachment to male favourites. James, we are told, did not indiscriminately choose men of all ages but, rather, those men who were 'fresh blooming and lovely'. Indeed, James exceeded many examples from ancient history in his advancement of beautiful young men at court. There follows a list of such youths who were catapulted to the highest honours by James because of their good looks. The greatest of these were Somerset and another 'adolescent of incomparable form',

Buckingham, who was 'introduced by the Queen herself into your bed-room'. Among James's most remarkable achievements, the author claimed, was his ability 'to mix pleasure with religion'. Like Christ, who had said that the little children should be allowed to come to him, James summoned the most handsome boys. The strong implication here is that James was a pederast. No wonder he tried to track down the author of *Corona Regia*! He did succeed in having Schoppe located and beaten up, but apparently for another of his writings. As late as 1623 James was still looking for the elusive author of *Corona Regia*.[20]

There may have been other books of this sort published on the continent which have not survived.[21] In 1618 the Spanish ambassador Gondomar reported that James, who was still greatly upset over *Corona Regia*, had been informed that there were plans to publish another book entitled *Jacobeidas* which would treat him 'much more ignominiously'.[22] James was right to worry that such publications damaged his reputation. Sir Simonds D'Ewes records in his diary that he spent an evening talking with friends about *Corona Regia* and two other books which were 'terrible and whollye against the King himself, accusing him of athisme, sodomye etc.'[23]

One way of avoiding reprisals was to criticize James only by implication, that is by writing about a different king who had ruled badly by entrusting too much power to homosexual favourites. The obvious example from earlier English history was Edward II (1307–27). The late historian John Boswell called Edward 'the last overtly homosexual monarch of the Middle Ages'.[24] Early in Edward's reign, the barons forced him to banish his sexual favourite, Piers Gaveston. When Gaveston returned to England, open rebellion broke out and Gaveston was killed. Later in his reign Edward ruled with another favourite, Hugh Despenser, until at last both Edward and Despenser were executed after a rebellion led by the queen. Historians routinely omit the details of Edward's murder, but it was widely believed that a red-hot poker was forced up his rectum (in a gruesome parody of sodomy). The parallel between Gaveston and James's first love in Scotland, Lennox, is really quite remarkable. In both cases the nobility took possession of the king and forced him to banish the favourite, though in Lennox's case there was no question of his returning because he died shortly after fleeing. Joseph Cady has shown that the story of Edward and Gaveston was used in France in the 1580s to criticize Henry III and his minions. It appears that 'the Edward II–Gaveston story functioned widely in informed European Renaissance culture as a symbol of male homosexual attraction'.[25] Certainly this was the case in England.

Interest in Edward II's reign increased in England immediately preceding and during James's reign. The playwright Christopher Marlowe completed a play entitled *Edward II* shortly before his death in 1593. It has been suggested that he was prompted to write about the subject because of the similar events observable in Scotland a few years earlier. Marlowe's Gaveston resembles Lennox – a 'sly inveigling Frenchman' who 'came lately out of France'. He has a proclivity for frivolous pastimes, 'wanton poets' and 'pleasant wits'. King Edward is described as 'bewitched' by Gaveston and 'love-sick for his minion'. The nobility resent the power and status accorded Gaveston. The queen resents the loss of her husband's affection. Gaveston, she says, 'hath robbed me of his love'. She wishes she had died on her wedding day rather than suffer Edward's rejection. 'In vain I look for love at Edward's hand', she explains, because his 'eyes are fixed on none but Gaveston.' Indeed, 'never doated Jove on Ganymede So much as he on cursed Gaveston.'[26] Marlowe's *Edward II* was printed two or three times before and twice (in 1612 and 1622) after James's accession.[27] Similarly, Michael Drayton kept revising and publishing his historic poem 'Piers Gaveston' (in 1593, 1596, 1605 and 1619); and Sir Francis Hubert's poem on 'The Deplorable Life and Death of Edward the Second' was revived in 1628 just before Buckingham's death.[28]

Playwrights and poets were not the only ones thinking about the example of Edward II during these years. As Gregory Bredbeck observed, 'a number of anecdotal summaries of the king's life, all written between 1590 and 1650, were widely reprinted'.[29] One of these anecdotal summaries was apparently written by Elizabeth Cary, Viscountess Falkland. She was well acquainted with the Jacobean court because her husband occupied several important positions there. In her historical sketch of Edward II's reign, she refers to Gaveston as 'the Ganymede' of Edward's affections. She interprets Edward's reign as a moral tale. It is, she says, one error for a king 'to be dissolute or wantonly', but a king who shares power with his sexual favourite invites his own destruction by committing this 'second error, which makes more kings than one in the self-same kingdom'. Did Lady Falkland have King James in mind when she wrote about King Edward? She certainly intended her story to have contemporary relevance. As she explained to her readers, 'the histories of these times are plentifully stored' with 'examples of this nature', but she chose the reign of Edward II to hold up as 'a perfect mirror, wherein ensuing kings may see how full of danger and hazard it is, for one man's love, to sell the affections and peace of the whole kingdom'.[30]

Historical analogies were not just scholarly exercises. They were political statements, and in the case of Edward II they betrayed disaffection not only towards the notorious favourite but also towards the king who loved and advanced him to power. James himself appreciated the implications inherent in any comparison between his own reign and Edward II's, as the case of Sir Henry Yelverton demonstrates. In 1621 Yelverton appeared in the House of Lords to defend himself in a matter involving Buckingham. Yelverton was carried away by the moment, and in the words of one contemporary, he 'rashly, or madly rather, fell in[to] most bitter speeches against Lord Buckinghame, charging him with assuming regal power, and admonishing him to read the articles of Hugh Spencer's conviction in the time of Edward II, thus wonderfully offending His Majesty as pointing at him as another Edward II'.[31] The well-known correspondent John Chamberlain, too, reported that Yelverton was 'comparing these times in some sort to those of Edward the second wherein the Spensers did so tirannise and domineer'. Chamberlain added that Prince Charles intervened and 'asked leave of the Lords to interrupt him [Yelverton] as not able to indure his fathers government to be so paralelled [*sic*] and scandalised'.[32]

Another historic parallel to James and Buckingham was the Roman Emperor Tiberius and his favourite Sejanus. As early as 1610 it had been suggested in Parliament that anyone who fostered division between the king and his subjects 'did either look for a Tiberius or Sejanus'.[33] James's contemporaries were familiar with these figures through their reading of the major Roman historians. In the *Annals* of Tacitus, readers would have found the story of Sejanus, who early in his career 'had sold his person to Apicius, a rich debauchee'. Later 'he won the heart of Tiberius'. With the Emperor's unqualified support, Sejanus proceeded to destroy anyone who might conceivably oppose him. He established, says Tacitus, a 'grinding despotism'. Meanwhile Tiberius, at the urging of Sejanus, retired from Rome to Capri, where he indulged in a life of debauchery. Eventually Tiberius did turn against Sejanus, and the royal favourite was killed, although the Emperor continued his life of debauchery on Capri.[34] In *The Lives of the Twelve Caesars*, the Roman historian Suetonius provided more detail about the kinds of licentiousness Tiberius enjoyed. For example, Tiberius had a room at Capri which was 'dedicated to the most arcane lusts'. In this room Tiberius gathered 'girls and perverts...who invented monstrous feats of lubricity, and defiled one another before him, interlaced in series of threes'. Much more outrageous than this voyeurism, Tiberius 'taught children of the most tender years, whom he called his *little fishes*, to play between his legs while he was in the bath'. The children who 'had not yet been weaned, he set at fellatio'. Finally, Suetonius tells us that one day Tiberius 'was so smitten by the beauty of a boy...that he was hardly able to wait till the rites were over before taking him aside and abusing him as well as his brother'.[35]

The story of the Emperor Tiberius and his overmighty favourite, Sejanus, haunted James from the very outset of his reign. In 1603, the year James succeeded to the English throne, Ben Jonson staged a new play in London entitled *Sejanus*. The timing was incredibly bad. Jonson was summoned before the Privy Council to defend himself against a charge of treason. Unfortunately, we have no way of knowing the exact nature of this charge. One recent commentator suggests that Jonson's play got him into trouble because he appeared to express sympathy for Sir Walter Raleigh, whose famous trial had just occurred.[36] This makes more sense than earlier commentators who thought that Jonson was alluding to the abortive rebellion and execution of the Earl of Essex at the end of Elizabeth's reign. In either case, there is no reason to believe that Jonson's *Sejanus*, unlike Marlowe's *Edward II*, was originally inspired by the episode between James and Lennox in Scotland. Jonson was not averse to taking risks. He was impertinent enough to co-author *Eastward Ho* in 1605, a play that ridiculed the Scots and earned Jonson a brief imprisonment.[37] And in 1621 he produced a masque, *The Gypsies Metamorphosed*, in which Buckingham himself was appropriately cast as the leader of a band of thieving gypsies.[38] But to produce *Sejanus* in the very year of James's accession as an overt commentary on James's relationship with Lennox would have been practically suicidal. Besides, one of the paradoxes in the history of literary patronage is the fact that Jonson lived in the home of Lennox's second son and namesake for several years. Indeed, when he published *Sejanus* in 1616, he added a letter of gratitude 'To the no less noble by virtue than blood: Esmé L[ord] Aubigny.'[39] On the other hand, no matter what Jonson's original intention, the summons before the Privy Council (and perhaps subsequent events at James's court) taught him that the public was capable of finding subversive meanings in his work. Consequently, when Jonson published *Sejanus* for the public to read in 1605 and 1616, he took great pains to assure readers that he had taken his story strictly from classical sources, particularly Tacitus and Suetonius.[40]

Nevertheless, the longer James ruled, the more uncanny Jonson's selection of Sejanus seemed. 'Actual history overtook staged history,' as Jonathan Goldberg observed.[41] Thus Jonson's *Sejanus* 'became subsequently, and in ways that Jonson could not possibly have intended, a metaphor for the career of George Villiers, duke of Buckingham'.[42] In Jonson's play, Sejanus, like Buckingham, began his career as a 'serving boy'. He 'prostituted his abused body' to a rich Roman and became 'the noted pathic [i.e. passive homosexual] of the time.' When Tiberius retreated to Capri, Jonson described him as a 'monster' who was 'forfeited to vice', an Emperor 'only in his lusts'. Among other things, Tiberius forced boys and girls to perform 'strange and new-commented lusts / For which wise nature hath not left a name'. Tiberius had 'become the ward / To his own vassal, a stale catamite'.[43] (A catamite was a boy in a pederastic relationship.) One is reminded that in 1623 Buckingham complained that his expressions toward James had been unfavourably interpreted as 'crude catamite words'.[44]

While Jonson's play acquired new meaning in the light of subsequent events, the French ambassador to England in the 1620s, Count Leveneur de Tillières, drew his own direct and lurid comparisons between the court of the Emperor Tiberius and the court of King James. Previous French ambassadors had been shocked by the tenor of James's court, even though they were acquainted with court minions from the history of their own country. Beaumont wrote that he felt 'as if the times of Henry III were before my eyes'. Just as Henry had his notorious minions, Beaumont observed, 'there are favourites here – as then'.[45] Desmarets sympathized with Queen Anne whom he described as 'an able woman' who realized 'that her husband cannot exist without a minion'.[46] But Tillières clearly exceeded these predecessors in the degree to which he was appalled by James's behaviour. He told his superiors in France that he had 'too much modesty' to report everything in graphic detail, and he struggled to find 'the most decent expressions' to inform them without giving offence.

What Tillières did include in his dispatches certainly makes us wish that he had been less inhibited. He reported that James was 'as good for nothing as possible, suffers himself to be walked in leading-strings like a child, is lost in pleasures, and buried for the greater part of his time in wine'. He described James as 'a King devoted to his own nothingness...plunging himself deeper into vice of every kind'. He referred to James's 'infamous licentiousness', his 'filthy and scandalous life'. Tillières reported that Buckingham 'advised the King to remain at Newmarket, where he leads a life to which past nor present times present no parallel'. But then a parallel did occur to the ambassador. James, he wrote, 'has made a journey to Newmarket, as a certain other sovereign once did to Capri'.[47] Tillières did not write in a vacuum. The stories he reported back to France were the stories he found circulating in London. Perhaps the most disturbing of these involved James's conduct with little children. There was to begin with James's interest in Buckingham's daughter Mall. According to Buckingham's modern biographer, the French ambassador 'reported that the King was enchanted by little Mall, whom he constantly fondled and embraced'.[48] However, the actual words used by the ambassador put the matter in a different light: 'It is true a report exists that his [James's] passion extends itself to Buckingham's wife, and to a little child which he passionately loves, tenderly embraces, and will always have in his sight; but I believe, that these and a thousand other particulars which one cannot venture to speak out, and which no man can believe who has not seen them, proceed simply from his friendship for Buckingham.'[49] Of course, we today would like very much to know those 'thousand other particulars which one cannot venture to speak out'. What exactly did James reportedly do that 'no man can believe who has not seen them'? Unfortunately, since the 'particulars' of these stories have not been conveyed to us, we are left with only the unsavory flavour. It is possible that there was no basis in fact for these stories. Active imaginations undoubtedly coloured what the French ambassador heard. Nevertheless, whether true or false, the stories did circulate, and James's image suffered accordingly.[50]

Not all the particulars have been lost, however. Tillières provided the details of one story involving a young niece of Buckingham; and if this story is at all typical, the rumours about James were very ugly indeed. As Tillières described this episode, James 'took a little girl, the niece of the Marquis, aged nine or ten years, felt her all that she would bear, then touched Buckingham's nose, and in the same place kissed him several times'.[51] What this story seems to be saying is that James touched this little girl in a very personal area of her body, then transmitted the smell from his hands to Buckingham's nose, then kissed the favourite's nose. The sexual implications of the story hardly require amplification. James was converting Buckingham into a feminized sexual object and expressing his attraction with a kiss. But is this story true? Tillières was not an eyewitness to the event he described, but he thought he had it on good authority. 'Had I not received this account from trustworthy persons', he wrote, 'I should have considered it impossible.'[52] We can never know whether the content of this story is true. Again, all that we can know for certain from Tillières' account of this alleged incident is that shocking stories involving James's sexual activities were circulating among his subjects, inflicting irreparable harm on his reputation. Given what else we know about James's behaviour, the story recounted here is not unbelievable. But if it was false, then James's love of Buckingham was being exaggerated and twisted by its observers into something ugly and perverse, converting him in this instance into a child molester.

In 1620 Tillières reported that the political situation in England was badly deteriorating: 'Audacious language, offensive pictures, calumnious pamphlets, these usual forerunners of civil war are common here.'[53] Criticism of James reached its zenith in the early 1620s, when he refused to engage England in the Thirty Years War on the Protestant side, hoping instead to affect the outcome of the war simply by agreeing to the Spanish Match between his son, Prince Charles, and the Spanish Infanta. Many English were exasperated with James's unrealistic negotiations and his aversion to war. Some combined their criticism of his foreign policy with criticism of his sexual morality.

One of the most outspoken attacks on James during this period was entitled *Tom Tell Troath*, which circulated around London in manuscript in 1622.[54] The anonymous author of this tract ridiculed James's love of peace as little more than cowardice. He charged that 'your Majesties courses are not onely inscrutable, but diametrically opposite to poore mans understanding'. More importantly for our purposes, in several places he raised the subject of James's sexuality. As the author explained to James, under normal circumstances, 'It is a part of supremacy, not to have your darling sinne layd open'. But these were not normal circumstances, and it was now time to acknowledge 'that which all the world sees'. At a later point in *Tom Tell Troath*, in a clever allusion to Somerset and Buckingham, the author told James that he could not achieve his dream of uniting Scotland and England merely 'by choosing the minion alternatively out of each nation'. Finally, towards the end of *Tom Tell Troath*, the author described a supposedly hypothetical king of a Protestant nation who obviously represented James. This Protestant king can 'make himselfe absolute and dissolute', knowing that his loyal Protestant subjects will endure anything without rebelling. He can be 'notoriously wicked in his person'. He can 'stampe vice with his example'. He can 'have lords spirituall for his mates, lords temporall for his eunuchs, and whom hee will for his incubus'. He can 'kisse his minions without shame, and make his grooms his companions without danger'. The only real danger this king need worry about is that his sexual favourites will gain great power over him because 'they are acquainted with his secret sins'. These companions are compared to a pack of dogs or 'sweete beagles'. James was fond of dogs, called the Earl of Salisbury his 'little beagle' and received letters from Buckingham signed 'your humble slave and dog'. In Jacobean England furthermore the word 'dog' could be used to denote a sodomite, or male prostitute.[55] Watching the king's subjects submit to this degenerate regime, the anonymous author of *Tom Tell Troath* lamented, we may 'cry with Tiberius, "O people prepared for servitude!"'[56]

Alexander Leighton, another advocate of war frustrated by James's inaction, published *Speculum Belli Sacri* in 1624. Leighton was subtler than the author of *Tom Tell Troath*, but he still made unmistakeable allusions to James's dependence on his sexual favourites. In an obvious reference to Buckingham, Leighton expressed the opinion that 'a King should have many Councellours, and that he should never commit the helme of affaires, unto one mans hand'. From the many historical examples of this phenomenon, wrote Leighton, 'take this one of Sejanus, whom Tiberius advanced'. Perhaps to strengthen the analogy with James's court, Leighton described Tiberius as a 'drunkard'. It is not enough to employ several counsellors; they must also be good counsellors. History again provides many examples of kings who relied on bad counsellors. One was Edward II, who followed 'the Counsell of the *Spensers* and *Gaveston*'. These analogies between James / Buckingham, Tiberius / Sejanus and Edward II / Gaveston are familiar to us by now. To these familiar analogies, Leighton added: 'One instance more in *James* the third, King of Scottes' who ruined his promise by 'addicting himselfe to the beastly humors of a few base fellowes'.[57]

James III was our James's great-great-grandfather who had ruled Scotland a century earlier. Although the facts are not clear, a legend had developed around the memory of James III to the effect that he fell under the influence of young counsellors or base-born familiars who became his favourites. According to the legend, a rebellion in 1482 culminated in the hanging of these men. It was, therefore, uncanny when the Ruthven Raid under James VI drove the Duke of Lennox out of Scotland exactly one hundred years later. History appeared to be repeating itself. The example of James III was used as a precedent by people unhappy with James VI. The minister Andrew Melville was forced to flee Scotland after drawing this analogy in a sermon in 1583. By the same token, knowledge of conditions under James VI tended to influence the way people looked back upon the distant reign of

James III, exaggerating the importance of his favourites in light of more recent experience with royal favourites.[58]

Judging from all the foregoing examples, it is apparent that people in Jacobean England were quite capable of recognizing and criticizing sexual relations between males. Some dared to use the vocabulary of sodomy despite its prohibition, but sodomy was not the only word or concept available to them. There were other ways of discoursing about or encoding sex between males, and we are capable of interpreting these allusions or decoding these past messages. Sir Simonds D'Ewes, who wrote in one place about James's 'sodomy', wrote more obliquely in another place about 'his vices and deviations'.[59] As we have seen from other authors, male lovers could be referred to as 'base fellows' or 'darlings' who engaged in 'the darling sin'. The classical relationship of Jupiter to Ganymede could be used as an analogy. And finally there were historical precedents (Edward II and Gaveston, Tiberius and Sejanus) that could be employed. James's contemporaries, therefore, were not as limited in their capacity to talk and write and think about sexual relations between males as is sometimes assumed.

The more fundamental question is whether these alternative words imply alternative constructs. Are all these other vocabularies simply circumlocutions, alternative ways of alluding to the same thing, denoting sodomy without actually naming it? No matter how oblique the allusion, the underlying construct may still have been sodomy. Even if that were the case, the very act of using these alternative expressions tended to modify the construct, make it seem less unspeakably monstrous, reduce it to human proportions, bring it down to earth, and rob it of its supernatural associations. Put another way, even if people were still talking indirectly about sodomy, because they were forced to talk about it in other terms, they were reconceptualizing it in the process. Some readers will continue to believe that the monstrous spectre of sodomy only appears here in another guise. Other readers will see these alternative modes of discourse as evidence that the construct of sodomy was already changing into the construct of homosexuality before 1700. Still other readers will see a distinctly different construct underlying all these alternative terms and analogies – the construct of pederasty. From Ganymede, through *Corona Regia*, to Sejanus, the implication was not simply that James had sex with other men, but that he had sex with decidedly young men or boys. As we shall explain more fully in the concluding chapter, this way of viewing James is consistent with the theory that prior to 1700 sexual relationships between males were age-differentiated or pederastic.

None of these alternative words and historical analogies implied toleration or even Bray's 'tacit acceptance'. All of them were ways of expressing active disapproval of James and his favourties. What lay behind this disapproval? To be sure, as Michel Foucault would have emphasized, power was an issue. James's favourites were resented because they wielded too much power. Buckingham under James, like Gaveston under Edward II or Sejanus under Tiberius, was attacked by people who resented his power, especially his power to dispose of lucrative court offices. One verse of the period that was ostensibly about Sejanus was really about Buckingham. It complained that he had the power to bestow whichever office 'doth befalle' and 'he is soundlye paide for all'.[60] James's favourites were also resented because they were social upstarts. According to the Venetian ambassador, Members of Parliament in 1621 'aimed at depriving him [James] of his principal favourites, who are usually the butts for accusations and universally hated, more especially because they are not intended by nature to rule, and many cannot endure to have a favourite over them, who is usually of low or scarcely noble birth'.[61]

No doubt criticism of James and his favourites was, in part, politically motivated. Money and power were at stake. Allegations of sexual impropriety were one easy means to discredit James, his favourites and his policies. For those allegations to have any effect, however, there had to be a shared community of opinion about what constituted an impropriety. When authors hinted broadly about James's 'darling sin' or alleged that he loved 'against nature', they assumed their readers would be able to decode these words, and they assumed their readers would be repelled. Despite what many modern commentators influenced by Foucault claim, the central issue in Marlowe's *Edward II* is not power; it is sex. As one scholar has correctly observed, the revolt against Edward arises from 'the barons' intensely phobic reaction to homosexual relations...a culturally-conditioned nausea'.[62] Likewise, insinuations that James and his favourites engaged in sex were not just convenient and unfounded accusations deployed for purely political purposes. The phenomenon was real, and the prejudice against it was real, a prejudice grounded as much in conventional and Christian morality as it was in politics.

This potent combination of politics and prejudice helps to illuminate specific events in James's reign. Take, for example, the impeachment of the Lord Chancellor, Sir Francis Bacon, in the Parliament of 1621.[63] Why did Parliament turn against Bacon seemingly out of the blue and revive an ancient constitutional procedure to ruin him? There are good objective explanations. Bacon was widely disliked. He was associated with monopolies which were under attack at this time and the Duke of Buckingham whom it was too dangerous to attack directly. Regarding the specific charges against him, it was true that he had accepted gifts which could be construed as bribes, though it is also true that these did not appear to affect the judgments he rendered in the Court of Chancery. Yet, having said all this, the sudden and violent turn against Bacon in Parliament is still puzzling. No less an authority than Conrad Russell observed in his history of the period that it is not clear where the initiative came from, and 'the case remains remarkably obscure'.[64]

At least part of the animosity towards Bacon may have arisen from the suspicion that he was sexually involved with his male servants. John Aubrey, the seventeenth-century antiquarian, has passed along the gossip to us that Bacon was a pederast whose servants were his 'Ganimeds'.[65] Sir Simonds D'Ewes was more expansive on the subject. Of all Bacon's 'stupendous and great' vices, D'Ewes singled out this one as his 'most abominable and darling sin'. Although Bacon was humbled by his fall from power, D'Ewes alleged that the former Lord Chancellor did 'not relinquish the practice of this most horrible and secret sin of sodomy, keeping still one Godrick a very effeminate-faced youth to be his catamite and bedfellow'. Since Bacon was no longer a man to be feared, 'men generally after his fall began to discourse of that his unnatural crime, which he had practised many years'. According to D'Ewes, there was even talk of bringing Bacon to trial and executing him for 'that horrible villainy'.[66] This admittedly is gossip. One recent scholar, attempting to defend the Lord Chancellor's reputation, asserted that 'there is no evidence that Bacon was a practicing homosexual', which is technically true if we discount hearsay testimony and circumstantial evidence such as Bacon's sterile relationship with his wife, who married again less than two weeks after his death.[67] By contrast, Bacon's most recent biographer concluded that 'the likelihood that he may have been a homosexual is undeniable'.[68] Whatever the truth may be about Bacon, what remains indisputable is the fact that these rumours concerning him did circulate among his contemporaries; and given the context in 1621, that may help explain why Parliament turned against him so suddenly and mercilessly. He was fined, imprisoned at the king's pleasure, barred from ever holding office or sitting in Parliament again, and forbidden to come within twelve miles of the court. The Earl of Southampton suggested that banishment would not have been too harsh a sentence.[69]

Southampton, who was one of Bacon's most zealous prosecutors, soon got a dose of his own medicine. The Earl was arrested by order of the Crown and kept under house confinement for almost a month. Why? Again one does not have to look hard for objective explanations. Long excluded from any major office under James, Southampton had become one of the leaders of a 'patriot' faction in Parliament that repeatedly thwarted the king and his ministers. His adherents were rumoured to be meeting at his house to plan each day's strategy in Parliament. Most recently Southampton had personally offended the powerful Duke of Buckingham and lobbied for England to enter the Thirty Years War against the wishes of the king.[70] No doubt James and Buckingham thought that Southampton needed to be shown who was in charge. But here, too, the reasons may go deeper.

Although Southampton had been belatedly admitted to the Privy Council in 1619, he refused to be a team player on that body. Upon his arrest in 1621 he was accused of having expressed disrespect for the Council 'there being so many boys and base fellows there'.[71] Historians have not paid much attention to those words. What do they mean? Both 'boys' and 'base fellows' had sexual connotations. A boy could be an ingle or catamite – that is, the passive sexual partner of an older man. The same connotation may have been implied in contemporary verses that lampooned James and his 'merry boys'.[72] The word 'boys' carried extra sexual connotations, too, because of the boys who played female roles on the stage. As Lisa Jardine explains, the 'womanish boy', the 'wanton female boy', the 'beardless boy' on the stage served as an alluring 'object of *male* erotic attention'.[73] The other phrase attributed to Southampton – 'base fellows' – is not new to us. We have already seen George Wither refer to 'base fellowes (whom I must confesse, I cannot find words able to expresse)' and Alexander Leighton refer to 'the beastly humors of a few base fellowes' associated with James III.[74] If Southampton really complained that the Council contained too many 'boys and base fellows', therefore, he was alluding to more than their youthfulness and lack of nobility. Of course, it is possible that Southampton did not make this complaint, but the fact remains that he was accused of making it, quizzed by the government for allegedly making it, which is interesting in itself.

The Parliament of 1621 is also the one in which Sir Henry Yelverton raised the comparison with Edward II's reign; and the Earl of Southampton was one of the peers who urged that Yelverton be given an opportunity to explain himself. There is a theme running through all these events. The spectre of a sodomitical court loomed over the events of 1621. Lawrence Stone wrote that with the accession of James to the throne, the English court 'became a haunt of homosexuals'.[75] Today's scholars might prefer to call it a homosexual subculture. Whatever we call it, James's contemporaries recognized the phenomenon, too; and they were alarmed by it. At another time under different circumstances, this spectre may not have seemed so threatening. What heightened apprehension in the 1620s was the combination of a sodomitical court with the outbreak of the Thirty Years War, James's unwillingness to join the fight and the effeminacy of his favourites. The Earl of Southampton may seem an unlikely figure to oppose this trend since he himself has sometimes been romantically linked with Shakespeare. But far more important was the fact that Southampton enjoyed a reputation as a military man.[76] In Elizabeth's reign, he had accompanied the second Earl of Essex in campaigns against Spain and Ireland. In James's reign, he and the third Earl of Essex continued to embody the ideal that the nobility should provide political and military leadership.[77] By the 1620s both men were major advocates of England's entry into the Thirty Years War. When Southampton was arrested, the Venetian ambassador observed that the Earl 'was considered here to be almost the only person capable of commanding an army'. As the ambassador viewed it, the struggle over the nation's foreign policy pitted a pacifist king against people like Southampton who advocated 'virile, spontaneous and forceful action'.[78] Another contemporary referred to this policy as 'vigorous and masculine'.[79]

Southampton stood for war and virility. By contrast, James was associated in the public mind with peace and effeminacy. The king's foreign policy and personal conduct contributed to a growing apprehension that Englishmen were becoming effeminized by peace and ease; and then, to make matters worse, he refused to lead them into war, thereby effectively denying them the best arena in which to test and affirm their own manhood. This chain of events would not have been set in motion if male homosexuality had not yet been linked in the public mind to effeminacy, as some historians of homosexuality maintain; but it was.

Chapter 4

Effeminacy and Peace

Effeminacy is a controversial topic in the history of homosexuality. Several historians have alleged, first, that the word 'effeminate' had a different meaning in the seventeenth century and, secondly, that it was not particularly linked to male homosexuality.[1] Let us begin with the question of meaning. It is true that the meanings of words were not as fixed in the seventeenth century as they later became. The word 'effeminate' was sometimes applied to a man in two ways that would seem odd to us today. It could be used to suggest that a man was excessively attracted to women; it could also be used to suggest that a man was wanton or oversexed (as women were presumed to be). Both of these meanings suggest heterosexuality – indeed robust heterosexuality – not homosexuality.[2] By emphasizing these two alternative meanings of the word, some scholars have managed to create the impression that effeminacy could not have been associated with male homosexuality in the seventeenth century. Jonathan Goldberg, for example, wrote that 'effeminacy was more easily associated with, and was a charge more often made about, men who displayed excessive attention to women than taken as an indication of same-sex attraction'.[3]

If effeminacy was not associated with male homosexuality in the seventeenth century, then when exactly is that connection supposed to have been made? Some scholars answer that it was established in the eighteenth century. Bruce Smith, for example, asserted: 'The first evidence we have of homosexual acts being associated with *our* sense of effeminacy does not occur until the eighteenth century.'[4] Alan Sinfield delayed the connection until even later. He located it at the time of the Oscar Wilde trials, that is, at the very end of the nineteenth century. Prior to that, according to Sinfield, 'it is unsafe to interpret effeminacy as defining of, or as a signal of, same-sex passion.' What did effeminacy connote before the Wilde trials? 'Mostly', claims Sinfield echoing scholars like Smith, 'it meant being emotional and spending too much time with women.'[5]

The truth is, although the word 'effeminate' was sometimes used in Jacobean England to imply that a man was excessively attracted to the company of women or sexually wanton, in a great many more cases it meant precisely what it means today. The first English dictionary was not published until 1656, but prior to that time there were other printed works, especially bilingual or foreign-language dictionaries, which do disclose the meanings of English words; and these clearly show that the predominant meaning of effeminate was 'womanish' in the sense of soft, weak or tender.[6] In the next two chapters we will encounter numerous authors who alleged that the nation was becoming effeminate because its men were becoming weak (not wanton, oversexed or unduly attracted to women). The propagandist Thomas Scott was typical when he complained in 1623: 'Some sinnes which we practise are too abhord to find matches, and therfore I must speake plainly. Are men ashamed to resemble women both in their apparaile, & in their effeminate fooleries?'[7] Scott's complaint is that men are looking and acting like women, not that they are lusting after women or spending too much time with them.

Anthony Fletcher, who has written one of the most extensive studies of gender in early modern England, came to the right conclusion about effeminacy. 'Contemporary usages of the term effeminate', he explained, 'refer to unmanly weakness, softness, delicacy, self-indulgence.' Despite his better understanding of what effeminacy meant, Fletcher made the mistake of repeating the conventional wisdom when it came to the relationship between effeminacy and homosexuality: 'There was not yet any association of homosexual behaviour with effeminate activity. Sodomy was not yet a vice understood in gendered terms.'[8] No matter how often this supposed truism is repeated, however, it is not true. Sodomy *was* understood in gendered terms. Of course, effeminacy was not yet interpreted as an infallible sign or definite marker, indicating in all cases that a man was a sodomite. In Jacobean England men were often accused of becoming effeminate, and that did not necessarily mean they were suspected of becoming sodomitical. Effeminacy did not always imply sodomy. But sodomy did imply effeminacy.

Sodomy was *always* understood in gendered terms. Dating as far back as the invention of the word 'sodomy' in the Middle Ages, it had been linked to effeminacy. Mark Jordan has shown that medieval condemnations of sodomy by Roman Catholic theologians were invariably predicated on the assumption that it made men surrender their masculine superiority, become soft and revert to 'an essentialized feminine'. For this reason, he writes, effeminacy was 'regularly alleged as a consequence of same-sex copulation'.[9] This stigma would have been especially attached to the male who took the 'female' role, that is the passive or receptive role, the penetrated rather than the penetrator. Martin Duberman emphasizes that this was the case in age-structured or pederastic relationships which involved a passive boy and an active adult man.[10] Always somewhere lurking in the background of prejudice against sex between males there was a revulsion against – or rather a fear of – effeminacy.

In the late sixteenth and early seventeenth centuries, the fear that effeminacy led to sodomy and became a sign of sodomy was spelled out in anti-theatrical tracts which argued that when boys dressed in women's clothing on the stage, it threatened to make the actors themselves more feminine; it even threatened to effeminize male observers in the audience. One possible consequence of this effeminization would be sodomy. Philip Stubbes made the connection between effeminacy and sodomy in his *Anatomie of Abuses* (1583). Stubbes defined effeminacy in the modern sense. He believed that when males dressed in fine clothing, it 'transnatureth them, makinge them weake, tender, and infirme'. Englishmen used to be strong, but 'now through our fond toyes and nice inventions, we have brought our selves into suche pusillanimitie, and effeminat condition, as we may seeme rather nice dames, and yonge gyrles, than puissante agents, or manlie men, as our Forefathers have bene'. Stubbes was most horrified by the spectacle of boys who pretended to be women on the stage. As a result of their cross-dressed, sexually provocative behaviour – their 'wanton gestures', 'wanton eyes', kissing, bussing, winking, glancing – Stubbes concluded that afterwards 'every mate sorts to his mate, every one bringes another homeward of their way verye friendly, and in their secret conclaves (covertly) they play the *Sodomit[e]s*, or worse'.[11] In *Th' Overthrow of Stage-Playes* (1599), John Rainolds issued a similar warning against attractive young boys dressing as women on the stage. 'Sodomy, homosexuality, sadistic flagellation and male marriage were all, he thought, likely consequences of such behavior,' as Marjorie Garber recently observed.[12]

The connection between effeminacy and sodomy was spelled out again in a well-known work of the early Stuart period, William Prynne's *Histriomastix* (1633). Effeminacy was a theme throughout Prynne's thousand-page diatribe against the theatre, and in one place he devoted a section of nearly forty pages to it. Prynne specifically charged that when male actors play female roles, it 'instigates' both actors and spectators to commit 'that unnaturall Sodomiticall sinne...not once to be named, much lesse then practiced among Christians'. Prynne cited numerous examples to support his charge, including 'Jupiter and his Ganymedes'. Ancient sodomites, wrote Prynne, clothed their Ganymedes 'in womans attire, whose virilities they did oft-times dissect, to make them more effeminate, transforming them as neere as might be into women, both in apparell, gesture, speech, [and] behaviour'.[13]

Stubbes, Rainolds and Prynne were all ardent Protestants or Puritans. Writing against the backdrop of Europe's religious wars, they saw Roman Catholicism in general and Spain in particular as the enemy.[14] Their writings constituted a partisan call to arms, especially for Stubbes and Prynne, who were writing during frustrating intervals when England was not involved in the fighting. Consequently, when these polemicists raised the twin spectres of effeminacy and sodomy, they were doing it to advance a cause. It was part of their discursive strategy to foster a more martial spirit and shame Englishmen into joining the fight. We cannot be certain, therefore, how much of this was mere rhetorical pose and how much genuine alarm. What we can know, however, is that these authors already defined effeminacy as we do and linked it to male homosexuality. More importantly, unless they had the bizarre intention of writing works that would be unintelligible to their readers, they must have assumed that the public thought in the same terms.

These anti-theatrical tracts were published shortly before and after James's reign. What was happening during his reign?[15] Again, England was at peace, and again, the alarms were raised over effeminacy and sodomy. The alarms were more widespread and insistent this time, however, not only because James obdurately refused to be drawn into the Thirty Years War, but also – and perhaps more disturbingly – because he allowed blatantly effeminate favourites who were his known lovers to dominate the court. Under James there was more graphic evidence than there had been under Elizabeth or would be under Charles that England was truly slipping into effeminacy and sodomy. In this context, effeminacy became a more highly charged political term. It was a code word. It was a way of alluding to James's sexual behaviour without attacking it head-on.

Fear of effeminization fuelled the demand for war. People who wanted to reverse James's pacifist foreign policy and purge his court of effeminate favourites fought back by reasserting the opposite values of manliness and militarism. At the court these malcontents were urged on by Queen Anne; in the nation at large they were urged on by polemicists such as Scott. In the end, they all got what they were asking for: war.

The problem began with the court. The kind of refined behaviour and ostentatious clothing that flourished at the typical Renaissance court threatened conventional views of manliness. Castiglione had wrestled with this dilemma in his classic work on *The Courtier*. He reminded his readers that 'the principal and true profession of the Courtier must be that of arms'. A courtier should be 'exceedingly fierce, harsh, and always among the first', while 'avoiding ostentation'. Granted that the ideal courtier should be endowed with a certain beauty and grace, his aspect should still 'have something manly about it'. In particular, the courtier's face should not be 'so soft and feminine as many attempt to have who not only curl their hair and pluck their eyebrows, but preen themselves in all those ways that the most wanton and dissolute women in the world adopt'. Courtiers who behaved in this womanly manner, Castiglione thought, should be driven not only from the court 'but from the society of all noble men'.[16] Although Castiglione did not address it directly, the problem was compounded when courtiers and their monarchs were further suspected of sodomy. As the modern scholar Randolph Trumbach observed, 'whenever homosexual behavior surfaced at the royal courts, from the 12th to the early 17th centuries, it was accompanied by what contemporaries viewed as markedly effeminate behavior'.[17]

The Jacobean court crossed the line drawn by Castiglione. It combined the twin fears of effeminacy and sodomy; and it thereby jeopardized manliness. James himself had not been unaware of this danger. Like Castiglione, in his own *Basilikon Doron*, he had advised his son, 'specially eschew to be effeminate in your cloathes, in perfuming, preening, or such like'.[18] Yet this is precisely what James himself preferred in the young men around him at court. Thomas Howard explained to a friend that the king 'doth admire good fashion in cloaths'. To succeed at court, Howard advised, 'I would wish you to be well trimmed; get a new jerkin well bordered, and not too short; the King saith, he liketh a flowing garment; be sure it be not all of one sort, but diversely colourd, the collar falling somewhat down, and your ruff well stiffend and bushy.' These might seem superficial matters, but Howard knew from experience that they were not: 'We have lately had many gallants who failed in their suits, for want of due observance of these matters. The King is nicely heedfull of such points, and dwelleth on good looks and handsome accoutrements.' Howard specifically cited the example of Robert Carr, who 'hath changed his tailors and tiremen many times, and all to please the Prince'. Physical appearance was the new key to success. Learning, wit and discretion were 'not the thinges men live by now a days'. Howard asked sarcastically, 'You are not young, you are not handsome, you are not finely [attired]; and yet will you come to courte, and thinke to be well favoured?'[19]

Both James's detractors and his defenders agree that his choice of favourites was based on their good looks. Howard described Somerset as 'straight-limbed, well-favourede, strong-shoulderd, and smooth-faced'.[20] A smooth face was particularly important. As the French ambassador Tillières explained, James did not choose his favourites based on any reasons of state, but rather 'the king simply allowed himself to be carried away by his passion'. And nothing appealed more to James's passion than a man who was still in the flower or prime of his youth with a beautiful face (*beau de visage*), preferably without facial hair. The way Tillières told the story, Somerset originally possessed these attributes, but he fell from favour when he lost his good looks and acquired an older man's beard (*beaucoup de barbe*).[21] Although Tillières did not spell it out, he implied that James was attracted to young androgynous men. Francis Osborne, one of James's harshest critics writing later in the century, was more explicit. Osborne wrote that 'handsomness' was the chief criterion for a favourite, and James loved these men 'as if he had mistaken their Sex, and thought them Ladies'. 'Which', Osborne added, 'I have seene *Somerset* and *Buckingham* labour to resemble, in the effeminatenesse of their dressings.'[22]

The word 'handsome' should not confuse readers; it had not yet acquired its modern connotation of 'rugged handsomeness'. In Renaissance England, the word 'handsome' meant comely, seemly, well trimmed or pleasing to the eye.[23] It was perfectly natural, therefore, to describe a man as both handsome and effeminate. For example, in 1564 when Elizabeth inquired whether Mary Queen of Scots might become romantically interested in Lord Darnley, the Scottish emissary recorded in his memoirs: 'My answer was that no woman of spirit would make choice of such a man, who more resembled a woman than a man. For he was handsome, beardless, and lady-faced.'[24] The emissary turned out to be mistaken about Mary's interest in Darnley, but his words survive to show us that Osborne was simply speaking the idiom of his day when he applied the word 'handsome' to a man who was so effeminate that he looked more like a woman than a man.

Returning to the Duke of Buckingham, we see other authors describing him as both handsome and effeminate. For example, Sir Simonds D'Ewes attended a social function in 1621 where his prime objective seems to have been to spend at least half an hour observing the fascinating young favourite. D'Ewes, who habitually referred to Buckingham as 'the beloved', described him as follows: 'I saw everything in him full of delicacy and handsome features; yea his hands and face seemed to me especially effeminate and curious.'[25] Similarly, Bishop Godfrey Goodman, one of James's supporters, observed that Buckingham 'had a very lovely complexion; he was the handsomest bodied man of England; his limbs so well compacted, and his conversation so pleasing, and of so sweet a disposition'.[26] John Hacket, who was one of James's chaplains and later became a bishop in the reign of Charles I, described Buckingham as a perfect physical specimen: 'From the Nails of his Fingers, nay, from the Sole of his Foot, to the Crown of his Head, there was no Blemish in him.' In Hacket's opinion, Buckingham's 'Looks, every Motion, every Bending of his Body was admirable'.[27] The royalist Sir John Oglander wrote that Buckingham 'was one of the handsomest men in the whole world'.[28]

When the great royalist historian the Earl of Clarendon looked back on the Jacobean age from his vantage point later in the century, he acknowledged James's weakness for attractive young men. James was an impressively learned man, wrote Clarendon, 'yet, of all wise men living, he was the most delighted and taken with handsome persons and with fine clothes'. In the particular case of Buckingham, 'his first introduction into favour was purely from the handsomeness of his person'. Indeed, Clarendon allowed that no man in any country had ever risen 'in so short a time, to so much greatness of honour, fame and fortune, upon no other advantage or recommendation than of the beauty and gracefulness and becomingness of his person'.[29] Opponents of Buckingham, observing his 'Delicacy and Beauty', the 'Decency and Grace of his Motion', were tempted to underestimate him. In Clarendon's words, these adversaries 'intended by some affront to discountenance his Effeminacy, till they perceived he had masked under it so terrible a courage as would safely protect all his Sweetnesses'. Clarendon hastens in this passage to defend Buckingham's character and portray him as courageous, but in the process he admits that the Duke's adversaries misjudged him precisely because of 'his Effeminacy'.[30]

Two of Buckingham's most outstanding physical assets were his long slender legs and his childlike face. These attractive physical qualities are very evident in what is probably the most well-known painting of

Buckingham. The historian Caroline Bingham described Buckingham in this painting as follows:

> Although he had been born in 1592 he still looks like an adolescent youth. He is clean-shaven and apparently perfectly smooth-faced. His dark hair is combed back from his forehead, and curls forward around his temples and ears.... The red velvet and white satin panels of the mantle separate to display his legs clad in white stockings. They are extraordinarily long and slender, like the legs of a thoroughbred colt.[31]

Buckingham accentuated his feminine appearance by wearing elaborate clothing. As Malcolm Smuts observed, portraits of the Duke sometimes made him look 'like an ivory-faced doll stuffed inside huge concoctions of diamond-studded fabric'.[32]

On at least two occasions, Buckingham's opponents tried to topple him by fighting fire with fire, enticing the king with an alluring alternative of their own choosing. The Howard family tried this strategy in 1618 with Sir William Monson; and the Earl of Middlesex tried it in 1622 with his brother-in-law, Sir Arthur Brett. Both failed. When Middlesex put forward Brett, it was described as an attempt 'to set up a new ydoll' or 'Darling'. It looked briefly as if it might succeed when Brett was knighted and appointed Groom of the Bedchamber, but he failed to advance any further in the king's favour.[33] Monson made even less headway, although we have an illuminating description of his effort written by John Chamberlain, the assiduous court observer. The way Chamberlain described it, Monson's promoters had not been very subtle. James quickly tired of the game and sent a message informing Monson 'that the King did not like of his forwardnes, and presenting himself continually about him'. James ordered Monson to stay away from the royal presence, and preferably to leave the court altogether. Chamberlain's letter discloses that Monson was not the only young aspirant hanging around the court at this time because, upon hearing of the king's anger, 'most of our younge court-gallants are vanisht like mushrooms'. Monson's rebuff had a chilling effect on his promoters. In Chamberlain's words: 'This was a shrewde reprimende and crosse-blow to some who (they say) made account to raise and recover theyre fortunes by setting up this new idoll, and took great paines in tricking and prancking him up, besides washing his face every day with posset-curd.'[34] (Posset-curd was a sweet drink made out of milk that was curdled by adding beer or ale.) Chamberlain makes the Howards look rather foolish, but the fact is Buckingham had won the king's affections in precisely the same way only a few years earlier in his capacity as James's cup-bearer, though his face apparently did not require the daily application of posset-curd.

The behaviour at James's court was drastically contrary to the values of his more zealous or puritan subjects. Take, for example, Thomas Beard, a minister and author of *The Theatre of Gods Judgements* (1597). In 1612, when he was a schoolmaster and Oliver Cromwell was one of his students, Beard published a second edition of his book which contained a chapter entitled 'Of effeminate persons, Sodomites, and other such like monsters'. The chapter begins by describing an Assyrian king who 'was so lascivious and effeminate, that to the end to set forth his beautie, hee shamed not to paint his face with ointments, and to attire his bodie with the habites and ornaments of women'.[35] It was not just puritan divines who disapproved of courtly effeminacy, however. In 1613 Barnaby Rich published a pamphlet condemning courtiers who 'creepe' into the king's opinion. To win the king's favour, wrote Rich, these aspirants 'will so curle their haire, picke their browes and so metamorphise themselves aswell in their atire as in their demeanures, that they rather make show to be demy-harlots, then men'.[36]

Rich was an outsider expressing a low-brow revulsion at the role played by high fashion at court. The Earl of Arundel was an insider who used a fashion statement of his own to register his disgust. In contrast to the ostentatious and upstart Buckingham, Arundel adopted an austere style of clothing that harkened back to the days of Elizabeth and affirmed his descent from the genuine old nobility. Many years later, in a play performed on the eve of the Civil War, there was a character modelled on Arundel who dressed in sombre clothing. Others in the play mocked this character who looked like the ghost of the Earl of Leicester 'in Leisters habit'. But he defended himself on the grounds that 'these things were worne when men of honor flourish'd, that tam'd the wealth of Spaine', and it 'was never a good time since those cloaths went out of fashion'. The name of this character based on Arundel was – Master Manley.[37]

James's favourites were effeminate. But what about James himself? It would have been possible to think of James as still dominant, still 'masculine', as opposed to his submissive favourites. James's critics, however, began to question his own manliness. The problem was not just that James allowed effeminate favourites to dominate the court; his foreign policy, too, seemed effete. In reality, it had been an act of great statesmanship for James to terminate the protracted and expensive war against Catholic Spain. As the war receded into memory, however, it was easy for zealous Protestants to romanticize it and to question James's motives for retreating into peace. James was proud to be styled *Rex Pacificus*, king of peace; and he often invoked the words from Christ's Sermon on the Mount: *Beati pacifici*, blessed are the peacemakers.[38] To his critics, however, his pacifism looked like passivity or, worse, cowardliness.

Many observers commented on James's pacifism, and few saw it as a virtue. Indeed, one of James's harshest critics on this subject was the ardent royalist, Sir John Oglander. Oglander began his character sketch of James with this terse condemnation: 'King James the First of England was the most cowardly man that ever I knew.' As Oglander described him, James 'could not endure a soldier or to see men drill, [and] to hear of war was death to him'.[39] In 1604 the French ambassador also commented on James's 'extraordinary weakness' and 'unmeasured love of peace'. The ambassador judged that James 'will on no provocation, commence a war, but will endeavour to maintain peace, even by bad, foolish, and disgraceful means'. James's aversion to war was probably a natural product of his insecure and violent childhood. The French ambassador realized how deep-seated this aversion was: 'He hates war from habit, principle, and disposition, and will (to use his own words) avoid it like his own damnation.'[40] The Venetian ambassador similarly observed that James 'loves quiet and repose, has no inclination to war, nay is opposed to it, a fact that little pleases many of his subjects'.[41] A later Venetian ambassador wrote more bluntly, 'Fear is, and ever was, his ruling passion!'[42]

The combination of effeminacy and pacifism at the Jacobean court generated a countervailing movement. This movement championed the opposite values of manliness and militarism. Evidence of this cultural backlash is ubiquitous. For example, Sir Fulke Greville wanted James to resume Elizabeth's militant anti-Spanish foreign policy. Greville was a man of both action and contemplation, a poet and a courtier, a friend and follower of the Elizabethan hero Sir Philip Sidney and the charismatic second Earl of Essex. Suddenly, in the early years of James's reign, Greville found himself alienated from the court and excluded from office (just as the Earl of Southampton had been). It was during this enforced idleness, sometime prior to 1612, that Greville conceived the idea of writing a history of Elizabeth's reign. When he asked the Earl of Salisbury for permission to consult the official records, Salisbury tried to discourage him from the project and denied him access. Greville's account of this rebuff shows that Salisbury was worried that a glorification of Elizabeth's reign 'might perchance be construed to the prejudice of this'.

Greville never wrote the projected history of Elizabeth's reign, but he did write a life of Sir Philip Sidney; and what he wrote fully justifies Salisbury's concern. The sub-title of Greville's work declared that 'The True Interest of England' consisted in 'suppressing the power of *Spain*'. Of course, Greville's paramount motive was religion, but worries about manliness and effeminacy bubbled to the surface in his argument. In Elizabeth's reign there were real men who understood the need to attempt 'Heroicall Enterprises abroad'. These were men of worth, stature, substance, not mere 'creations of chance'. And Elizabeth prized such men. She did not 'bring the children of favor, and chance, into an equall ballance of comparison with birth, worth, and education'. She let the whole world know that she would not be captivated by favourites or fall prey to the 'Monopolous use of Favourites'. She did not allow the business of the kingdom to fall 'within the narrownesse of a young fraile mans lustfull, or unexperienced affections'. Just in case his readers might miss these implied comparisons with James, Greville instructed them to notice the 'differences, between the reall, and large complexions of those active times, and the narrow *salves* of this effeminate age'.[43] Greville's imagery hardly seems accidental here. Real men of action have natural complexions; effeminate men soften their complexions with salves (like posset-curd).

There was a widespread opinion that the longer the peace with Spain lasted, the weaker England became. Another minor literary figure, Richard Brathwaite, published a poem in 1615 using imagery similar to Greville's. Brathwaite compared a 'good Souldier' with a 'carpet-Knight'. He associated the good soldier with cannons, steel and iron, clattering armour, the battlefield and marching. He associated the carpet-knight with perfumes, powders, down-filled beds, nimble capering and the voice of 'Amorous Ganimedes'.[44] Brathwaite published these words at the same time that Buckingham was gaining favour, partly through his nimble dancing. On one occasion when James lost patience with a dull masque at court, Buckingham saved the day. In the words of a Venetian observer, 'the Marquis of Buckingham, his Majesty's favourite, immediately sprang forward, cutting a score of lofty and very minute capers'. Other dancers joined in, one performing thirty-four capers, 'but none came up to the exquisite manner of the marquis'. When this celebration was finally over, James 'embraced and kissed him tenderly and then honoured the marquis with marks of extraordinary affection, patting his face'. The Venetian observer left the entertainment at half past two in the morning, describing himself as 'half disgusted and weary'.[45]

England's failure to join the fighting in The Thirty Years War intensified this concern that the nation was becoming soft. John Everard preached a sermon in 1618 only a few weeks after the outbreak of war. Everard bemoaned 'this effeminate age', 'these *wanton* and *womanish* times'. From these few words it might appear as if Everard did equate effeminacy with wantonness, but he had much more than this in mind. He elaborated on the theme of 'nice and delicate wantonnesse' by using the example of the ancient city of Nineveh where peace and prosperity had made the residents 'wanton, effeminate, base, drunken, coward-like *Carpet-Knights*' (the same term that Brathwaite used). Everard glossed the words of God's judgment against Nineveh in the Bible (Nahum 3.13) that 'thy people in the midst of thee are women'. Everard interpreted these words to mean that the men of Nineveh:

> Are *women*, proud as *women*, foolish and voide of counsell as *women*, fantasticall and new-fangled as *women*, feare-full and coward-like as *women*, nice and effeminate as *women*. ...[46]

By 1620 even Ben Jonson had captured some of the enthusiasm for war in a poem entitled 'An Epistle to a Friend, To Perswade Him to the Warres'. Jonson decried the man of his time who was obsessed with his fine clothing, 'his Combes, his Curling-irons, his Glasse, Sweet [perfume] bags, [and] sweet Powders'. 'This', Jonson explained, 'hath our ill-us'd freedome, and soft peace Brought on us'.[47]

Overt criticism of James's foreign policy and effeminate favourites appeared only sporadically on the public stage. Much recent scholarship has been devoted to the question of whether early Stuart drama glorified or undermined the monarchy, whether it served to contain criticism or had the opposite effect of delegitimizing authority.[48] Anyone looking for criticism of the overall ethos surrounding the royal court can find examples in the plays and, to a lesser extent, even the masques of the period. Only rarely, however, can one find direct unambiguous criticism of the king himself, especially criticism calling attention to his sexuality. Few playwrights were so foolhardy. This was an especially tricky issue for Jonson who, in his efforts to entertain and amuse the king, sometimes stepped over the line. Jonson got into trouble early in the reign for creating a character in *Eastward Ho* (1605) who implied that the Groom of the King's Bedchamber functioned as a pander.[49] Beaumont and Fletcher may have been satirizing James more subtly when they wrote *The Woman-Hater* (1606). One of the characters in this play expresses his desire to 'be a Favorite on the suddain'. Impossible, replies a more experienced courtier, 'you have not the face to be a Favourite on the suddain'.[50] There are indications that James was openly ridiculed on the stage for a brief period after arriving in England. As we saw in the previous chapter, the French ambassador reported that as late as 1608 James was depicted on the stage accompanied by his favourites, swearing, obsessed with hunting, bemoaning the loss of his phoenix and 'drunk at least once a day'.[51] Unfortunately, no plays this outrageous have survived, and even secondhand accounts of this sort disappear after the early years of the reign. Later criticism of the king was subtler, though satirists did not spare his court and favourties.[52] For example, Margot Heinemann observed: 'Attacks on over-powerful effeminate favourites are common in [Philip] Massinger's plays. The parallels with Buckingham, though not necessarily exclusively with him, would readily be drawn by the audience.'[53]

James's foreign policy did keep drawing him into the limelight. His peace with Spain was controversial from the outset. Thomas Dekker's *The Whore of Babylon* (1606) can be read as 'a form of Elizabethan nostalgia and an implicit critique of James's pacifism'.[54] Here too, however, there was a quiescent period through the middle years of the reign. More strident attacks resumed in the 1620s after the outbreak of the Thirty Years War. As he had done at the beginning of his reign, James again reacted by strengthening government censorship.[55] Of course he could not entirely succeed in stifling criticism, but even the most dissident drama of these later years made only cautiously oblique references to the king himself, and there was very little of the sexual and gendered language we are interested in.[56]

Queen Anne was a prominent participant in the criticism of her husband's conduct at court and in foreign affairs. In 1604, when the French ambassador reported that James was a king 'whom the comedians of the metropolis bring upon the stage', he also reported that the king's 'wife attends these representations in order to enjoy the laugh against her husband'.[57] Recent historians have shown that Queen Anne reacted to 'the homosexual and partriarchal ethos' of her husband's court by establishing a vibrant court of her own that served as a locus for resistance. Anne befriended the very people James viewed with suspicion because of their eagerness for war. Most notable was her ultimately unsuccessful effort to spare the life of Sir Walter Raleigh, the great Elizabethan foe of Spain, whom James executed in 1618. More successful and important in the long run was her contribution to the evolution of the masque. In contrast to the all-male acting companies of the day, Anne and the women of her court performed key roles in these masques; and often they played assertive, militant, even martial women. In one of these Anne played 'War-like Pallas, in her Helmet drest'. Another masque featured a queen who led the women of her realm in the slaughter of their husbands. Anne and the women of her court must have been as pleased to perform these gender-bending roles as James was uncomfortable to view them.[58]

Although these dramatic productions may have been satisfying, therapeutic and reaffirming for Anne, her best practical chance of retaliating against James and ultimately vindicating herself was by turning her son against his father. The contest being fought in society at large was thus carried out within James's nuclear family. Anne, who had been 'bitten' by James's favourites or 'dear ones', to use the words of Archbishop Abbot cited earlier, bit back. She focused her attention on Prince Henry, fashioning him into the opposite of his father, determined that if she could not make a man of her husband, then she would make a man of her son. Above all, he would have to be a warrior. The French ambassador reported that Anne 'says aloud, she hopes her son will one day overrun France as well as his ancestor Henry V'.[59] The victories of Henry V in the Hundred Years War against France, particularly the famous battle of Agincourt, had made him the epitome of the warrior-king. Only a few years earlier Shakespeare's stirring *Henry V* had played before London crowds.[60] Anne knew very well what she was doing when she asserted that Prince Henry 'is like that king'. She compared the prince to a paragon of manliness, not to his own father. Anne's efforts to mould Henry into a warrior-king were part of the continuing battle she had fought against James for possession of her children.[61] After the move to England, when she was at last able to exert more influence over Henry, it was observed that she 'never lets him away from her side'.[62] James was upset with this turn of events. The ambassador described him as 'perplexed by fear and jealousy respecting the alteration that is observable in the Prince of Wales, and produced by his mother'.[63]

Prince Henry did become fervently militaristic. He developed a keen interest in the military arts, arms, armour and the navy.[64] Like his mother, he used the vehicle of the court masque to express his oppositional values, casting himself in the role of an Arthurian knight on a mission to revive the nation's military glory.[65] But it was not only in his more pronounced militarism that Henry distinguished himself from his father. James was a prodigious swearer; Henry made anyone who swore in his presence pay a fine into a box he had built for the purpose.[66] James's court was notoriously disorganized; Henry insisted on a greater degree of order and propriety in his own. There is no way to know how much Henry would have developed along these same lines if he had been left to himself. Like many a teenager, he was creating an identity for himself, engaging in what we might call an act of 'self-fashioning'. Obviously the queen did what she could to influence the fashion, but Henry was not putty in her hands: Henry, for example, rejected her Roman Catholicism in favour of a militant Protestantism. What Henry and his mother had most in common was a shared destestation of King James's lifestyle. Roy Strong, the author of a wonderfully rich study of Henry, observed that even in his choice of clothing the prince was making 'a statement against the follies of his father's court', and 'he clearly abhorred the homosexuality of his father'.[67] Henry's ostentatious repudiation of his father's values put him in an awkward position since it was also imperative for him to maintain an outward appearance of obedience and respect. Meanwhile James, who understood what was going on, grew resentful. As the Venetian ambassador explained, James was not particularly pleased 'to see his son so beloved and of such promise that his subjects place all their hopes in him; and it would almost seem, to speak frankly, that the King was growing jealous'.[68]

Sometimes the tension or jealousy between father and son came to public notice. At Henry's investiture as Prince of Wales, for example, James ordered that the prince not be seen on horseback.[69] Naturally, James tried to make a scholar of his son. The Venetian ambassador reported that Henry 'studies, but not with much delight, and chiefly under his father's spur, not of his own desire'. This led to another telling incident when James scolded the prince for neglecting his studies. Although Henry held his tongue while still in his father's presence, he is supposed to have said afterward: 'I know what becomes a Prince. It is not necessary for me to be a professor, but a soldier and a man of the world.'[70] The queen's hand is particularly evident here because, according to the French ambassador, she had endeavoured 'hourly to corrupt the spirit and disposition' of the prince, drawing him away from his studies on the grounds that they were 'unworthy of a great commander and conqueror'.[71]

As Prince Henry grew older, a veritable cult developed around him with the expectation that he would lead England into war against the enemies of Protestantism. These hopes were dashed, however, when Henry died in 1612. The role of 'commander and conqueror' now fell to James's younger surviving son, Charles – or 'Baby Charles', as both his parents routinely called him. Anne appears to have been more interested in her sons than her daughter. Perhaps that is because it was only through her sons that she could express her abhorrence of James's conduct. They could become 'real' men and repudiate the values of their father; her daughter Elizabeth could not. In Charles, Anne had fewer natural abilities to work with, but he was her last chance at vindication. But her final years were marked by depression and illness. 'She is unhappy', explained the Venetian ambassador, 'because the king rarely sees her and many years have passed since he saw much of her.' These were the years when Somerset and Buckingham gained ascendancy in the king's affections. Trapped in an unhappy marriage, Anne could only become more despondent and resentful.

As in the case of Henry, it is impossible to prove that Anne shaped Charles to her own ends, but the results are uncannily similar. Like Henry, Charles would define himself as the opposite of his father. Like Henry, Charles would pride himself on order and decorum.[72] Like Henry, Charles tried to become the warrior-king that Anne and many others wished for. By the summer of 1620, Charles was, in the words of his biographer, 'a very young man growing in vigour, his childhood frailties overcome, showing off his military prowess in the tiltyard'.[73] Because he survived and married, Charles would have one more way to distinguish himself from his father. Charles, as we shall see, was determined to become a paragon not only of manliness, but also of uxoriousness and heterosexuality.

Queen Anne died in 1619 – too soon to see Charles demonstrate his manhood in the tiltyard, too soon to witness a raging public debate over the very concept of 'manhood' and too soon to see her dream of a warrior-king turn into a nightmare.

Chapter 5

Manliness and War

In the 1620s the war of words escalated. Advocates of war, increasingly exasperated by England's failure to enter the Thirty Years War, berated their fellow Englishmen for refusing to fight. More and more, the issue of manliness came to the foreground. To be more precise, the issue of King James's manliness came to the foreground.

As we saw in the previous chapter, James's effeminate favourites and his policy of pacifism raised questions about his manliness. The traditional concept of manhood, to quote one recent historian, required a 'willingness to engage in violence with other men'.[1] 'Sheer physical courage', in the words of another, 'was central to the chivalric code from which the early modern concept of honour evolved.'[2] Real men, perhaps especially real kings, were supposed to be physically strong, inclined to war and courageous. James, by contrast, suffered from a weakness in his legs, avoided war and appeared – at least to his more bellicose subjects – to be cowardly. A real king was supposed to be dressed in armour, mounted on a rearing horse, poised on the brink of heroic combat. James was often on horseback. In fact, his love of the chase was the most conspicuously virile activity he engaged in. Jenny Wormald, surprisingly, concedes that James was a coward, but she adds that his 'cowardice in military matters was not paralleled by cowardice on the hunting-field'.[3] On the other hand, James did not so much hunt as follow the hounds on horseback while they ran down their exhausted prey. A German visitor in 1613, observing that 'the king hurries incessantly after the dogs until they have caught the game', concluded that there could be 'no particular enjoyment in this sport'.[4] In any case, no matter how much bravery this activity required, James's contemporary critics preferred to interpret it as a sign of decadence, a self-indulgent escape from the serious responsibilities of the real world into a world of play.

The very characteristics James prided himself upon most, his love of peace and his scholarship, were viewed as liabilities by his detractors. As one person sympathetic to James lamented, his critics took his love of peace and turned it round 'to his dishonour'. They made it appear as if 'his peaceable disposition hath not proceeded so much out of his Christian pietie and justice, as out of mere impotencie, and baseness of mind'.[5] James's scholarship was turned against him in the same way, interpreted as another sign of his impotence. John Reynolds wanted James to put down the pen and take up the sword. He called for James to heed the advice of an ancient Spartan king 'that words are feminine, and deeds masculine, and that it is a great point of honour, discretion, and happinesse for a Prince, to give the first blowe to his Enemies'.[6] Thus the narrow political issue of whether or not England should join in the Thirty Years War widened into a debate over gender. The argument over war and peace became an argument over what it meant to be a man. James had one concept of manliness, his critics another; and integral to that difference was the disposition to fight.

James eschewed violence at precisely the time there was enormous public pressure for him to embrace it. In 1618, when the Thirty Years War was erupting on the continent, a tract appeared in England entitled *The Peace-Maker: or Great Brittaines Blessing*. The authorship of *The Peace-Maker* is disputed. The tract was published with royal favour, began with a preface 'To all Our true-loving, and Peace-embracing SUBJECTS', and mirrored James's views so much that it has often been attributed to him. It is true that James gave the work his blessing and may have influenced its contents, but the actual author appears to have been Thomas Middleton.[7] In *The Peace-Maker*, England was described as an island of peace (*Insula pacis*), the 'Land of Peace, under the King of Peace'. One purpose of this work, as the subtitle indicated, was to demonstrate the foolishness of duelling and quarrelling among excitable young men 'wherein consists neyther MANHOOD nor WISDOME'. The link between manhood and wisdom would certainly have appealed to the king. James was a scholar, an intellectual, who thought that true manliness required reflection, not impulsive violence. He had, for example, made several efforts to suppress duelling.[8] According to *The Peace-Maker*, honour does not consist in rashness, revenge or bloodshed. The truly wise man will ignore insults and 'embrace Humanitie'. Unfortunately, most men are too worried about their reputations, too quick to take offence, too eager to seek revenge. 'All they venture for, is to bring the bloudinesse of their Action into the compasse of Honour (as if Honour consisted in destruction).'

Why should people want war? 'When was Warre sent as a Blessing, or Peace as a punishment?' Instead, *The Peace-Maker* concluded by exhorting the 'Sonnes of this Age' to practise humility, mercy, charity, faith and piety, for only through these qualities could they hope to attain eternal peace.[9]

At the end of 1619 James published *A Meditation Upon the Lords Prayer,* which he dedicated to Buckingham as a 'Newyeers gift from me, as a token of my love'. This work echoed the ideas in *The Peace-Maker.* Its most important message, James said, was to practise charity and forgive those who offend you. Valour is commendable, wrote James, but 'all is in the right use of it'. It is not valourous to be overcome by rancour, revenge and malice. These emotions arise from baseness, not from 'true courage'. At one point in the *Meditation,* James reflected on his own reputation. 'I know not by what fortune, the *diction* of PACIFICUS was added to my title, at my comming in England ... but I am not ashamed of this addition', for Solomon was a king of peace, and Christ himself 'said nothing, wrote nothing, did nothing: yea in a maner breathed nothing all the dayes of his life, but Love and Charitie'.[10]

James was not alone in eschewing violence. Some members of the clergy espoused peace. Our view can too easily be distorted by a handful of puritan zealots clamouring for a holy war.[11] Furthermore, James's reconceptualization of honour and courage can be seen as part of a wider reformation of manners occurring at this time.[12] Humanists such as Sir Thomas Elyot and Sir Philip Sidney had refined the old martial and warlike cult of honour, placing less emphasis on violence and more on intellectual and moral qualities.[13] One modern scholar has gone so far as to argue that James's pacific policies had a 'liberating' influence on Shakespeare. 'The king's consistent theory and successful practice of peace between 1603 and 1613 encouraged Shakespeare to continue in the direction he was already heading, stimulated his investigations into the pathology of socially sanctioned violence, and motivated him to use the theater to reeducate his audience.'[14] All this having been said, however, the fact of the matter is that the outbreak of the Thirty Years War constituted a huge setback for the proponents of non-violence. The English 'Sonnes of this Age', including the king's own son, would soon be longing to go into the action, and even the King of Peace would be powerless to stop them.

James himself was confused on the subject. Although he wished to refine his culture's conception of manhood, he stoutly opposed any redefinition of womanhood. Although he was personally attracted to men who resembled women, he took the lead in condemning women who resembled men – an irony that has often been remarked upon. By instructing his clergy to denounce women who defied conventional dress codes, James helped provoke the most famous literary controversy over gender in Jacobean England, a controversy that began with the publication of a tract entitled *Hic Mulier: or, The Man-Woman* in 1620.[15] This polemical tract warned against the effects of gender inversion: as the men of England became more effeminate, the women were becoming more masculine. According to the anonymous author of this tract, women were dressing and acting like men to an unprecedented degree, for 'since the daies of *Adam* women were never so Masculine'.[16] One thing these masculine women did was to cut their hair short; another was to trade their sewing needles for swords. How were these insolent women to be controlled? The author offered a simple solution: husbands and fathers must lay down the law and, for good measure, cut off the supply of money that financed this waywardness.

Later in 1620, a more imaginative solution appeared in *Haec Vir: or The Womanish-Man*. The anonymous author of this tract (who may have been the same person who penned *Hic Mulier*) alleged that the root of the problem lay not with the women but with the men. The women of England would not have become more masculine if the men of England had not started the process by allowing themselves to become more feminine. Speaking in the voice of a woman, the author of *Haec Vir* complained to her male readers:

> you have demolish'd the noble schooles of Horsmanship ... hung up your Armes to rust, glued up those swords in their scabberds that would shake all Christendome with the brandish, and entertained into your mindes such softnes, dulnesse and effeminate niceness, that it would even make Heraclitus himselfe laugh against his nature to see how palingly you languish in this weake entertained sinne of womanish softnesse.

For this author, the solution to the problem was not just for men to issue orders and cut off allowances. They had to refashion their whole behaviour. Only when men started acting like men again could they expect women to act like women. Put on your armour, wrote this author, issuing a challenge: 'Be men in shape, men in shew, men in words, men in actions, men in counsell, men in example: then will we love and serve you; then will we heare and obey you.'[17] Women should wield sewing needles; men should wield swords. As we shall see, this linkage between manliness and the sword is ubiquitous in the writings of the early 1620s. There no doubt is some phallic significance in this imagery, but the more practical conclusion was that men had to use their swords to prove their manliness. As the author of *Haec Vir* implies, it was time for the men of England to strap on swords and take them out of their scabbards. It was time to go to war.

John Everard used remarkably similar language in 1618 when he delivered the sermon which, as we saw in the previous chapter, tried to resurrect a martial spirit in an 'effeminate age'. Everard exhorted his listeners to embrace war and to detest 'these baser and effeminate *viro rum feminae, feminarum viri*'. What endangered the nation, according to Everard, was not just effeminacy but effeminization. To make his point, he used the biblical example of Sesostris who decided that the best way to secure his rule over Egypt was 'to impose upon women the workes of men, and upon men the workes of women'. The men sat at home, learned to spin, carried burdens on their heads, wore double garments against the cold and grew their hair long. By requiring the men of Egypt to behave this way, Sesostris was able to 'weane them from all man-like thoughts and exercise of Armes'. As Everard explained the process, men who behave this way not only lose their martial spirit but '*un-man* themselves'. Lest this example be lost on his English audience, Everard drove home the point. If Solomon were alive today and observed the condition of the English, 'he could not say as once he did, "I have found one man amongst a thousand, but a woman amongst them all have I not found"; more truly might he say, "I have found a thousand women ... in the shape of one man, but a man indeed have I not found."'[18]

Where were the men of England to be found when the Thirty Years War broke out? Indeed, if they failed to join the battle, were they men at all? One modern scholar, Laura Levine, has gone so far as to argue that men were not assumed to be men at this point in history unless they demonstratively acted like men. If a man failed to behave in a manly manner, then he would revert to his basic nature, which was thought to be dangerously feminine. As Levine saw it, 'there is no masculinity except in the performance of masculinity'. Masculinity needed 'to be performed in order to exist'. When this did not occur, then 'femininity seems to be the default position, the otherness one is always in danger of slipping into'.[19] Looked at this way, the fear of effeminization was the fear of men reverting to women for lack of manly action. The single best arena in which masculinity could be performed and hence affirmed was war, and James took away that arena. By refusing to 'fight like a man', he jeopardized the masculinity of all Englishmen and cast special doubt upon his own manliness.

Neither the author(s) in the *Hic Mulier* controversy nor Everard placed any personal blame on King James for the 'un-manning' of English men (though this did not prevent Everard from being imprisoned more than once in the 1620s).[20] The numerous plays that questioned James's foreign policy on the public stage in the 1620s were similarly circumspect about indicting James personally.[21] They put his policy on trial but not his person. For direct criticism of James, one has to look elsewhere.

The question of James's manliness (or rather its lack) was raised most prominently in the polemical tracts designed to humiliate and exhort him into war. *Tom Tell Troath* is an excellent example. As we saw in an earlier chapter, this work, which began circulating in manuscript in the streets of London in 1622, came dangerously close to accusing James of sodomy. It also made a pointed issue of his manliness. What the anonymous author of this tract wanted, in effect, was for James to remake or refashion himself. Whereas James prided himself on being a man of letters and a peacemaker, this author wanted him to become precisely the opposite. He told James he could obtain 'with the sword, [that] which you have so often in vaine desired with your pen'. He mocked the motto *Beati pacifici*. He even resorted to a male sports analogy, telling James that if he would take up arms, then 'the footeball will presently be on your side'. According to this anonymous author, James's subjects were exasperated with him. They 'wish Queen Elizabeth were alive again'. Under James, they had 'lived to see that brave stock of soveraigne reputation, which our greate Queen, your predecessor, left us, quite banisht, and brought to nothing'. In a more explicit reference to James's questionable manhood, the author reflected, 'who would have thought, that wee should have lost, but rather infinitely gained, by changing the weaker sexe, for your more noble [sex], to be our commanders'? The implication is clear: Elizabeth had been more of a man than James was. Two opportunities now presented themselves for James to vindicate himself and prove his manhood. He could enter the war in Germany on his daughter's behalf, and he could join the cause of the embattled Protestant minority in France. These are described as 'two faire occasions, that come, as it were, a-woinge to your Majestie', and James is exhorted to take up his 'mayden armes'.[22]

No one has ever established who the author of *Tom Tell Troath* was, but in style and content it bears a remarkable resemblance to the many works of Thomas Scott published in the early 1620s.[23] Historians have recognized Scott's importance as the 'controversialist *par excellence* of the 1620s', but they have not examined the powerful role played by sex and gender in his writings.[24] In a previous chapter, we saw Scott's insinuations about James's sexuality. Not surprisingly, Scott also complained about the effeminacy of the times and the loss of manliness. Scott's complaints about contemporary England fit well with Levine's argument that if men fail to do manly things, they lose their manliness. Adopting the voice of Count Gondomar in *Vox Populi* (1620), Scott taunted Englishmen. He accused them of becoming 'effeminate and cowardly'. He boasted that the Spanish need not fear these English soldiers because 'their bodies by long disuse of armes were disabled and their mindes effeminated by peace and luxury'. England, he declared, never had 'more people and fewer men'. Scott tried to maintain an air of respect for James in *Vox Populi*, but his disrespect kept slipping through. In one place, for example, he managed to ridicule both James's passion for hunting and his love of peace when he wrote that James 'extreamly hunts after peace'. James, wrote Scott, 'so affects the true name of a Peacemaker' that he will 'doe or suffer anything' to maintain peace. James was not Scott's kind of man. Scott wanted a man of action, not this 'King of Schollers'. Even Elizabeth had been more of a man than James was. Scott described her as 'that deceased English *Virago*'.[25] No wonder Scott was forced to flee the country.

James issued a series of proclamations during the 1620s to suppress seditious writings, punishing both authors and printers who evaded government censorship.[26] But there was no stopping the flow of works published abroad. In the tracts Scott wrote from his continental refuge, he continued to berate his fellow Englishmen for their effeminacy and to cast aspersions on James's manliness. In *The Belgicke Pismire* (1622), Scott bemoaned the 'effeminate fashions and mollifying pleasures' of the times. He was not impressed by men who were trained 'to hunt, to hawke, or daunce, or drinke, or court, or play, (the ordinarie exercises of these degenerate times)'. He yearned instead for the old days when Englishmen engaged in 'shooting, running, wrastling, and the like strennuous and manly sportes'.[27] In reaction against the 'courtly and effeminate braverie of perfuming and powdring', Scott declared his preference for perfume and powder of a different sort. In his opinion, 'a Souldier never smells sweeter, and lookes better ... then when he is perfumed with sweat, and powdred with dust, and painted or besmeared with bloud'.[28]

Scott was not a subtle writer, but his criticisms of James were oblique enough to escape the notice of some modern historians. One historian has even made the amazing claim that Scott 'was never, throughout his works, critical of the King in anything but the mildest way'.[29] Nothing better proves the fallacy of that statement than *The Belgicke Pismire*, where Scott's criticism of James was anything but mild. Knowing that James liked to think of himself as the British Solomon, Scott mocked him with a parable from the Book of Proverbs in which Solomon compared the industrious ant (pismire) to the lazy sluggard.[30] Scott spent several pages implying that James resembled the sluggard of this parable. He is 'a prater that never doth any thing', 'a couragious coward', 'a wise foole', 'a resolute waverer', 'a constant changeling', 'a longing, prating, prodigall, cowardly, slow, selfe conceipted, certaine-uncertaine foole, who sleepes away his time, and thinkes all men are borne to worke, that he might play ... sleeping out his life in solitarie retirement and brutish sensuality'. Scott exhorted the sluggard to abandon 'thy sensuall pleasures, thy bewitching pastimes, thy brutish passions, thy beastly companions'. We can sense Scott's mounting exasperation in this series of denunciations. The sluggard resembles James in one more respect: he prides himself on his book learning; whereas true wisdom requires action. Action, unfortunately, was not forthcoming from a sluggard who was 'rockt asleepe ... with a lullabie of peace'. Given all these characteristics of the sluggard, Scott doubted 'if he bee worthie to bee called a man'.[31] Scott wanted a real man of action, not an effete intellectual.

Scott's view of war and peace was the exact opposite of James's. The peace that James prized Scott found contemptible; the war that James abhorred Scott earnestly longed for. For Scott, war produced manliness, and he mustered examples from the past to convince his readers. In *The Belgick Souldier* (1624), Scott assumed the voice of a veteran soldier to shame the English into war. To the Belgick soldier, peace was not a blessing but an 'iniquitie' that 'hath made us drunke with ease and carelesnesse'. War was the antidote, the 'cure', to these ills. England flourished in times of war, in the Elizabethan days of real men like Sir Francis Drake, Sir Walter Raleigh, and the Earl of Essex. Those were the days of 'fiery spirits', not 'effaeminate Courtiers'.[32]

In yet another tract, Scott spoke through the voice of *Robert, Earle of Essex His Ghost* (1624). Essex has no patience for James, who is 'baffled and abused' by the Spanish. The virile ghost instructs his English compatriots to exhort James, 'perswade and stirre him up ... to go forth against the *Romish wolves*, and *Spanish foxes*'. To those who might object that James loves peace, the ghost gives an answer loaded with sarcasm. Yes, says the ghost, 'your King himselfe is much affected with the very name of PEACE, alleadging, that hee hath beene a peaceable

King from his Cradle; that *BEATI PACIFICI* is his happy destined *Motto*; and with such like selfe-pleasing songs, hath a long time sung a *Requiem* to himselfe'. God, by contrast, was '*a man of War*'.[33] Alexander Leighton echoed Scott's view: '*Jehovah is a man of war*.'[34] These divines took their cue from Scripture (Genesis, 15.3) which assured them: 'The Lord *is* a man of war.'[35]

Two other polemical tracts which appeared in 1624 are so similar in style and content to Scott's that they are often attributed to him, but they were the work of John Reynolds, who spent several months in prison for writing them.[36] In *Vox Coeli* Reynolds portrayed a consultation in heaven among Henry VIII, Edward VI, Mary I, Elizabeth I, Prince Henry and the recently deceased Queen Anne. They debate the pros and cons of the Spanish Match, and, not surprisingly, the Catholic Mary is the only one who favours it. Throughout the debate Queen Elizabeth appears to be the most manly of them all. She repeatedly reminds the reader how she stood up to Spain when she ruled England. She is dismayed at the pusillanimous policy of her successor. Meanwhile Prince Henry makes it clear that if he had lived he would have done a better job of defending England. Through the voices of these various ghosts, Reynolds, like Scott, portrayed James as an effete intellectual. Philip of Spain, wrote Reynolds, 'loves King *James* his Gowne & Pen, yet no way feares his sword'. After all, why should Philip fear James's sword since 'hee never yet knew the way to draw it'? Indeed, it is apparent to the whole world that there is no reason to fear the English because 'the element and delight of their King, is bookes, not battailes, the pen not the Pike'. And again the effeminacy has spread to the nation at large. Englishmen would command more respect 'if they wore worse cloathes, and had better hearts and swords, and if they were more martiall and lesse ef[f]eminate'. Even after the other five rulers vote against her, Queen Mary holds out hope for Spain because 'the *English* are Effeminate, and you *Spaniards* Souldiers'.[37]

In *Votivae Angliae* Reynolds repeated the same themes, but he attacked James more directly. He lectured James on the true state of affairs: 'the King of Spayne plays the Practike with your Majestie, whiles you professe the *Theorie* to him; you give him contemplation for action, hee returns you action for contemplation'. Spain and the Empire 'feed your Majestie with the emptie ayre of hoapes, and with the bitter sweet sugar of maine flattering and false promises'. Reynolds, like Scott, charged that Gondomar has 'lulld'd your Majestie asleepe'. (This image persisted through the middle of the century when James appeared in John Harrington's *Oceana* as the monarch Morpheus, named after the Greek god of dreams.[38]) In Reynolds's opinion, James's reputation was so tarnished it could only be redeemed by the sword. Again and again, he exhorted James to 'drawe his Royall Sword'. By taking up the sword, Reynolds argued, James could convert shame into honour and restore the face of England to 'her old one, which was ever woont to looke more Martiall, and lesse Effemynate'.[39]

Scott and Reynolds were far from alone in wanting James to be less a man of contemplation and more a man of action. In 1622 the Venetian ambassador likewise reflected that early in his reign James had been 'as anxious for reputation with his pen and tongue as reluc- tant now with the sword'.[40] James was proud of his accomplishments with the pen, but his critics did not believe in the power of the pen, and they certainly did not believe that the pen was sufficient by itself to make a man. To prove his manhood and to vindicate the nation's, James would have to use his sword.

In 1622 an anonymous work entitled *The French Herauld* appeared in England and was promptly banned. This work repeated many of the now familiar arguments for war, including the telling comparison between King James and Queen Elizabeth. In contrast to James, Elizabeth had been a monarch to reckon with: 'her people loved her, her subjects feared her, her courage made her redoubtable, her neighbours received great blowes for seeking to offend her.' *The French Herauld* exhorted James to 'cut out the tongues' of the flatterers who surrounded him, make his name feared and erase the blame he incurred for failing to help his daughter. In words that came closest to what we have seen before, the anonymous author of this pamphlet exhorted: 'Wake out of your slumber, give your servant the pen, and take the sword in hand.'[41]

If Thomas Middleton was the true author of *The Peace-Maker*, the semi-official justification for James's foreign policy published in 1618, it did not prevent him from switching points of view to suit the times or his patron. In 1620 he helped dramatize the opposite view that James was too much a scholar and too little a man of war. Middleton and William Rowley co-authored a *Courtly Masque: The Device Called, The World Tost at Tennis*, in which the two principal characters are a scholar and a soldier. The goddess Minerva, who represents both wisdom and war, tells these characters that the complete man must be both scholar and soldier: 'Thou art no soldier unless a scholar, Nor thou a scholar unless a soldier.' To prove her point, Minerva (with the help of her father, Jupiter) conjures up historical examples of men who achieved greatness by combining both qualities, including Julius Caesar, Charlemagne and King Arthur. Alas, however, these precedents have not been followed, and in the present world, Jupiter laments: 'Men strive to know too much, too little do.' There is a king in *The World Tost at Tennis* who presumably represents King James. At one point in the masque, this king shirks his responsibility. He takes an orb representing the world and hands it to a land-soldier. 'I cheerfully resign it', says the king, his sole ambition being 'the quiet calm of peaceful days'. At the end of the masque, of course, the king is converted. He faces up to his responsibilities, takes back possession of the orb representing the world and issues a command that henceforth there should be cooperation and mutual respect between the scholar and the soldier. Having achieved their objective, Jupiter and Minerva can now ascend from the stage, but not before Jupiter takes one last opportunity to drive home the moral: 'Scholar and soldier must both shut in one, / That makes the absolute and complete man.'[42]

When they wrote *The World Tost at Tennis*, it appears as if Middleton and Rowley were more concerned to represent Prince Charles's point of view than King James's. As the 'Induction' to the masque stated, it was originally 'prepared for his Majesty's Entertainment at Denmark-House'. Prince Charles was presumably behind these preparations because he had recently been granted Denmark House, which had been the prized residence of his late mother. As the title-page of the masque indicates, it was expected to be performed 'by the Prince his servants', that is by Charles's own company of actors. For reasons that remain obscure, however, the play was never performed at Denmark House. Perhaps James objected to the masque's content, or Charles anticipated that James would object. One can only assume that the purpose behind the masque was to put subtle pressure on James to adopt his son's more warlike policy. It is surely no accident that the masque ends with a reference to Charles's first tilt, describing him as 'Minerva's valiant'st, hopefull'st son' who 'early in his spring puts armour on'. Similarly, the soldier of the masque is last seen declaring that he will go 'over yonder [to the Continent] to the most glorious wars / That e'er fam'd Christian kingdom'.[43] The zeal for war was so great among some of James's subjects that they were taking matters into their own hands. *The World Tost at Tennis* was composed for performance during the winter of 1619–20 and printed the following summer, just in time to coincide with the departure for the continent of a volunteer army of about 2,000 men financed by private contributions.

The forces swirling in Jacobean England converged in the poet Michael Drayton. As we saw in an earlier chapter, Drayton's historic poem about Edward II and his favourite, Gaveston, helped to keep that apt comparison in the foreground. Drayton was a friend of George Wither and John Reynolds. He shared their views but, unlike them, managed to stay out of prison. One of Drayton's strangest poems was *The Moon-Calfe*, which voiced the same anxieties that surfaced in the controversy over *Hic Mulier* and *Haec Vir*. *The Moon-Calfe* describes the birth of 'monstrous Twins' fathered by the Devil. These twins are 'A Fem'nine man, a woman Masculine'. The man who is 'too much woman' is a sodomite, proof again that effeminacy was already linked to sodomy. This feminine man bathes in milk and 'lookes like' the kind of person the ancient Jews put in male brothels ('a Pathique in their Malekind Stewes'). But he is capable of playing the dominant role, too, for nothing delights him more than his own 'smooth-chind, plump-thigh'd, Catamite'. Appalled by the sight of this sodomite, his own off-spring, the Devil asks: 'Is she [sodomy] new risen, and her sinne agen Imbrac'd by beastly and outragious men'? Like the Devil, through whose voice he speaks here, Drayton was appalled by the new-risen sodomy of the Jacobean age and the effeminacy that accompanied it. What Drayton yearned for was the return of heroic, martial men. That is why he admired Prince Henry and was loosely associated with the young prince's circle. That is why he wrote poems celebrating Henry V and his military triumphs. The counterpoint to Drayton's *Piers Gaveston* was his *Ballad of Agincourt* (and the less famous *Battaile of Agincourt*). Like many of his compatriots, Drayton did not want another Edward II; he wanted another Henry V.[44]

Events in the real world did not stand still while the poets, play-wrights and pamphleteers waged their war of words. Parliament met twice in the 1620s, and in both cases the rhetoric and ideas we have observed in the polemical writings of the period were reflected in the debates at Westminster. We have already seen the Parliament of 1621 as the scene of Sir Francis Bacon's impeachment and Sir Henry Yelverton's provocative allusion to the reign of Edward II. This Parliament, the first to meet since 1614, provided advocates of war (such as the Earl of Southampton) with the forum they needed to rally the king and nation to war. Circumstances, too, added an air of urgency to their proceedings. By this time the plight of James's son-in-law, the Elector Palatine, and James's daughter Elizabeth had grown desperate. Frederick had utterly failed to make good his claim to the crown of Bohemia, and his own lands in the Palatinate were all but lost. 'The foxes have holes and birds their nests', said one Member of Parliament in 1621, but poor Elizabeth had nowhere to rest her head. If England did not rescue Frederick and Elizabeth, another

MP concluded, the nation's honour would 'lye in the dust'. Sir Edward Coke cited the precedent of Edward III's reign when the Commons were able to dissuade the king 'from peace and persuade him to take his sword in hand because a just war was better than a dishonorable peace'. Others agreed that James had 'been too long with his sword in his sheath'. If now James would take up the sword, one exasperated MP declared, 'I wish the skabbard were throwne away.' Sir James Perrott, anticipating Scott's metaphor in *The Belgicke Pismire*, exhorted his colleagues: 'Lett's not be like Sallomon's sluggard.'[45]

On the subject of war, however, there was no united front in the Parliament of 1621. Some members wanted to fight directly on Frederick's behalf with a land army in the Palatinate itself. Others who viewed the Palatinate as a dangerous quagmire preferred what they called a 'diversionary' war at sea against Spain. Furthermore, there were many in the Parliament of 1621 who were wary of any war at all. Most important, James's position remained baffling. While he seemed to encourage talk of war in Parliament, it was not clear what kind of war, if any, he was willing to pursue. The result was nothing like a convergence of viewpoints. Instead, the Parliament of 1621 ended with the debacle of the 'Great Protestation', Parliament urging James to undertake a war and to marry Charles to a Protestant, James angrily ripping the 'Protestation' from the Commons' journal. By the time James dissolved this Parliament, he was less inclined to embark on war and more determined than ever to pursue the peaceful alternative of the Spanish Match.[46]

Not until 1623 did the stunning turn of events occur that advocates of war had been waiting for. It was then that Prince Charles and Buckingham went to Spain in person to expedite the marriage with the Spanish Infanta. After six months of futile bargaining, they returned empty-handed, smarting from their failure and determined to embark on a war of revenge.[47] To accomplish this end, they needed to enlist the support of James and of Parliament. We need not relate here all the details of the ensuing political events that culminated in England's ill-fated entry into the Thirty Years War.[48] What is of interest to us, however, is the personal transformations that were involved in this dramatic change of policy.

The resumption of war gave both Charles and Buckingham an opportunity to declare their independence from the king. Indeed, this mutual desire was probably one of the reasons the two men had grown closer. Although Buckingham still used sexual imagery to express his affection for James, physical relations between the two had probably ended years earlier.[49] This would also help to explain Buckingham's surprising success in gaining Charles's trust.[50] The trip to Spain sealed the friendship. Now only death could separate James's son and favourite. They had become comrades-in-arms, first in their struggle to shake free of the king, next in the bloodier struggle of the Thirty Years War. Charles was now free to pursue the militant Protestant cause that had been frustrated in England since the death of Prince Henry. Buckingham, in his capacity as Lord Admiral, assumed the chief responsibility for executing the war. For both, this turn of events was an affirmation and a test of manhood.

Witnessing these transformations, Thomas Scott could hardly believe his eyes. Charles had not returned to England with a Spanish bride. He had instead, wrote Scott, 'returned *alone*, and shewed by his single returning *alone* that he loved us...God be praysed that he is come home ALONE'. In Scott's estimation, Charles had become a veritable Hercules. And Buckingham, who had previously seemed like a gourd because he shot up so suddenly, now assumed the stature of a mighty oak. Charles and Buckingham were men after all, but what of James? Even James now won effusive praise from Scott. He was an oracle whose writings deserved admiring attention. It was true that in the past James had 'over-loved peace', but now 'His angry Sword Drawes, and to Armes, the signall gives'.[51]

How far could James be transformed? Could he become, like God, a man of war? Failing in health and spirit, he still tried to resist the combined demand of Charles and Buckingham for war. He prudently reminded Parliament in 1624 that war would be a very expensive proposition. But Charles and Buckingham manipulated and badgered him into accepting war. James was still emotionally dependent on Buckingham, who used that dependence, exercising a kind of emotional blackmail over James to hold him to the war cause, expressing his pique and threatening to withdraw his affection whenever the king resisted.[52] As the Venetian ambassador described it, James 'now protests, now weeps, but finally gives in'.[53] Under this pressure, James told Parliament that he was ready to engage in war, but MPs who knew his record on this subject doubted his resolve. The king, as one MP complained, was 'a great lover of peace'. It would require 'an extraordinary Overture' to 'draw the King from Peace'.[54] For many MPs, as for Buckingham and Charles, peace had grown contemptible; war had become 'the most manly and English way'.[55]

The text of the parliamentary debates in 1624 is well known; but the sub-text has been little examined. Taking the speeches of MPs at face value, historians have attributed England's resumption of war to simple political and religious causes. If MPs had subconscious or ulterior motives, if there were less visible motives embedded in the culture or mentality of the time, these have remained hidden from historians. This unimaginative literalism for the 1620s contrasts with the fascinating work of recent cultural historians regarding the outbreak of the First World War. In *Nationalism and Sexuality*, for example, George L. Mosse wrote, 'A variety of motivations were at work as the generation of 1914 rushed to the colors at the outbreak of the war, but the quest for masculinity cut across them all.'[56] Similarly, Mark Girouard's *Return to Camelot* illuminates the crucial role played by concepts such as manliness, chivalry and honour in predisposing Englishmen to embrace war in 1914.[57] The same analysis can be applied to events in 1624. Sir Benjamin Rudyerd, the person who advocated war as 'the most manly and English way', came closest to the naive optimism of 1914 when he envisaged war as an opportunity where 'every younger brother may have hopes to fish out some future fortunes'.[58] Rudyerd reflected a widespread disinclination in Parliament to contemplate the bloody realities of the battlefield. King James tried to remind MPs that war entailed 'the effusion of Christian blood', but most of his listeners preferred to dream of a relatively bloodless naval war – a war, in effect, without battlefields.[59] Graphic realities were swept aside in 1624 by bombastic appeals to injured male pride and lofty exhortations to restore national honour.

The Thirty Years War offered an excellent opportunity for Englishmen to prove their manhood by rescuing a damsel in distress – Elizabeth of Bohemia. This chivalrous impulse ran through English society on the eve of war. At a Christmas dinner in 1622, for example, one of the lawyers at the Middle Temple 'took a cup of wine in one hand, and held his sword drawn in the other, and so began a health to the distressed Lady Elizabeth, and, having drunk, kissed his sword, and laying his hand upon it, took an oath to live and die in her service'. The sword and cup were then passed around for the other men to do the same. When news of this ritual reached James, we are told, 'his Majesty was highly displeased'.[60] The author of *Tom Tell Troath* informed James that in the taverns 'for one healthe that is begun to your selfe, there are ten drunke' to Elizabeth and Frederick. Abandoning this poor couple to 'reele up and downe, without hope of recovery, is the scorne and opprobry of the nations of the earth'.[61]

Parliamentary debates in 1624 made this same appeal to chivalry and national honour. One of the stories that circulated among MPs, for example, was that when Charles was in Spain, he had sent word to

James that if the Spanish decided to hold him hostage, then James should 'forget you have a son, & look after your daughter'.[62] When Dudley Carleton retold this anecdote, he described Charles's apparent willingness to sacrifice himself as an act of 'heroic resolution'.[63] There is no evidence that Charles ever sent this message to James, but MPs eagerly accepted the Prince's new image as the crusader who could rescue his sister and restore England's reputation.[64] Considering his abysmal failure in Spain, it was not logical to think that Charles was now the man who could get the job done. Sir Robert Phelips observed that the last Prince of Wales who went to Spain, the illustrious military commander known as the Black Prince, 'did go with an army and did return with victory'.[65] This sharply contrasted with Charles, who went practically alone and returned empty-handed. But Phelips did not make this historical comparison to be critical. He was expressing the expectation (or hope) that next time Charles would get it right. Sir Benjamin Rudyerd tried to reinforce the impression that Charles was a new man since the trip to Spain. This transforming experience, said Rudyerd, 'hath actuated and produced those excellent parts which are naturally in him and enabled him for great counsels and resolutions'.[66] Charles wanted another chance to prove himself, and he challenged MPs to prove themselves too. If they shrank from war, Charles told them, 'it would be dishonorable unto yourselves as well as unto me who am now first entering into the world'.[67]

Numerous speakers in the House of Commons combined the theme of national dishonour with a manly call to arms. Sir Robert Phelips lamented that the loss of the Palatinate 'hath made us a scorn to all'. He urged his listeners to 'take the ancient English way to recover what we have lost by the sword'.[68] Christopher Brooke complained that while Prince Charles was in Spain, he 'received great indignities and was made cheap amongst them'. Territory could be recovered, said Brooke, 'but honor cannot so well'.[69] Sir John Walter bemoaned the fact that 'we have been famous heretofore; now our honor is in the dust'. A commitment to war would 'declare us to be the offspring of the ancient English'.[70] Sir Humphrey May urged the Commons, 'Not to do anything as might diminish our ancient fame of being a valiant nation.'[71] Sir William Beecher agreed that England had been considered 'a nation valiant but blunted in a long if not improvident peace'.[72] Sir John Walter, too, called for a return to England's former greatness: 'Let us remember whose offspring we are and endeavor to make our reputation equal to that of our ancestors.'[73] Sir Thomas Jermyn went further back, comparing contemporary Englishmen to the

Old Testament figure Samson. (Was Gondomar Delilah?) In any case, it was now time for the English to show their strength.[74] Even the most deeply revered intellect in the House of Commons, Sir Edward Coke, displayed his male nature in 1624: the mere thought of war, Coke boasted, made him feel seven years younger.[75]

Bombastic speeches about war may have boosted the egos of male MPs, but mere words did not frighten the Spanish. As the Venetian ambassador reported, the Spanish 'despise this kingdom as unwarlike, poor, disunited, under a timid king with an inexperienced prince'. The Spanish derisively called the clamour for war in 1624 'the revolt of the mice against the cats'.[76] Now only time would tell whether Englishmen were mice or men.

The political and religious reasons for England's resumption of war are well known. Indeed, historians never seem to tire of dissecting the parliamentary debates and foreign negotiations of this period in the minutest detail. But could it be that they have missed something? Could it be that another reason many Englishmen welcomed war in 1624 was because they felt the need to prove their nation's manhood after twenty years of rule by a king who did not act like a traditional man, who seemed afraid to fight, who was suspected of committing sodomy and who was known to dote on his effeminate favourites? We have seen abundant evidence to suggest that this was indeed the case.

Women and war – James would have preferred to live without them both. As he explained in one of his last speeches to Parliament:

> First, it is true that I, who have been all the days of my life a peace-able King, and have had the honour in my titles and impresses to be styled *Rex Pacificus*, should without necessity embroil myself in war, is so far from my nature and from the honour which I have had at home and abroad in endeavouring to avoid the effusion of Christian blood … that, unless it be upon such a necessity that I may call it, as some say merrily of women, *malum necessarium*, I should be loth to enter into it.[77]

James curiously coupled his aversion to war here with his aversion to women; they were two 'necessary evils'. It was precisely these aversions in their king that had made Englishmen worry about their nation's manhood. In 1624 it was too late to alter the king's sexual preference, but there was still time to vindicate English manhood by forcing him to embrace war.

Chapter 6
Legacy

James I died in 1625, but the repercussions of his homosexuality did not die with him. The trend in recent years has been to interpret the disintegration of Charles's regime in the 1640s as the product of immediate circumstances, unrelated to what occurred earlier in his own reign, let alone to anything that occurred in the reign of his father. In this chapter, therefore, we are bucking the trend in suggesting that James's homosexuality continued to have repercussions long after his death, repercussions that were evident in the war on the continent, the continuing ascendancy of Buckingham, the marriage of Charles, the deteriorating reputation of the monarchy and eventually even the outbreak of civil war.

First there was the war on the continent. Thomas Scott, the pamphleteer who had so fervently advocated war, was delighted with the transformation of the English into a fighting people. Speaking now through the manly voice of Sir Walter Raleigh, Scott observed that 'Englishmen, who for the space of twenty-two yeares before, had but as it were dallyed and plaied with Armes, rather seeking to affect it for novelty then necessity, were now, in one yeares deliberate and materiall exercise, become so singular and exquisite' that they excelled the Netherlands in military prowess. Under James, England's 'ease had made her grow idle', but now every child aspired to be a Hercules, and the whole island had become a 'Nurcery of excellent and exquisite Souldiers'.[1] In 1626 Scott was murdered by a soldier.[2] Life does have its ironies.

Scott's fate serves as a metaphor for the war effort in general. The war expanded to include Spain and France. It brought the nation to the point of bankruptcy and political breakdown, and it led to the death of approximately 20,000 British fighting men.[3] James would not have been surprised. In the words of Sir John Oglander, James 'was a good king and, in his death, said that our nation could not be contented for they desired war, and he prophesied that, when he was dead, they should have more war than they knew how to manage'.[4]

Then there was Buckingham. By returning from Spain empty-handed and advocating war, he had temporarily made himself popular. In John Hacket's words, 'he was St *George* on Horseback, let the Dragon take heed, that stood in his Way'.[5] The worse the war effort went, however, the more resentment was focused on Buckingham. His popularity evaporated so rapidly that by 1626 Parliament attempted to impeach him. Shielded by Charles, he escaped impeachment and a second parliamentary attack in 1628. But he could not escape the assassin's knife. In the summer of 1628, while preparing to lead another naval expedition, he was murdered by John Felton. Buckingham's most recent biographer portrays him as a valiant figure, struggling to win a war that was doomed by Parliament's short-sighted refusal to provide enough money. Buckingham is made to seem a hero, and Parliament 'neurotic' for attacking him.[6] Meanwhile, Felton has been depicted as merely a disgruntled soldier who was passed over for promotion. In time, however, the traditional view of Buckingham is likely to prevail. He was hard-working and even courageous, but he was too young and inexperienced to master the situation he had got himself into. He did not have the political and diplomatic skills, let alone the wisdom, James had possessed; and he was utterly unrealistic in his military enterprises. Felton was encouraged by popular opinion to kill Buckingham, and frankly the populace had good reason to rejoice in his murder.[7] Charles withdrew from the continental conflict shortly thereafter, and for a while at least his subjects were spared further bloodshed.

Buckingham's reputation had fluctuated wildly during the war. At the outset, by championing the war, he had temporarily made himself seem more manly. Perhaps the most famous example of this transformation appeared in Thomas Middleton's *A Game at Chess*. This enormously successful play represented Buckingham and Charles upon their return to England as heroes who had outwitted the Spaniards. Buckingham's character in the play personally dispatched the Spanish Duke of Olivares to Hell. Olivares was described as an 'olive-coloured Ganymede'.[8] Thus the most famous Ganymede of his age was briefly transformed into a destroyer of Ganymedes. The transformation was not irreversible, however. When the war turned into one unmitigated disaster after another, Buckingham was again depicted as a man who had gained power through his 'Ganimedean looks'.[9]

Derision of Buckingham's manhood was a recurring motif in libels written during the war. He had achieved the office of Lord Admiral not on the basis of ability but physical attractiveness; 'shape was all the cause'. But good looks and dancing ability could not win wars. When Buckingham personally led an expedition to France, one poet remarked, 'Our Duke of Buckingham is gone / To fight and not to daunce.' When he returned in defeat, another wit wrote that instead of the ancient Argonauts, he was the 'great commander of the al-goe-naughts'. To conquer Spain and France 'Requires a soldiers march, not courtiers daunce'.[10] Perhaps the unkindest cut of all came in a poem from this period in which Buckingham was compared to a capon – that is, a castrated cockerel.[11] Even the verses produced at the time of Buckingham's assassination mocked his manhood. A recent historian who studied these libels found that Felton, the assassin, was usually portrayed as a strong and brave figure, 'the opposite of the effeminate, foppish coward Buckingham'.[12]

Just as Buckingham could not escape the comparison with Ganymede, so could he not escape the comparison with Sejanus. In 1626, when Sir John Eliot presented the impeachment charges against Buckingham to the House of Lords, he resurrected this comparison. Eliot cited Tacitus and referred specifically to the 'solecisms' and 'veneries' of Sejanus, which in the language of the day implied abnormal sexual pleasures. When King Charles heard about this, he was reported to have said, 'If the Duke is Sejanus, I must be Tiberius.'[13] Likewise, in 1628, just before Buckingham's assassination, the story of Sejanus circulated in England in the form of a tract entitled *The Powerful Favorite, Or, The Life of Aelius Sejanus*. Earlier in the century, Ben Jonson's *Sejanus* had inadvertently become applicable to contemporary events. The reappearance of Sejanus in this popular tract in 1628 was no accident.

The war cannot be blamed on James, except in so far as it was a reaction against his foreign policy and personal practices. Buckingham, on the other hand, was all James's making. He lifted Buckingham from obscurity, made him the most powerful man in the country, and passed him along to Charles. This was arguably the worst part of James's legacy. Buckingham's biographer alleges that royal favourites served a useful purpose by deflecting criticism away from the king. The favourite could be blamed for anything that went wrong, and he could even be removed from office, while the king escaped unscathed.[14] What this ignores is the way the choice of a favourite reflected the king's judgement. A bad favourite implied bad judgement on the part of the king who favoured him. Furthermore, the inordinate power of a favourite upset the natural order of things, which again threatened the king who depended on that natural order for his authority. Buckingham's ascendancy was especially suspect because its origins no less than its effects seemed unnatural.

All of these themes ran through *The Powerful Favorite*. The tract began by asserting that kings should not be free to let their passions dominate affairs of state: 'Seeing that Princes dispose soveraignely of their hearts... Wee had need therefore to desire that their affections to particular men might be just and well regulated.' It ended with the lesson 'that no man can ever use power well which is ill gotten'. When a king's affections are not well regulated, trouble will ensue, 'for it cannot goe well when the people perceive that favour transferreth soveraigne honours of superiours upon an inferiour, and that the Prince suffereth a companion in the kingdome to assist him to governe'. Companions (especially 'beastly companions', as Thomas Scott called them) had no rightful claim to power, and kings who forgot this fact were forgetting their own place. The king 'who so neglects to play the part of a Master, shall finde servants bold enough to command him'. One of the most perceptive comments in *The Powerful Favorite* explained that 'Princes are offended when we blame their favorites, because it seemes we accuse the weaknesse of their judgments in the election of a Subject unworthy their favour.' In other words, kings understand that assaults on their favourites constitute assaults on themselves. For this very reason, Tiberius punished the assailants of Sejanus as rigorously as if he himself had been their target.[15] This is precisely how Charles reacted to attacks on Buckingham. He was especially vindictive towards Sir John Eliot. In 1626, when Eliot compared Buckingham to Sejanus, Charles had him imprisoned. Three years later, after Buckingham was murdered, Charles imprisoned Eliot again, this time keeping him there till he died.

Kings will naturally favour one servant over another. That is to be expected. It is quite another matter, however, for a king to give inordinate power to a lover. The historical sketch of Edward II's reign written by Lady Falkland emphasized this same point: It is not 'proper (if the sovereign's affections must dote) that the object of their weakness should sway the government of the kingdom. Such an intermixtion begets confusion and error, and is attended by perpetual envy and hatred.'[16]

Malcontents did not accuse Charles, as they had James, of engaging in a sexual relationship with Buckingham. But they knew that Charles somehow loved Buckingham, that the Duke had used sex to gain power and that he might use it again. As one poem of the period declared: 'You love the king, he you...and you Solely, for your looke.' Another poem referred to Buckingham as 'a monarch's minion' who danced and charmed his way into his 'soveraignes heart' and 'deare affection'. Another poem referred specifically to Charles: 'Our Charlemaine takes much delight/In this great beast soe faire in sight/With his whole heart affects the same/And loves too well *Buck-King* of *Game*.'[17] One unfortunate poet whose name we know, Alexander Gill, expressed his concern about Charles and Buckingham all too clearly. He got into trouble with the authorities for writing a poem in which he prayed 'God, to save/My sovereign from a Ganymede,/Whose whorish breath hath power to lead/His Majesty which way it list:/O! let such lips be never kist.'[18]

Images of sexual inversion were mixed with images of political inversion in the satirical verses of the period. To many observers it appeared as if Buckingham was more the ruler of England than Charles: 'The subject is more soveraigne then his king.'[19] In one poet's words, the ship of state was 'Not govern'd by the master, but his mate.' The word 'mate' was probably intended here to convey a sexual connotation. Similarly, the king's sceptre served as a phallic image in another poem where Buckingham was made to admit that he 'Undid that king that let mee sway/His sceptre as I pleas'd.' Another poet said of Buckingham, 'Hee shall be king there, sitt in the kings throne,/Or els commaund the king, and that's all one.' Another observed that what gave Buckingham power was his ability to conjoin the king's authority to his own: 'My power shall bee unbounded in each thing,/If once I use these words *I and the king*.'[20] Buckingham became a virtual co-ruler. The higher he rose, however, the more it upset the social order. As the Venetian ambassador explained, people 'cannot endure that one born a simple gentleman, a rank slightly esteemed there, should be the sole access to the Court, the sole means of favour, in fact one might say the King himself'.[21]

The whole state was turned topsy-turvy by Buckingham's ascendancy. One poem declared that his paramount sin was his 'affection of a higher state'. Several others declared that he 'mounted' too high. Again the sexual innuendo is obvious. James had elevated Buckingham to the peerage, but he could not make him the equal of the other hereditary peers. One poet put this view in the mouth of Buckingham himself, referring to 'my peeres (they were not my com-peeres, Though farr my betters both in blood and yeares)'.[22] Another poet, dismayed by the spread of rebellious sentiments, tried to defend

the Duke; but his words verified how much the natural order had
been upset:

> The wisest king did wonder, when hee spy'd
> The nobles march on foot, their vassals ride.
> His majestie may wonder more, to see
> Some that will neede bee kinge as well as hee.
> A sadd presage of danger to this land,
> When lower strive to get the upper hand ...[23]

James had set this process in motion when he first allowed
Buckingham to get the upper hand. Once ancient distinctions of rank
were overturned, there was no telling where the process might end.
The shock of Buckingham's assassination drove one poet to warn:
'God's siccle spares not either king or crowne.'[24] That was an ominous
prophecy when one considers that, two decades later, Charles was
beheaded. (The implement employed on that occasion was an axe
rather than a sickle, but as prophecies go, it was not far from the
mark.)

Alan Bray has argued that there was a fine line between intense male
friendship and sodomy in Renaissance England. Kisses, embraces and
strong emotional bonds were ordinary signs of male friendship. However, men were suspected of crossing over the line to sodomy if one of
them came from a significantly lower level of society and profited conspicuously from the relationship. 'If someone had acquired a place in
society to which he was not entitled by nature and could then because
of it perhaps even lord it over those who were naturally his betters', it
conjured up the spectre of sodomy.[25] Of course, the spectre was not
always the reality, and Bray proceeds to argue that we should not necessarily believe accusations of sodomy that arose in such circumstances,
even in the case of Buckingham. But why not? Generally speaking, in
the circumstances Bray describes, suspicions of sodomy would be reasonable. And in Buckingham's case they would seem especially reasonable. What catapulted Buckingham to dizzying heights, what gained
him stupendous wealth and power, was – more than anything else –
his sexual relationship with the king. That is not simply what people
suspected; that is what they knew.

Charles inherited his one and only favourite from James. After the
death of Buckingham, Charles never had another. What he did have
were reasonably competent officials. His chief officials – Archbishop
Laud, the Earl of Portland, the Earl of Strafford – were not faultless, but

they were industrious and efficient administrators; and no one familiar with these characters would claim that they achieved their positions by virtue of their good looks, charm or dancing ability. One can only wonder, therefore, how much better Charles's reign might have begun if he had not inherited Buckingham from his father.[26]

Of course, Charles had happily accepted Buckingham. He had no such fondness for other aspects of his father's legacy. Indeed, he tried to reverse many of its aspects. The modern historian Kevin Sharpe has provided the most thorough analysis of Charles's campaign to reverse the effects of his father. 'After the bawdy decadence of James I's reign', Sharpe explains, 'Charles sought to establish a well-regulated court as a shrine of virtue and decorum.' When Charles ascended to the throne, the 'licentiousness, ribaldry and drunkenness of James I's court were rapidly out of season'. Instead, Charles set out 'to reform a licentious court into a moral community', to establish 'a very different moral tone for his court to that of his father'. The difference began at the top, for Charles was 'in many respects a complete contrast to his father'. Instead of indulging himself as James had done, Charles 'was an ascetic figure of great personal control'. In some ways he could justly be described as puritanical. He did not swear; he was abstemious about food and drink; he 'set an example of decorum, upright behaviour and self-control'.[27]

Why did Charles make such a concerted effort to be so different from his father? The obvious answer is that Charles felt a deep revulsion for the lifestyle of his father and wanted to make it as clear as possible that in these matters he was not his father's son. The reforms Charles promoted in his court were identical to the ones that his brother, Prince Henry, had implemented in his. Perhaps, therefore, we are seeing the hand of Queen Anne at work here. It would appear that she had indeed managed to turn her sons against their father and set the wheels in motion to purify the court of all she detested after James's death.

Homosexuality was one of the practices Charles tried to purge. With Buckingham out of the way, Charles was free for the first time to focus all his emotions on his wife. Charles, one observer noted, 'has now so wholly made over all his affections to his wife, that he dare say they are out of the danger of any other favourites'.[28] Charles and Henrietta Maria had been married for three years, but it was only now, after the death of Buckingham that they fell in love. A few weeks later the queen was pregnant for the first of several times. In contrast to his father, Charles became conspicuously heterosexual and uxorious. His large and loving family served, like his court, as a model for his subjects to admire and emulate. Charles made a conscious effort to ulitilize art and literature to project this image of conjugal happiness. As Roy Strong observed, 'Charles and Henrietta Maria were the first English royal couple to be glorified as husband and wife in the domestic sense'.[29] This glorification of domestic love can be seen in the surviving paintings of Charles and his family and perhaps most pointedly in Thomas Carew's masque entitled *Coelum Britannicum*, which was performed at court in early 1634. According to Sharpe, when Carew wrote *Coelum Britannicum*, 'he evidently framed his masque in accordance with the king's tastes and values – and possibly under royal direction'.[30] It is important to bear this in mind when examining the contents of the masque.

Coelum Britannicum begins with the god Mercury congratulating Charles and his wife on the transformation they have effected in England. The old days of 'wanton love' are gone. Charles and Henrietta Maria are leading an 'exemplar life' that serves as a 'patterne' to the whole world. The example set by Charles and his queen is so spectacular that it has risen to heaven and inspired even the gods to emulation. Jupiter especially has decided to lay aside his 'wild lusts' and reform himself according to this earthly example. As Mercury explains to Charles and Henrietta Maria, 'When in the Chrystall myrrour of your reigne / He view'd himselfe, he found his loathsome staines.' Thus had the British royal couple radiated 'a pure refined influence'. At this point in the masque, Momus (the spy, tattle-tale and mocker of the gods) arrives to report the details of Jupiter's conversion. From Momus we learn that Jupiter, who was decaying in his natural abilities, 'recanted, disclaymed, and utterly renounced all the lascivious extravagancies, and riotous enormities of his forepast licentious life'. One product of Jupiter's forepast licentious life was the constellations. Whenever Jupiter had had extramarital affairs, his wife, Juno, had turned his lovers into beasts. Then Jupiter, having superior power, turned these beasts into stars which formed the constellations of the heavens. (It was part of classical mythology that Ganymede became the constellation Aquarius.) When Jupiter decided to reform his behaviour, he also gave orders 'that this whole Army of Constellations be immediately disbanded and casheered, so to remove all imputation of impiety from the Coelestiall Spirits, and all lustfull influences upon terrestriall bodies'. Jupiter issued many other orders, too, for a full-scale reformation of the heavens. 'Heaven is no more the place it was', Momus says. It has become a 'Monastery of converted gods'. Among these converted gods is Bacchus, who 'hath commanded all Tavernes to be shut, and no liquor drawne after tenne at night'. Then Momus announces what, from our point of view, must be the single most interesting reform:

> *Ganimede* is forbidden the Bedchamber, and must only minister in publique. The Gods must keepe no Pages, nor Groomes of their Chamber under the age of 25, and those provided of a competent stocke of beard.

'In briefe', Momus concludes, 'the whole state of the Hierarchy suffers a totall reformation, especially in the poynt of reciprocation of conjugall affection'. Jupiter is so impressed by Charles and Henrietta Maria that he has decided 'to eternize the memory of that great example of Matrimoniall union which he derives from hence'. He has engraved an inscription on the door of his own bedchamber: 'CARLOMARIA'.[31]

The meaning of *Coelum Britannicum* should be obvious to anyone acquainted with the facts of Charles's life.[32] Jupiter represents King James. In *Coelum Britannicum* Carew not only announced to the world that Charles's values were different from his father's; he actually gave Charles the satisfaction of accomplishing in the fictionalized world of the masque what he was never able to accomplish in the real world – the reformation of his father's behaviour. The banishment of Ganymede from the bedchamber (as well as any young, smooth-faced grooms or pages) represents the banishment of homosexuality, or more precisely the banishment of pederasty. At about this same time, Sir Robert Naunton looked back nostalgically to the reign of Elizabeth, when there were 'only favorites not minions'; and John Suckling expressed similar longings for a time when there were 'No smooth-fac'd Favorites' at court.[33] The mood of *Coelum Britannicum* is celebratory and triumphant, but when we consider the personal family background, it acquires a pathetic quality. It suggests that Charles had been embarrassed by his father's 'loathsome staines' and 'riotous enormities'. It suggests that he was unhappy not only about his father's behaviour but about the effect that behaviour had on his mother. If Jupiter represents James, then Juno must represent Queen Anne. Here at last in Carew's masque, she gains the satisfaction of obliterating all the constellations, all the painful reminders of Jupiter's infidelities. Here at last marital strife and extramarital lovers are replaced by 'conjugall affection'. Charles could not make his mother happy in her own lifetime, but through *Coelum Britannicum* he was able to imagine her in heaven enjoying the 'conjugall affection' of a reformed husband.

Part of James's legacy to Charles was a damaged reputation. In *Basilikon Doron*, where James (in theory) condemned sodomy, swearing, drunkenness and effeminacy, he also cautioned against the loss of reputation. James instructed his son to govern so well that his people could not indulge in 'idle and unreverent speeches' about him, so well that '*Momus* himselfe may have no ground to grudge at'. James understood the importance of reputation. Even the gods could be hurt by Momus, who peaked through key-holes and exposed their faults to public scorn. How much more, then, did a king have to guard his reputation? A king, wrote James, 'is as one set on a stage, whose smallest actions and gestures, all the people gazingly doe behold'. A king's subjects see only his 'outward appearance', and from this they draw conclusions about his inward character. Consequently, 'if his behaviour bee light or dissolute', they will assume the worst about his 'inward intention'. This is no small matter because, if the people form a low opinion of the king's character, it will 'breed contempt, the mother of rebellion and disorder'. James knew it was important to maintain respect for the monarchy. He knew a king was constantly in the public eye. And he worried about the public's ability to see straight through to their king's innermost thoughts. He expressed this concern elsewhere in *Basilikon Doron*:

> ... Kings being publike persons, by reason of their office and authority, are as it were set (as it was said of old) upon a publike stage, in the sight of all the people; where all the beholders eyes are attentively bent to looke and pry in the least circumstance of their secretest drifts: Which should make Kings the more carefull not to harbour the secretest thought in their minde, but such as in the owne [end] time they shall not be ashamed openly to avouch....[34]

What 'secretest drifts' might James have had in mind? The modern critic Jonathan Goldberg detects a guilty conscience at work in these passages. He writes that it is not clear what James feared most – that his subjects would jump to the wrong conclusions about his innermost thoughts or that they would guess those thoughts all too well.[35]

When James wrote *Basilikon Doron*, his reign in England still lay ahead of him. Of course James could be justly proud of a great deal he accomplished in that reign. But his solid accomplishments were overshadowed by persistent scandal – the drinking, the profligate spending, the boyish sexual favourites, the notorious Frances Howard, the Overbury murder, the corruptions of the Howard family in the Treasury and the navy, the even greater rapaciousness of Buckingham and his family, the rumours of sodomy and the aura of effeminacy. All these were a far cry from the days of Elizabeth. James may have known how to behave as king, but he was either too weak or too strong to follow his own advice. He lived his life as he pleased. That was part of his prerogative. But he paid a price. Or, rather, his son who inherited a crown of diminished majesty paid the price.

Unlike his father, Charles tried very hard to follow the advice in *Basilikon Doron*. Masques such as *Coelum Britannicum* were performed on a private stage, but to promote public perceptions of a reformed and respectable court. (They were also printed for public consumption.) Charles took 'painstaking care with the dissemination of his image'.[36] Through literature, painting, sculpture and architecture, he tried to repair the image of the crown. He was part of the cultural backlash against the values of his own father's court. Unlike others in that cultural conflict, however, he had more at stake. It was his crown that was tarnished and his authority that was threatened. For him, more than anyone else, it was imperative to restore the crown's reputation and counteract 'contempt, the mother of rebellion and disorder'. In 1631 the sensational trial of the Earl of Castlehaven gave Charles a concrete opportunity to show the world he would not countenance sodomy. Castlehaven was convicted and beheaded for assisting in the rape of his own wife and engaging in sodomy with his servants. Attorney General Heath in his opening statement to the court declared that the Earl's crimes were worse than those of the Roman Emperors as described by Suetonius. If Heath was thinking particularly of the Emperor Tiberius, he was tactful enough to omit the name. Instead, he assured the court that Charles, 'who is the pattern of virtue, not only as king, but in his person also...when he first heard of it [Castlehaven's case], he gave strict command, that the truth should be searched out, that his throne and people might be cleared from so heavy and heinous sins'.[37]

Nearly thirty years ago Perez Zagorin popularized the idea that there was a cultural conflict in early Stuart England between *The Court and the Country*.[38] The court–country thesis has fallen on hard times since then.[39] Certainly it is no longer possible to think of court and country as two monolithic entities diametrically opposed to one another, villains on one side, heroes on the other. Many individuals who were part of the court agreed with the 'country' critique of the court, and it is not far-fetched to say that Charles was one of them. Indeed, he made a concerted effort to reshape the practices of the court so that they would more closely approximate 'country' ideals. While political historians have virtually abandoned the court–country thesis, it continues to hold some value for historians who deal more with culture and literature. Malcolm Smuts and Kevin Sharpe are especially noteworthy in this respect. Smuts has written that 'complaints against the court and the city were a prominent motif in court culture itself'.[40] And coming even closer to the mark, Sharpe has observed that criticisms 'of what was perceived as a degeneration from courtly ideals were articulated within the court itself, even from the throne'.[41]

While few historians continue to speak in terms of court and country, even fewer appreciate the association between these two mentalities and sexuality. One of these few is Lawrence Stone, who provided the most succinct and memorable list of alleged court and country attributes: 'the Country was virtuous, the Court wicked; the Country was thrifty, the Court extravagant; the Country was honest, the Court corrupt; the Country was chaste and *heterosexual*, the Court promiscuous and *homosexual*; the Country was sober, the Court drunken'.[42] These stereotypes of court and country might have developed no matter who was on the throne, but certainly James contributed far more to them than Elizabeth had. As Smuts observed, 'Although the traditional portrait of a slovenly, homosexual king presiding over a debauched court is grossly exaggerated and one-sided, it does contain a significant core of truth.'[43] James did not single-handedly cause the English court to be viewed as wicked, extravagant, corrupt and drunken; but he did lend credence to this caricature. Above all, it was James who made the charge of homosexuality credible.[44] None of James's Tudor predecessors, especially the ostentatiously heterosexual Henry VIII and defiantly virgin Elizabeth, had given any reason to believe that the very throne of England was a seat of homosexuality.

How much did James's sexual life colour the whole perception of his court? It seems likely that it had a disproportionately adverse effect. If James's extramarital affairs had been heterosexual (as Charles II's were, for example), they would not have hurt his reputation so badly. They might even have enhanced it among those who interpreted sexual prowess as one of the marks of a real man (though some historians claim this attitude did not develop until the eighteenth century). In Stone's opinion, the 'greatest damage to the reputation of the Court and the aristocracy was done by their association in the public mind with homosexuality'.[45] If this was true of the court and the aristocracy, it could not have applied with less force to the person of the king.

Despite Charles's most strenuous efforts to restore the reputation of his family and the dignity of the crown, he could not erase the negative image inherited from his father's reign. As Stone remarked: 'By 1640 there was not much left of "the divinity that doth hedge a King".'[46] Of course Charles, too, contributed to the erosion of respect for the crown. Although his personal life was commendable, he failed miserably in the arena of politics. Eventually he blundered into a civil war that engulfed his three kingdoms and brought his own head to the executioner's block.

The trend in recent years has been increasingly to see Charles as the author of his own ruin. In his detailed analysis of the *The Fall of the British Monarchies*, Conrad Russell expressed surprise to discover how active a participant Charles himself was in the story.[47] Complicated though that story was, Russell concluded, 'I find civil war without him almost impossible to imagine.'[48] The more central Charles becomes to the story, the more important it is to understand what made him the kind of person he was. Charles was combative. In Russell's words, he was 'a king who invited resistance' and 'got what he was asking for'.[49] What made Charles so quick to stand on his honour, so inflexible, so deaf to criticism and resistant to good counsel, so ready to fight rather than compromise?[50] As we have seen, Charles came to the throne with an agenda. He set out to remove the aura of disorder and dissolution that hung over James's court. But he also set out to be different from his father in ways that proved more destructive.

The hallmark of James's reign was peace; the hallmark of Charles's reign was war. Charles discarded his father's pusillanimous and pacifist foreign policy, embarking instead on an adventurous war. He tried to become the warrior his mother and others had hoped for in Prince Henry. It is true that Charles withdrew from the Thirty Years War, and during the ensuing decade of the 1630s his court glorified peace. But that was merely making a virtue of necessity. Peace had been forced on Charles by the exhaustion of his Treasury and the collapse of political support. And even while he was at peace in the 1630s, Charles culti-vated the image of the warrior on horseback, the commander's baton in his hand, a radically different iconography from that of his father's reign. The court culture of the 1630s made it appear as if Charles was a knight who could fight if he wanted to fight, but chivalry and the influence of his loving wife turned his attention to domestic bliss instead.[51] This idyllic pose was shattered, of course, by Charles himself when he seized the first opportunity that came along in 1639 to pick another fight, this time with the Scots. There soon followed the First Bishops War, the Second Bishops War and the Civil War – year after year of needless, ruinous war. Godfrey Goodman perceptively observed that 'never man did desire wars more than King Charles, and never man was more unfortunate in all his wars than King Charles'.[52] Charles spent nearly half his reign at war. He was not *Rex Pacificus*; he was *Rex Bellicosus*. In the end his opponents called him 'that man of blood'. Charles was determined to be different from his father, and in this respect – unfortunately – he was.

When the civil war broke out, the man chosen to lead the parliamentary forces against Charles was the third Earl of Essex. He, too, was part of the legacy from James's reign. Heir to the title of his illustrious father who was executed under Queen Elizabeth, Essex had been a companion of Prince Henry and a prominent advocate of England's intervention in the Thirty Years War who chafed under James's policy of peace. Perhaps more importantly, he was the man who had been accused of sexual impotence by his wife, Frances Howard, in the scandalous divorce trial that cleared the way for her to marry James's favourite, the Earl of Somerset. In the words of his biographer, Essex 'would find it difficult indeed to forget the humiliating divorce'. He bore a grudge for the rest of his life; he needed 'to avenge himself'.[53] As Captain-General of the parliamentary army, he got the belated chance he had been waiting for to vindicate his name and demonstrate his manhood. Once again he proved a disappointment. In 1644, when Charles chased him into Cornwall to the town of Lostwithiel, he ran away.

Chapter 7

Memory

While James lived, he was subjected to countless unfavourable comparisons with Queen Elizabeth 'of blessed memory'. In the reign of his son Charles there was no such nostalgia for James. For the most part, there was discreet silence. After the civil war and execution of Charles, however, memories of James and his court did resurface in a series of historical and polemical works. These works afford us an opportunity to examine how James's sexual relations with other males were remembered and represented. Of course, the factual accuracy of these representations is suspect, but in some ways that only makes them more interesting. What we want to examine is how these works treat the subject of King James's sexuality. What aspects do these polemical tracts choose to exaggerate, omit, distort? What attitudes do they reveal? What words do they use? What constructions of sexuality are implied by these words? In these tracts we find people discoursing about, or (in today's jargon) 'writing', sex. By examining these works as discourse, we can learn more about the way in which sex between males was construed or constructed in the middle of the seventeenth century. This will help us to determine how much sodomy dominated the discourse, what other less monstrous ways there were for thinking about sex between males, and whether supposedly 'modern' constructions were already taking shape.

By far the most notorious of these works is Sir Anthony Weldon's *Court and Character of King James*. Weldon had occupied two minor offices under James (Clerk of the Kitchen and Clerk of the Greencloth), and he was knighted in 1617. In that same year he accompanied James on his visit to Scotland. It would have been more prudent for Weldon to stay at home. The trip to Scotland inspired him to write a tract ridiculing the Scots, and the discovery of this manuscript appears to be the reason why James removed him from office. Not surprisingly, in his later years Weldon was an enthusiastic supporter of the parliamentary side in the civil war. He died near the beginning of 1649, and his *Court and Character of King James* appeared the following year.[1]

There are reasons why Weldon should be considered a good source of information. He was placed in an advantageous position to observe James at a distance or to hear firsthand accounts of his behaviour from others around the palace. But the insider information in Weldon's *Court and Character* is mixed indiscriminately with quirky interpretations and misinformed gossip. For example, Weldon repeats the farfetched story that James had begun to hate Buckingham, who retaliated by poisoning the king. This has made it easy for modern historians to discount Weldon as a mere scandalmonger who had an axe to grind. Robert Ashton described Weldon's *Court and Character* as a 'scurrilous and spiteful account', warped by Weldon's 'pathological hatred of the Stuarts'.[2] Maurice Lee Jr called Weldon 'that foul-mouthed discharged office-holder'.[3] Neil Cuddy dismissed Weldon's work as a 'rabidly xenophobic denunciation'.[4] Jenny Wormald likewise wrote that Weldon's character sketch 'arose out of hatred for the Scots'. She, too, emphasized that Weldon had a score to settle with James. The 'consequences of the loss of his job have lasted to the present day', she wrote; 'few men in history have had quite such revenge'.[5] Christopher Durston referred to Weldon's work as a 'poisonous piece of literary revenge' and claimed that it was 'almost entirely responsible for James's "black legend"'.[6] These caricatures of Weldon are more truly venemous than anything Weldon wrote about James.

Considering how bitterly historians condemn Weldon, one must be surprised on reading him to discover that his analysis of James, though biased and marred by errors, was also in some places perceptive and favourable. Weldon wrote, for example, that James 'was a King of mercy as well as peace, never cruell'. The execution of Sir Walter Raleigh is described as 'the only marke of Tyranny upon this good Kings reigne ... and even against that good Kings will'.[7] Even Weldon's detractors practise selective use of evidence from his writing. Lee, who advised that historians 'can, and should, ignore the venomous caricature' provided by Weldon, concluded his own book on James with a quotation from Weldon in praise of James![8] Likewise, S.J. Houston, who described Weldon's *Court and Character* as 'salacious backstairs gossip' and 'a portrait smeared with malice because its author had been sacked', could not resist concluding his book on James with the same quotation from Weldon.[9] Here is Weldon's epitaph on King James which Lee and Houston thought fit to quote: 'In a word, he was (take him altogether and not in peeces) such a King I wish this Kingdom have never any worse, on the condition, not any better; for he lived in peace, dyed in peace, and left all his Kingdomes in a peaceable condition, with his own Motto: *Beati Pacifici.*'[10] Does that sound like a venomous caricature, a portrait smeared with malice?

Fortunately, for our purposes, it is not necessary to assess the reliability of all of Weldon's *Court and Character.* We are only interested in what he says about James's sexual habits, and even if all of this turns out to be 'salacious backstairs gossip', so much the better. Robert Ashton deserves credit for recognizing the usefulness of gossip. Although Ashton criticized the writings of Weldon and others like him because they were motivated by 'spiteful and indiscriminate animus against the king', he nevertheless understood that these works 'present a view of the king which came to be held by many of his subjects'; and therefore, no matter how 'unreliable and unfair these accounts may be, they are material which no historian can afford to neglect'.[11]

What, then, did Weldon say about James's sexual relationships? Not much. He described James's first English favourite as 'the first Meteor of that nature appearing in our climate' and another as 'a kinde of Favourite, but not such as after appeared with young Faces, and smooth Chins'. Weldon claimed that the Countess of Suffolk 'did looke out choyce young men, whom she daily curled', 'perfuming their breaths' to attract James's attention, but she ceased her 'curling and perfuming' when Somerset became the established favourite. When Buckingham appeared on the scene, Weldon says the king 'cast a glancing eye towards him,which was easily perceived by such as observed their Princes humour'. Buckingham was manoeuvred into the position of cup-bearer, so 'that he might be in the Kings eye' and dressed in more attractive clothes to make a better impression. After Buckingham achieved his objective, Weldon observed that James's 'passion of love to his new Favourite…was more impatient, then any woman to enjoy her love'. After a while, however, James grew 'weary' of Buckingham, and the principal reason for this 'staleness' was the Duke's marriage, 'after which the Kings edge was ever taken off from all Favourites'. These descriptions of James and his favourites are coloured by a mildly mocking tone, but they are not outrageous distortions.[12]

Weldon's *Court and Character* is mistaken in places, as, for example, in suggesting that James grew tired of Buckingham, and it sometimes exaggerates. In one well-known passage Weldon remarked upon the change in James's behaviour late in life when he involved himself in

Buckingham's growing extended family. 'King *James*, that naturally in former times, hated women, had his Lodgings replenished with them.' Now 'children did run up and downe the Kings Lodgings, like little Rabbit-starters'. This 'was a strange change, that the King, who formerly would not endure his Queen and children in his Lodgeings, now you would have judged, that none but women frequented them'. What Weldon wrote here was only a slight exaggeration of the truth; he stopped far short of the French ambassador, who suggested that James was molesting the little children.[13]

These allusions to James's odd relations with men and women add to the general air of ridicule in Weldon's portrait of the king, but they do not dominate. Such allusions are even less prominent in the twelve-page, overall character sketch at the end of Weldon's work. Here (among several items of praise) is where one finds all the features of Weldon's familiar portrait – that James was constantly 'fidling about his Cod-piece', wore padded clothing for fear of assassination, had a tongue too big for his mouth which made him drool, never washed his hands, rarely changed his clothes, cursed liberally, and was generally 'the wisest foole in Christendome'. The closest Weldon came to mentioning James's sexual practices in this character sketch was when he observed that the king was fond of changing favourites and 'was not very uxorious'.[14]

On balance, then, how did Weldon treat homosexual relationships in his *Court and Character*? There is no doubt that James's love of male favourites counted against him. Weldon used the issue to denigrate James, and he presumably expected his readers to respond accordingly. But Weldon was very far from exaggerating the issue. Perhaps what is most interesting about Weldon is what he did *not* say. He did not use the word 'sodomy'. It is a curious fact that this portrait of James, which is routinely described as a venemous, poisonous, scurrilous, malicious and spiteful act of revenge did not try to get more propaganda value out of James's love affairs with other males. Weldon mocks James's displays of affection for his favourites, but he does not recoil in horror. He recognizes the existence of sex between males, but he does not seem to view it through the monstrous category of sodomy.

Of course, it could be objected that the only reason Weldon did not speak more openly about sodomy was because of the Christian prohibition against naming it overtly. This objection collapses, however, when one examines how Weldon treated another man who appears to have been homosexual. One of the ways Buckingham had exerted his influence was by arranging marriages for several of his single relatives.

What Weldon found remarkable about these arranged marriages was that they included even men 'that naturally hated women'. Among these, Weldon found the case of Sir Anthony Ashley, who had been persuaded to marry one of the Duke's female relatives, especially note-worthy. Weldon described this particular marriage as 'above all the Miracles of those times' because Ashley 'never loved any but boyes'.[15] There is not the slightest indication that Weldon thought of Ashley as a hideous sodomite. There is no suggestion of devils, witches, papists, monsters or total moral depravity. Ashley just 'never loved any but boyes'. In fact, Ashley belonged to a whole class of men in Weldon's mind whom he characterized as 'those that naturally hated women'. Weldon did not say that it was perfectly natural for some men to love boys, but this would seem to be a logical implication of what he did say. If Weldon did take such a broad-minded view of nature where sex-ual relations were concerned, he was remarkably ahead of his time.

There is one other passage from Weldon's *Court and Character* that complicates the picture. The scene described in this passage is the final parting between King James and the Earl of Somerset. The charges in the Overbury murder case were just coming to light, and Somerset must have derived false reassurance from James's effusive farewell:

the King hung about his neck, slabboring his cheeks; saying, for Gods sake when shall I see thee againe? On my soul, I shall neither eate, nor sleep, untill you come again. ... Then lolled about his neck; then, for Gods sake, give thy Lady this kisse for me. ...

According to Weldon, James behaved in this manner 'at the stayres head, at the midle of the staires, and at the stayres foot'. As soon as Somerset was out of earshot, however, James declared, 'I shall never see his face more.'[16]

This episode may have transpired very much as Weldon depicted it. Weldon claimed he was an eye-witness to the scene, and one of Somerset's servants instantly informed him of James's final remark. Moreover, James's alleged behaviour on this occasion is consistent with several other reports we have already encountered that describe him hanging about the necks of and kissing his favourites, reports that extend over a forty-year period from 1582 to 1622. In any case, for our purposes, it makes no difference whether the story is true or false. What is interesting is how Weldon tells the story. He did make James look more disgusting by using words like 'slabboring' and 'lolled', but ostensibly the point of the story had nothing to do with sex.

The moral of the story, according to Weldon, is simply that James was a consummate dissembler. As we have seen, James was proud to take as his motto *Beati Pacifici*, but Weldon thought an equally apt motto was *Qui nescit dissimulare, nescit regnare* (he who knows not how to dissemble knows not how to rule). Indeed, this motto appeared on the title page of Weldon's *Court and Character*.[17] James knew that a king was an actor on a stage. He was indeed a skilful dissembler who knew how to keep people, especially foreign ambassadors, guessing about his intentions. He himself might not have objected to Weldon's point here.

It is possible, however, that contemporary references to James's capacity for dissimulation were a coded way of referring to his sexual practices. To crack this code we must read Weldon's book alongside Arthur Wilson's *The History of Great Britain, Being the Life and Reign of King James The First* (1653). Wilson had been employed by the Earl of Essex from about 1614 and accompanied him on several military adventures on the continent in the 1620s. He was, therefore, in an advantageous position to pick up court gossip, but he would also have seen events through the prejudiced eyes of the noble faction including the Earls of Essex and Southampton who were hostile to James's foreign policy and his favourites.[18] Wilson wrote about James:

> Some Parallel'd him to *Tiberius* for *Dissimulation*, yet Peace was maintained by him as in the Time of *Augustus*; And Peace begot *Plenty*, and *Plenty* begot *Ease* and *Wantonness*, and *Ease* and *Wantonness* begot *Poetry*, and *Poetry* swelled to that *bulk* in his time, that it begot strange *Monstrous Satyrs*, against the King's own Person, that haunted both *Court*, and *Country*. ....[19]

Wilson here hints at a fact that Weldon did not spell out: the motto regarding dissimulation was associated with the Roman Emperor Tiberius. Many readers of Weldon and Wilson would have known this from their reading of the Roman historian Tacitus who had made Tiberius a byword for dissimulation. It will be remembered that Jonson's chief authority for the play *Sejanus* was Tacitus. Sir Francis Bacon helped to popularize Tacitus in England.[20] In his *Essays* Bacon cited Tacitus for his authority on Tiberius under the subject 'Of Simulation and Dissimulation'.[21]

Wilson's prose is less explicit or graphic than Weldon's; he does not describe James embracing or kissing, much less slobbering over, one of his favourites. But at the same time the passage quoted above from Wilson's history does manage to convey more lurid connotations.

The mere mention of Tiberius's name would have conjured up the images that had dogged James throughout his reign in England regarding Sejanus, the island of Capri and shocking sexual perversions. The word 'wantonness' had served as a code word since the Parliament of 1610 where the Lord Treasurer clumsily insisted that the king needed money to supply his wants, not his wantonness. And the phrase 'monstrous satires' perhaps comes closest to what Wilson really had in mind. Were the satires monstrous, or was the activity they satirized monstrous? Was Wilson here trying to insinuate the monstrous sin that is not supposed to be mentioned by name?

James was a puzzlement. Many of his English subjects found him doubly puzzling because he was both a Scot and a man who loved other males. They viewed him through the distorting lenses of xenophobia *and* homophobia. They saw him as not just a foreigner but the 'Other', a person in many respects like themselves and yet in other disturbing ways an alien presence. He was a man, but did not act entirely like a man. He was a king, but did not act entirely like a king. He had a wife and children, but reserved his greatest love for effeminate youths. He wrote learned treatises, but did 'beastly' things. He made peace, not war. As polemicists like Thomas Scott complained, Queen Elizabeth had been more of a man and king. This is probably the light in which James's reputation for dissimulation should be viewed. It was part-and-parcel of his inscrutability, his otherness, his ability to be known and yet remain a mystery. He was, in a word, queer.

In addition to the Tiberius analogy, Wilson made other oblique allusions to James's sexuality. For example, he explained that James was alienated from Queen Anne by his '*Masculine conversation* and *intimacy*'. The word 'intimacy' here was probably intended to carry a sexual overtone. When James first became interested in Somerset, Wilson again used words that conveyed a sexual overtone. He wrote that the king's '*fancy* ran with a violent *stream* upon a young Gentleman'. After spending time with the young man, James formed the opinion that he 'might be a good Anchorage, and a fit Harbor for his most retired thoughts'. Regarding Buckingham, Wilson wrote that 'the King cast his eye upon a young Gentleman, so rarely *moulded*, that he meant to make him a *Masterpiece*'. James was 'strucken with this new *object*', but he did not want 'to be thought changeable, and taken again with a sudden affection', so he was careful not to bring Buckingham into prominence too quickly. After Buckingham achieved prominence, 'lying all this while in the King's *bosom*, every man paid tribute to his *smiles*'. Buckingham so enthralled the king that he became 'not only Master of his Horse, and Ships, but his Heart also'. Like Weldon, Wilson commented on the transformation that occurred when James, who 'never much cared for Women', began to enjoy the company of the women and children associated with Buckingham's family. In the 1620s James's pacifism drew scorn upon him and the nation. On the continent he was pictured as having no sword in his scabbard or with a sword 'that no body could draw out, though divers stand pulling at it'. Wilson conceded that James was a wise ruler but questioned 'whether his Wisdom, and knowledge, exceeded his *Choler* and *Fear*'. Wilson's conclusion was that James's behaviour undermined his authority: 'So dangerous it is for *Princes*, by a *Remiss Comportment*, to give growth to the least *Error*; for it often proves as *fruitful* as *Malice* can make it'.[22] That is not only a reasonable conclusion; it mirrors what James himself had said in his *Basilikon Doron*.

Despite the reputation Weldon has for muckraking, actually, on the subject of King James's sexuality, neither he nor Wilson went very far beyond mild innuendo. The innuendo was more pronounced in a work that appeared in 1652 entitled *A Cat May Look Upon a King*. This work has been attributed to Weldon, but it appears to be the product of an imitator who tried to capitalize on the popularity of Weldon's work, which by this time had run through four printings. *A Cat* is not as subtle or balanced as Weldon's *Court and Character*. Its portrait of James is a harsher caricature with none of Weldon's occasional praise. Perhaps befitting a work composed after the execution of King Charles, *A Cat* is more of a hatchet-job. The author may also have felt the need to outdo Weldon, to ratchet up the rhetoric against James one more notch. Whatever the reason, *A Cat* relentlessly criticizes James for his 'hypocrisie, perjury, cowardise, blasphemy, malice... and base ingratitude'. How did it treat his sexuality? Like its predecessor, *A Cat* referred to James's 'slabbering expressions of affection'. It also alluded to his favourites as 'Fellowes of no merit... [who] do his foul pleasure'.

There is a theme running throughout *A Cat* – the recurring insinuation that James had something to hide. He 'durst not own, that [which] he would do by his Favourites'. Only his favourites knew for sure what they did to win the king's favour. Take Somerset, for example. James raised him from obscurity and gave him fabulous wealth, but 'can any man tel for what?' If Weldon did not write *A Cat*, then the person who did write it was guilty of lifting a story out of Weldon's *Court and Character* almost verbatim. According to this story, Somerset had proclaimed that the king did not dare put him on trial. Consequently, at the trial there were two men stationed beside Somerset 'with cloaks on their arms'. These men had been instructed, 'if *Sommerset* did any way flie out against the King, they should instantly hoodwink him wth their cloaks, take him violently from the Bar, and carry him away'.[23] What was James afraid Somerset would say? It may have been that James had poisoned his own son, Prince Henry, which was one of the many poisoning rumours of the time; or it may have been something else. We are reminded that the author of *Tom Tell Troath* charged that the king's favourites would be in a position to blackmail him because they were 'acquainted with his secret sins'.

The author of *A Cat* went further than Weldon and Wilson in implying that there was something counterfeit about James, something dishonest. In fact, at one point he challenged James's defenders to 'publish one cleare act of Honesty from him all the time of his reign'.[24] All these authors insinuated that James had something to hide. But what was it? Was it sodomy? That may be what Wilson meant to imply by 'monstrous satires' and the author of *A Cat* when he used the term 'foul pleasure'. Perhaps these authors were trying to imply what they were prohibited as Christians from expressing explicitly. On the other hand, what is missing from all of these authors, even the author of *A Cat*, is the exaggerated sense of stark horror that should have accompanied thoughts of sodomy. What they seem to imply but shrink from spelling out is simply that James had sex with his favourites. No more and no less. They are repelled by this truth and expect their readers to share their revulsion, but even the merciless author of *A Cat* does not go so far as to suggest that James was a hideous sodomite. It is hard to resist the impression that the phenomenon these authors have in mind, though they do not yet have the word to express it, is simply homosexuality.

This impression is reinforced by Francis Osborne's *Traditional Memorials on the Reign of King James*, first published in 1658. Osborne's salacious descriptions, far more than Weldon's or Wilson's, demonstrate how James's sexuality could be exploited for propaganda value. Osborne started out mildly enough. He provided one of the few descriptions of James kissing Queen Anne, but he accused the king of doing this only 'to shew himself more uxorious before the People at his first coming than in private he was'. Here again was the idea that James was not truly what he appeared to be, linked this time to the issue of uxoriousness, which was a sore point for James's defenders. Osborne also wrote that one of James's minor favourites in England, Philip Herbert, was 'a man carressed by King *James* for his *hansome face*'. In a similar vein, he stated that the Earl of Somerset was

in greatest favour with James 'before he had either *Wife or Beard'*.
Osborne saved his harshest language for his conclusion. Here he wrote
that James's bosom was 'a place reserved for younger men and of more
indearing Countenances: and these went under the appellation of his
Favorites or *Minions*, who like *Burning-glasses* were daily interposed
between him and the Subject'. These 'Golden Calves', as Osborne
called them, had no real merit:

> no other Reason appeared in favour of their choice but *handsomness*,
> so the love the K. shewed was as amorously conveyed as if he had
> mistaken their Sex, and thought them Ladies. Which I have seen
> *Somerset* and *Buckingham* labour to resemble, in the effeminateness
> of their dressings. Though in w[horish?] looks and wanton gestures
> they exceeded any part of Woman-kind my Conversation did ever
> cope withal.

Osborne complained that James was not discreet about his love for
these favourites, but rather his 'kissing them after so lascivious a mode
in publick, and upon the Theatre as it were of the World, prompted
many to imagine some things done in the *Tyring-house*, that exceed my
expressions no less than they do my experience'. Osborne emphasized
that James's favourites procured their advancement by agreeing to
accept conditions that others found repugnant. The Earl of Holland,
for example, dashed his chances of preferment 'by turning aside and
spitting after the King had slabbered his mouth'.

Osborne's language is more lurid and sensational than Weldon's or
Wilson's. His objective is to disgust the reader by creating images of
men labouring to look like women, men kissing each other in public,
men doing unspeakable things in private. Yet he could not penetrate
beyond the closed door. He had difficulty imagining what might constitute sex between men because, as he explains, such things 'exceed
my expressions no less than they do my experience'. The best he can
do is describe it as a kind of misguided heterosexuality where one man
mistakes another for a woman. Beyond that, he had his suspicions, but
he could not articulate them. Searching for a word to characterize the
relationship between James and his favourites, he could only hesitat-
ingly refer to it as 'love, or what else posterity will please to call it'.[25]

Osborne did not call it sodomy. He exaggerated and ridiculed the
behaviour between James and his favourites, but he did not inflate
the rhetoric by raising the monstrous spectre of sodomy. He neither
stated nor implied that James's offensive behaviour was related to

witchcraft, the devil, or papists. He obviously viewed it as unnatural, but he did not call it a sin against nature. Osborne found James's behaviour repugnant enough in itself without having to associate it with anything supernatural or monstrous. He had no name for this behaviour. When he did try to name it, the best he could do was 'love, or what else posterity will please to call it'. The word 'homosexual' was not yet in Osborne's vocabulary, but it would seem to be the word he was searching for. Furthermore, Osborne expected his readers to be repelled by the same things that repelled him. And here again there was no need to employ the ghastly discourse of sodomy. James's affection for other males and his physical contact with them were apparently sufficient in themselves to excite revulsion. Osborne's prose, therefore, hints not only at the familiar construct of homosexuality but also at the familiar prejudice of homophobia.

It is not just that references to James and his favourites lack the aura of horror that was supposed to have surrounded sodomy. Sometimes they show sex between men or even anal intercourse treated with levity. Take for example, the case of Sir Anthony Ashley, whom Weldon described as someone who 'never loved any but boyes'. Weldon was not the only person to comment on Ashley's surprising marriage to one of Buckingham's relatives, Phillipa Sheldon.[26] One commonplace book of the period contains the following verse about Ashley and his bride:

> Old Abbott Anthony
>   I thinke hath well done,
> Since he left Sodomy,
>   To marry Sheldon.
> Shee hath a buttocke plumpe,
>   Keep but thy tarse whole
> And sheele hold up her rumpe,
>   With her black arse hole.[27]

Unlike Weldon, the anonymous author of this verse did explicitly mention sodomy. Indeed, he went even further: the central subject of the verse is anal intercourse. Yet the tone is one of humour and ridicule, not horror.

The amusement value attached to anal intercourse may also explain an odd incident earlier in James's reign. When Buckingham became Lord Admiral, he implemented a plan to add two new ships to the navy every year. In 1619 King James personally christened the first set of ships, one of which was named *Buckingham's Entrance*. This name may have provoked too much comment because, for reasons that were never recorded, it was soon changed to *Happy Entrance*.[28]

Sir Edward Peyton also made light of anal intercourse in his *Divine Catastrophe of the Kingly Family of the House of Stuarts*, originally published in 1652. As history, Peyton's *Divine Catastrophe* is about as close as you can get to rubbish. He claimed, for example, that Queen Anne was forced to look for sex elsewhere and found it in a series of lovers; and he implied that James was not the true father of Prince Charles! Again, however, we are not interested in the factual accuracy of Peyton's history but rather the way it dealt with the subject of James's sexuality. Obviously Peyton tried to create the impression that James was no fit sexual partner for Queen Anne. In another place he spelled out that James was 'more addicted to love males then females', and he wrote that James 'sold his affections to Sir George Villiers, whom he would tumble and kiss as a mistress'. Altogether Peyton counted five 'minions and favourites' who at different points during James's reign were able to 'rule the kingdom in the person of the king'. Nevertheless, Peyton did not use this situation to concoct lurid descriptions of James and his favourites or to launch into a sermon on sodomy. Instead, he told a joke. It seems that the Spanish ambassador Gondomar lived next door to Lady Hatton, who was the estranged wife of Sir Edward Coke. Gondomar tried to get a key from Lady Hatton, so that he could pass through the back gate of her grounds to take the air in the nearby open fields, but she denied him access. When Gondomar explained his predicament to King James, he made light of it. Gondomar, 'observing how King James was addicted, told him that the Lady Hatton would not suffer the Lord Cook her husband to come into her fore-doore, nor he himself to come into her back-door'.[29] Peyton's story is not meant to horrify but to amuse. It is a joke capitalizing on James's alleged proclivity (his addiction), and it assumes that readers will laugh, not recoil in horror. Modern readers may not find the story amusing, but it is not because they fail to 'get' the joke. In fact, the familiar quality of stories like this makes the seventeenth century seem closer to our own than is usually supposed.

Of course there were royalist authors during the Interregnum who tried to defend King James's reputation against the libellous attacks of Weldon, Wilson, Osborne and Peyton. Weldon's work was answered within a year by William Sanderson's *Aulicus Coquinariae or A Vindication In Answer to a Pamphlet Entitled The Court and Character of King James pretended to be Penned by Sir A.W. and Published Since His Death*.

Another rebuttal compiled at this time by Godfrey Goodman, Bishop of Gloucester, was not published until the nineteenth century, when it appeared under the title of *The Court of King James the First*. These works gave alternative interpretations of key events such as the Gowrie Conspiracy and the Overbury murder trial that were often just as inaccurate as Weldon's, and they defended the character of many of James's courtiers whom Weldon had besmirched. Both authors made it clear that their goal was to discredit Weldon. Goodman went about this task in a fairly professional manner, but Sanderson adopted a no-holds-barred approach. His book is laced with *ad hominem* attacks on Weldon. The very title *Aulicus Coquinariae* (the court of the cook) was a pointed reminder of Weldon's lowly position in the royal kitchen. Sanderson called Weldon's book a piece of 'ribaldry and beastly bawdery', and he accused Weldon of 'peeping, pimping, into each petticoat'.[30]

James's love for his favourites constituted a major problem for Goodman and Sanderson. One can almost sense their discomfort in the passages where they addressed the issue. After all, what could they say? The existence of James's favourites was too well known to be denied. The only way to defend James against Weldon's most damaging accusations in this area was to minimize the sexual function of the favourites without descending too far into details. But when these royalist authors tried to do this, they were at their least convincing.

In his first mention of the issue, Goodman wrote that James extended favours to certain men 'according to the fancy of love therein, and he agreed with Weldon that the king altered his affections or 'was mutable in so many favourites'. Admitting that James loved a series of male favourites led Goodman to the awkward question of whether James loved the queen. Goodman drew attention to the pertinent fact that James and Anne produced children, but this fact in itself was not sufficient to rebut Weldon's charge that the king 'was not very uxorious'. Furthermore, Goodman was an honest enough man to acknowledge that James and Anne did begin spending a considerable amount of time apart from each other a few years after arriving in England. Goodman did his best to explain this behaviour: 'It is true that some years after they did not much keep company together. The King of himself was a very chaste man, and there was little in the Queen to make him uxorious; yet they did love as well as man and wife could do, not conversing together.' Besides, Goodman added, James 'was never taxed or tainted with the love of any other lady'. Goodman's strategy here was to shift the blame to Anne; it was her fault that she did not have what it took to make James more uxorious. In the process, however, Goodman conceded that James and Anne 'did not much keep company together' and were 'not conversing together', which seem his delicate ways of saying that the royal couple stopped having sex. It did not help Goodman's cause to emphasize that James never loved 'any other lady', especially when he proceeded to describe how much James did love Somerset and Buckingham. With respect to Somerset, Goodman explained that the Earl fell from favour because 'love and affection, though they are the strongest passions for the instant, yet they are not of longest continuance'. Just as a 'man may be glutted with one favourite, as he is feeding upon one food... so truly I think the King was weary of an old favourite'. As for the new favourite, in Goodman's estimation, 'it was impossible for one man to dote more upon another than the King did upon Buckingham'.[31] Goodman's honesty actually kept leading him towards a confirmation rather than a refutation of Weldon's portrait where the king's love of other males was concerned.

Sanderson did not grapple as extensively with the immediate issue of James's favourites or the underlying issue of sexuality. For example, writing about James Hay, one of the king's lesser favourites, he simply tried to brush the issue aside. According to Sanderson, 'it is no matter upon what score that the king gave his affection to this favorite'. Sanderson tried to be a little more forthright on the subject of Somerset, whom he described as 'the first favorite that we find, that is, one whom the king fancied meerly for his fashion'. According to Sanderson, therefore, James 'gave his affection' to one favourite and 'fancied' another. Such vague language raised more questions than it answered. Sanderson was not evasive, however, when it came to the final parting scene between James and Somerset described so graphically by Weldon. Goodman had wisely ignored this scene, but Sanderson felt compelled to address it. He began by arguing that it was only natural for James to express his affection and sadness towards Somerset on this occasion, knowing that they would never meet again and that the Earl was a doomed man. This was a plausible argument, but Sanderson could not leave it at that. He attempted to explain away the more provocative features of Weldon's story. Take Weldon's 'much forced story' at face value, wrote Sanderson, and what you actually see is a commendable 'strugling in the king to make justice and mercy kiss each other'. All Sanderson accomplished by this metaphorical addition was to remind readers of the concrete act of James kissing Somerset. Finally, Sanderson, like Goodman, tried to find an alternative explanation for the estrangement between James and Queen Anne. James had worked hard in Scotland, Sanderson explained. He needed a rest, and his natural inclination was to follow 'a sportfull life'. Besides, due to the weakness in his limbs, he needed the exercise. For all these reasons James tended to live apart from Anne at his various hunting lodges. This, Sanderson asserted, was the full and innocent explanation for James's separation from Anne, as opposed to Weldon's 'scandalous intimation of leaving his queen. Without any love or liking.'[32]

Both Goodman and Sanderson were deeply disturbed by Weldon's accusations and eager to defend James against them. Yet both authors had to admit that James loved or 'fancied' his favourites, and both authors realized that James's love of other males raised the question of whether he was truly capable of loving a female, namely Queen Anne. Since they did not explore the physical side of James's relationships, it is impossible to know whether they thought they were defending James against the charge of sodomy. If they did suspect that this is what Weldon had tried to insinuate, they were too prudent to confront the issue head-on. It is hard to tell, therefore, where to situate Goodman's and Sanderson's discourse with respect to pre-modern sodomy and modern homosexuality. Both writers tried to frame the argument in different terms, suggesting a kind of platonic love between males, what we today might call homoeroticism or homosociability without the sex. We have no way of determining whether this was a conscious or unconscious strategy on their part. They may have been very clever, or very naive. They may also have compartmentalized what they knew, placing their knowledge of James in one part of their minds and their knowledge of sodomy in another part, failing to make the connection, which Alan Bray claimed was typical of the seventeenth century.

Another royalist author, Sir John Oglander, used strikingly similar language. Unlike Goodman and Sanderson, Oglander did not set out to write a rebuttal of Weldon; he simply kept a diary or commonplace book. Because of that fact and because he was a loyal royalist who was twice arrested for his sympathies, he is considered a more credible source. Jenny Wormald, James's staunchest modern supporter, allows that Oglander provides 'a generally enthusiastic description of the king'.[33] Even on the subject of James's sexuality, Oglander tried to be positive. Like Goodman, who wrote that James was 'a very chaste man' who 'was never taxed or tainted with the love of any other lady', Oglander similarly praised James for being 'the chastest prince for women that ever was, for he would often swear that he had never known any other woman than his wife'. Oglander chose his words carefully here. He specified that James was 'the chastest prince for women' precisely because he knew very well that the people James loved outside his marriage were males. Like Goodman, who wrote that 'it was impossible for one man to dote more upon another than the King did upon Buckingham', Oglander wrote that Buckingham had 'the King's affection so tied unto him as to deny him nothing'. Oglander went further than Goodman, however, when it came to describing the nature of James's love. Indeed, Oglander's words came close to the anti-royalist rhetoric of Weldon and Osborne when he wrote that James:

> loved young men, his favourites, better than women, loving them beyond the love of men to women. I never yet saw any fond husband make so much or so great dalliance over his beautiful spouse as I have seen King James over his favourites. ...[34]

Oglander knew that James loved his favourites and treated them the way a man would treat a beautiful wife. Yet that knowledge did not stop Oglander from finding much else to praise in James or from enduring imprisonment for the Stuart cause. It would seem, therefore, that Oglander, like Goodman and Sanderson, was too naive to realize that James's physical relations with his favourites went beyond dalliance, or that he failed to make the connection, as Bray would argue, between James's sexual relations with his favourites and the spectre of sodomy. In Oglander's case, however, a third possibility suggests itself. Considering how graphically he described James's treatment of his favourites, it is possible that Oglander was capable of accepting sexual relations between males with equanimity without resorting to the ghastly discourse of sodomy. Whatever the reasons, all of these royalist authors acknowledged that James loved male favourites; yet none gave the impression of trying to cover up or explain away sodomy.

The gossip about James and his favourites did not end with the restoration of the monarchy in 1660. What is perhaps the most frequently quoted description of James's court was written by Lucy Hutchinson sometime during the 1660s (although her *Memoirs* were not published until the nineteenth century). Her view was certainly biased because her husband was a regicide, one of the judges who had voted for the execution of Charles I, and he died in prison in 1664. Nevertheless, her outraged attitude towards James's court is probably representative of the view that circulated through Stuart England by word of mouth among the more puritan or godly sort. Hutchinson described James's court as a 'nursery of lust and intemperance' where courtiers 'surfetted with riott and debaucheries'. The people of England were robbed to support this 'vice and lewdnesse', and the contagion spread until 'every greate house in the country became a sty of uncleannesse'. King James himself 'lay wallowing like a swine in the mire of his Lust', and Buckingham obtained the king's favour 'upon no meritt but that of his beauty and prostitution'. Hutchinson gave credit to Charles for trying to reform the court. She wrote that he 'was temperate and chast and serious; so that the fooles and bawds, mimicks and Catamites of the former Court grew out of fashion'.[35]

No one has called Lucy Hutchinson 'foul-mouthed', although she deserves the appellation more than Sir Anthony Weldon. In some ways her description of the Jacobean court harkens back to the earlier discourse of sodomy. She was more deeply religious; she still thought in term of an all-encompassing moral depravity. She used the term 'abominations', and she even asserted that 'a greate cause of these abominations was the mix'd marriages of Papist and protestant famelies'.[36] But that is as far as she went. She did not invoke images of witches or supernatural forces. She clearly thought the behaviour at court was sinful, but she did not label it a sin against nature. She did not actually employ the term 'sodomy', though she certainly was not inhibited about using other words to denote obscene behaviour. In her description of Buckingham as a man who used 'his beauty and prostitution' to succeed at a court peopled by 'Catamites', what she seems to be implying is pederasty. Hutchinson was a deeply religious person who perpetuated some of the old horror associated with sodomy, but even in her prose there are indications that sodomy was being brought down to earth and reduced to human proportions.

In his pioneering work on *Homosexuality in Renaissance England*, Alan Bray established the view that there was a huge gulf between the Renaissance and our own day on the subject of sex between males. 'It can hardly be stressed too strongly or too often', wrote Bray, 'that the society of Renaissance England is at an immense distance, in time and culture, from our own.'[37] According to Bray, the Renaissance construct for sex between males was sodomy, the twentieth-century construct is homosexuality, and the two are worlds apart. Most subsequent writing on the subject has been deeply influenced by Bray. With few exceptions, historians of homosexuality have assumed that a decisive reconceptualization, a shift away from the one construct towards the other, must have occurred in the eighteenth or the nineteenth or possibly even the twentieth century, but in any case not earlier.

Meanwhile a few sceptics have suggested that this alleged gulf may result at least in part from our lack of knowledge about the earlier period. As Stephen O. Murray phrased it, perhaps we just need to know more about the *status quo ante*.[38]

The polemical works written about the Jacobean court help to fill in the picture of the *status quo ante*. And they suggest that the more we learn about the earlier seventeenth century, the narrower the gulf between then and now will appear. The royalist authors we have examined (Goodman, Sanderson, Oglander) wrote about James's sexual relations with other males in a surprisingly matter-of-fact fashion. They do not appear to have thought that such love was shocking. Of course, there are explanations for this that would be consistent with Bray's ideas. Perhaps these royalists did not understand or wish to acknowledge that James's relationships involved a physical dimension. Perhaps they simply failed to make the connection with sodomy, or perhaps they thought that James and his favourites did not cross the line between simple 'male friendship' and sodomy.[39] The anti-royalist authors (Weldon, Wilson, Osborne, Peyton) offer more conclusive evidence about early modern attitudes towards sex between males because sex is more definitely what they wrote about. What is impressive in these authors is the degree to which they wrote about the subject without using the horrible discourse of sodomy. They were writing anti-Stuart propaganda. They had a perfect opportunity to smear James with the charge of sodomy, yet they failed to exploit the opportunity. The tepid descriptions they did give of James kissing and fussing over his favourites are intended to mock or ridicule him, not to consign him to hell as a sodomite. Three decades earlier, when Sir Simonds D'Ewes recorded comparable scenes in his diary, he was much more deeply shocked by the king's behaviour, and he specifically used the word 'sodomy'.

Nor is it simply a matter of these anti-Stuart propagandists being afraid to use the word that Christians were not supposed to mention. Rather, their whole way of thinking about the subject appears to have advanced beyond the primitive discourse of sodomy. Hutchinson admittedly harkened back to that older discourse, but the others did not. Despite all the scorn usually heaped on Weldon, he was arguably the most enlightened of the bunch. He apparently considered it natural for some males to love other males rather than women, as for example Sir Anthony Ashley who 'never loved any but boyes'. Osborne's descriptions were more lurid and suggestive, but the word 'sodomy' never apparently entered his mind. He left it to posterity to invent a new word for the phenomenon. Wilson's most direct reference to sex between James and his favourites is the facetious statement that the king's *'fancy* ran with a violent *stream* upon a young Gentleman'. In a similar vein, when Peyton raised the subject of anal intercourse, he did so jokingly, not in deadly earnest. Indeed, his description of James as a man who was 'more addicted to love males then females' is a rather bland statement of fact.

On the other hand, these anti-Stuart authors should not be made to seem too enlightened. They had abandoned the sodomitical associations with witches, papists, all-encompassing moral depravity, and other threats to the whole order of the universe. They had stripped the subject down to the bare fact of sex between males. But they still assumed that their readers would be repulsed by this behaviour alone. Weldon's description of James kissing and 'slabboring' over the Earl of Somerset was one of the most effective images in this rhetorical arsenal. It was not the classic rhetoric of sodomy, but it was a negative rhetoric none the less. There was still a stigma attached to male sexual relationships, even if it was not always the old, hideous stigma of the sodomite. Homosexual behaviour could now be identified and deplored in its own right on a human scale. New terminology had yet to be invented to describe this process. It would appear, however, that what we are witnessing here, well ahead of the eighteenth century, are early versions of homosexuality and homophobia. As the case of King James illustrates, in the early seventeenth century a man who engaged in sexual behaviour with other males could already be stigmatized without being demonized.

Conclusion: James and the History of Homosexuality

Our conclusions are of two sorts – those that pertain to James and those that pertain more generally to the history of homosexuality.

To begin with James: he did have sex with his male favourites, and it is nonsense to deny it. Maurice Lee Jr claimed that the question of whether James had physical relations with his favourites was 'unimportant', and that in any case he probably did not have such relations because he was 'one of those people ... who are simply not much interested in physical sex at all'.[1] Judging from all the testimony amassed in the preceding chapters, however, that was not the view of contemporaries. Nor does it constitute a satisfactory explanation for James's lifetime pattern of behaviour. Of course, we can never know precisely what James and his favourites did in bed, but certainly when he complained to Somerset about 'your long creeping back and withdrawing yourself from lying in my chamber', and when Buckingham said he would 'never forget at Farnham, where the bed's head could not be found between the master and his dog', they had more than sleeping in mind. Furthermore, when competitors paraded Monson and Brett at court to lure James away from Buckingham, what did they think James was interested in, if not sex? The preponderance of evidence thus shows not only that James was enormously interested in sex, but also that other people tried – with varying degrees of success – to take advantage of this fact.

Secondly, James's favourites traded sex for money and power. To take only the three most famous: Esmé Stuart became Duke of Lennox; Robert Carr became Earl of Somerset; and George Villiers became Duke of Buckingham. Along with these titles came money and power. During his brief ascendancy, Lennox was virtually the power behind the Scottish throne. Somerset aligned himself with members of the

Howard family to fill their pockets at the subjects' expense. Buckingham was so rapacious, garnered so many offices for himself, piled up such stupendous wealth and wrecked the political process so badly that he was eventually called by one Member of Parliament 'the cause of all our miseries' and 'the grievance of grievances'.[2] Roger Lockyer tried to vindicate Buckingham in his densely documented biography of the Duke, and Lee asserts that 'he was no lightweight'.[3] But neither was he a heavyweight. None of these men was. It is true that they possessed some ability; and it is true that if they had not seized wealth and power, the men who did so in their place might have been even worse. The fact remains, however, that what catapulted all three men to prominence was not merit but sex.

In a highly regarded article published in 1983, Jenny Wormald asked how a ruler who succeeded so admirably in Scotland could be judged a failure in England. Was he 'Two Kings or One'?, she asked. The answer is one king – one king who was a shrewd ruler in many respects, but not where his sexual relations were involved. James repeatedly alienated a sizeable portion of the political elite and jeopardized his reputation, if not his crown, by giving inordinate wealth and power to his undeserving sexual favourites.

Thirdly, James's relationships with his favourites generated a significant political backlash. The two best recent summaries of James's life argue that his favourites, with the obvious exception of Buckingham, had little political influence. In S.J. Houston's phrase, they were merely 'apolitical playthings'.[4] This hardly seems the case with respect to Lennox in Scotland or Somerset in England. More importantly, however, to say that James's favourites were apolitical is to exaggerate the distinction between the private and the public. The line between the private and public spheres is never clear-cut where political figures are concerned, and certainly not where royalty is concerned. James dangerously crossed that line when he raised his favourites from obscurity to prominence. James was not asexual; and his favourites were not apolitical. Even the favourites who had no political aspirations, held no major office and exerted no influence over the king's policies still played a significant role in politics. They may have been 'apolitical playthings' in a narrow sense, but that did not prevent them from becoming political liabilities.

To be sure, some of the political backlash against James and his favourites arose from older noblemen who simply resented these upstarts, but there was much more at stake here than aristocratic snobbery. Lennox was feared because he was known to be working on behalf of France and Roman Catholicism. A lesser Scottish favourite, the headstrong Earl of Huntly, was involved in treasonous correspondence with Spain and was a constant threat to law and order. Lennox precipitated an open rebellion, and Huntly came close to doing the same more than once. In England resentment over the cost of James's favourites had an adverse effect on the king's relations with Parliament. James Hay and Philip Herbert were quite minor favourites, but when James elevated them to the peerage and gave them large sums of money to pay off their personal debts, he created a political problem for himself. Parliament was not inclined to give the king more money if this was the way he chose to spend it. By the same token, it is true that during most of his lifetime James made his own foreign policy without interference from his favourites, but the existence of those favourites still had an adverse effect on the reception of his policy. James's devotion to peace was widely interpreted as a sign of weakness, as a by-product of his attachment to effeminate favourites. This, in turn, contributed to the formation of a war party, aided by Queen Anne, which pinned its hopes first on Prince Henry, then on Prince Charles, to take more manly action. This backlash came to a head in the 1620s when Sir Francis Bacon was impeached, Sir Henry Yelverton dared in Parliament to raise the disturbing analogy of Edward II's reign and James came under increasing pressure to abandon his peaceful foreign policy.

This was not politics as usual. It was politics tinged with homophobia. Wormald has said that the problem for James (as opposed to Queen Elizabeth) 'was not one of gender but of nationality'.[5] This highlights the xenophobic reaction against James but entirely misses the homophobic reaction. Gender *was* a problem for James. As David Cressy expressed it, the reigns of Elizabeth and James were 'the reigns of a manly queen and a queenish king'.[6] The Earl of Southampton and others who attacked Bacon and lobbied for war were tired of 'boys and base fellows' at court. They feared the nation was slipping into effeminacy. As the Venetian ambassador explained, they advocated a 'virile' foreign policy.[7] In the end they managed to drive the 'Land of Peace, under the King of Peace' back into war. Thus the backlash against James's favourites helped to destroy one of his greatest achievements.

Fourthly, apart from these specific political consequences, in a more generalized way, James's relations with his favourites damaged his reputation and eroded respect for the crown. Contrary to the impression created by recent historians, the chief person responsible for James's unflattering reputation was not Sir Anthony Weldon; it was James himself. Lawrence Stone was one of the last historians to state the obvious – that reports of James's 'blatantly homosexual attachments and his alcoholic excesses were diligently spread back to a horrified countryside'.[8] In Scotland the clergy compared the Duke of Lennox to the minions of the French court and invoked the image of Sodom and Gomorrah. In England James was criticized, even ridiculed, for his 'darling sin' on the stage, in underground verse, in political pamphlets and in Parliament. James prided himself on being a scholar. He wanted to be perceived as an Apollonian philosopher-king. But critics like Thomas Scott perceived him as a Dionysian party-animal. Scott lectured James: 'To eate, drinke, daunce, and rise up to play with the Sodomites; to abuse our bodies woorse then beasts in sinnes not to be named, there needs no other wisedome then to follow the sway of our owne corrupt concupiscence; a beast can do this.'[9]

Recent historiography has emphasized a desire for harmony and a common body of shared assumptions among people that made early Stuart England politically stable.[10] Conrad Russell's collected essays are entitled *Unrevolutionary England*. This line of argument grossly underestimates the level of instability that developed under James. Rebellious thoughts were in the air, and those thoughts arose at least in part in reaction to James's personal behaviour. As we saw in the underground poem 'The Warre of the Gods', the other gods set out to overthrow Jupiter (representing James) who 'with Ganimede lyes playing'.[11] In 1604 the French ambassador reported that James's 'reputation suffers much by base and feeble actions, which are remarked in his private conduct and life'. In 1620 another French ambassador was exaggerating but not hallucinating when he observed, 'Audacious language, offensive pictures, calumnious pamphlets, these usual forerunners of civil war are common here.'[12] The Earl of Clarendon described the years when Buckingham was ascendant as 'a busie querulous froward time' when disaffected people 'Extended their enquiries even to the Chamber and private Actions of the King himself'.[13] *The Answer to Tom-Tell-Troth* attempted to rebut the 'malicious' pamphlets that 'defame', 'scorne and disgrace' the monarch. The authors of these traitorous works were 'able to set the whole State on fire, imbroyle the Realm and aliene[ate] the hearts of people from their Prince'. Their goal was 'to undermine Loyalty, and either to ingage you abroad in forraigne wars or indanger Your person at home in Civill [wars]'. As a result of these subversive works, 'discontent runs with a seditious voyce over the kingdome'. From all the passages in all these scandalous works, the author of *The Answer* singled out the one that was most offensive, the one that ridiculed the king who 'may have Lords tempo-rall for his Eunuches, spiritu[al] for his mates, and whom hee will for his Incubus, and kisse his Minions without shame'.[14]

Prince Charles witnessed this erosion of respect for the monarchy and he tried to remedy the situation by being the opposite of his father. James had been *Rex Pacificus*; Charles would be *Rex Bellicosus*. James had been notorious for his male favourites; Charles would be notable for his devotion to his wife. The masque *Coelum Britannicum* glorified the 'conjugal affection' of Charles and Henrietta Maria at the same time as it celebrated the banishment of beardless young men from the Bedchamber. Charles cultivated a more dignified royalist cul-ture that helped to form a party on his behalf when his rule was put to the test. But it might never have been put to the test if he had not inherited Buckingham at the outset of his reign, if the majesty of the crown had not been diminished, and if he had not been so fiercely determined to be different from his father.

Finally, James's affairs with his favourites were hurtful to his wife. Political historians have not been very interested in this subject, and even social historians might think that sympathy for Anne is inappro-priate because she and her contemporaries in the seventeenth century would not have viewed the situation as we do. But they did. Take the example of Queen Isabella in Christopher Marlowe's *Edward II*. Isabella laments: 'In vain I look for love at Edward's hand, Whose eyes are fixed on none but Gaveston.' She complains that Gaveston has 'robbed' her of Edward's love, 'For never doated Jove on Ganymede So much as he on cursed Gaveston.' She even expresses the wish that she had been poisoned or strangled to death on her wedding day rather than live to see 'The King my lord thus to abandon me!'[15] What Marlowe's play demonstrates is that contemporary sensibilities did include sympathy for a woman whose husband loved a man. Of course, Anne was not as badly spurned as Isabella, but she did have sufficient reason to feel unhappy and resentful. The polemicists of the 1650s understood this. Weldon's accusation that James 'was not very uxorious' hit home. It was an accusation his opponents took seriously and tried to rebut by alleging that Anne was the one to blame or that James needed to aban-don her for long periods to go on hunting expeditions for the sake of his health. It is true that James took pride in the fact that he was not sexually promiscuous with other women. As the royalist Sir John Oglander observed, James 'would often swear that he had never known any other woman than his wife'. This might have salved James's con-science, but it did not satisfy Anne. Oglander himself had to admit that he 'never yet saw any fond husband make so much or so great dalliance over his beautiful spouse as I have seen King James over his favourites'.[16] Time and again Anne lost the battle for her husband's affection to a youthful male favourite. As Archbishop Abbot observed, she had 'been bitten with Favorites both in England and Scotland' and wanted no more 'dear ones'.[17] According to Abbot, Anne reached an accommodation with James, but surely she would have preferred to eliminate rather than accommodate these dear ones. The French ambassador sized up the situation correctly. He reported that Anne was an able woman who had to live with the fact 'that her husband cannot exist without a minion'.[18]

In recent years one set of historians has been labouring to rehabilitate the reputation of King James, but another set has been working on the rehabilitation of Queen Anne. Although apparently no one has noticed, these two sets of scholars are proceeding on a collision course. The dilemma is best illustrated by Barbara Kiefer Lewalski's study of Anne as an unhappy woman struggling 'to maintain her own worth and dignity' against her husband's 'attitudes, interests, and sexual proclivities'. Since 'the homosexual and patriarchal ethos of his court excluded her from any significant place in his personal or political life', Anne eventually went her own way. In Lewalski's words, 'James's homosexuality as well as other familial circumstances led to Queen Anne's progressive withdrawal to her own court and affairs'.[19] We have seen how Anne's 'oppositional' court acted as a countervailing force and how she also sought vindication through her sons. Indeed, Charles eventually gave her that vindication symbolically in the masque *Coelum Britannicum* where Jupiter, representing James, became a reformed husband who 'recanted, disclaymed, and utterly renounced all the lascivious extravagancies, and riotous enormities of his forepast licentious life'. He laid aside his 'wild lusts', and his wife laid aside 'her raging jealousies'.[20]

In view of the movement that has been underway for nearly two decades to rehabilitate King James's reputation, these conclusions may seem too harsh. However one judges them, they are not based on the prejudices of the past. Lee was right to complain that many previous historians allowed their accounts to be 'colored by their obvious distaste for James's lifestyle and their prudish revulsion at the sexual implications involved'.[21] And Wormald was right to assert that James's reputation has been hurt by a 'nineteenth-century distaste for his sexual morals'.[22] But it is time now to stop complaining and come to grips with this subject in a way that is coloured by neither smug Victorian moralizing nor an equally self-righteous determination to vindicate James. That is what we have tried to do in this book.

Turning to the more general history of homosexuality, this is a relatively new field of study in which the hypotheses of a few early scholars have tended to become doctrinaire viewpoints, several of which look less persuasive after examining the case of James VI and I. To begin with, there is the revolution alleged in Alan Bray's influential *Homosexuality in Renaissance England*. Although Bray briefly acknowledged the existence of alternative ways of denoting males who had sex with other males (Ganymede, for example), his approach quickly turned reductionist. He created the impression that sodomy was the only construct for sex between men in the early seventeenth century, and sodomy was a strange and monstrous construct. It was so horrible and alien that people were disinclined to recognize it when it existed right under their noses in themselves or their neighbours. Consequently, although in theory there was tremendous prejudice against sodomy, in practice there was a 'tacit acceptance'. By focusing exclusively on sodomy and emphasizing its monstrous dimensions, Bray buttressed his contention that people in Renaissance England inhabited a mental universe 'at an immense distance, in time and culture, from our own'.[23] Not until the very end of the century did a revolution in thinking occur. Only then did a new construct begin to appear that was closer to modern homosexuality.

Although James himself conforms to one part of Bray's thesis in so far as he did not recognize sodomy in himself, many of his contemporaries thought they recognized it in him. And despite the dangers associated with criticizing the king, they used a number of avenues to express their disapproval. Bray's argument that people in Renaissance England did not take notice of sodomy has become so firmly established, however, that even the best scholars have tried to force it onto the evidence. A dramatic example is Stephen Orgel, who wrote: 'King James's public and overtly physical displays of affection for young men are frequently remarked in the period; they are considered to be in bad taste...but not even the most rabid Puritan connects them with the abominable crime against nature.'[24] Oh, really? What about the ministers of Scotland who threw the biblical example of Sodom in James's face; Sir Simonds D'Ewes who recorded in his diary that James was suspected of sodomy; Thomas Scott who insinuated that James played with sodomites; and the anonymous author of 'The Warre of the Gods' who expressed the radical view that James should 'Be quite displaced / Or else disgraced / For lovinge so 'gainst nature'?[25] These critics were indignant, and what aroused their indignation was not mere 'bad taste'; it was sodomy.

Bray does make one exception to his own rule, and James might be thought of as conforming to that exception. Bray allows that people did sometimes take note of sodomy when it threatened hierarchy, patriarchy or the social order. Bray surprisingly ignores the example of James, but his case could be used to substantiate this claim. As noted earlier, the more money and power James gave to his favourites, the more he upset the social order, and consequently the more criticism he provoked, especially from the old nobility who felt threatened by these newcomers. On the other hand, concern about the social order was only one cause of the animosity directed against James and his favourites. It was probably one of the motives behind the Earl of Southampton's complaint about 'boys and base fellows' at court, but not the only motive. Southampton and others like Thomas Scott were concerned because they made an association between the king's suspected sodomy and his pusillanimous foreign policy. Sir Simonds D'Ewes was even less concerned about the social order; what upset him was the spectre of sodomy *per se*. Similarly, although their motives for writing about it were mixed, propagandists of the Interregnum who described James kissing his favourites were genuinely disgusted by the sight and expected their readers to share in that disgust. In other words, concern about the social order was only one motive, and by no means the principal motive, underlying complaints about James's sexual favourites.

James's contemporaries undoubtedly took notice of James's sexual relations. The really important question is, what did they think they were seeing? Some, such as D'Ewes and Scott, clearly thought they were observing the horrible spectre of sodomy; but others processed the information another way. A particularly fascinating example is George Abbot, the Archbishop of Canterbury. Abbot was a leader of the faction who opposed the Earl of Somerset by promoting an alternative favourite in the person of George Villiers, later Duke of Buckingham. Villiers was given appropriate clothes and manoeuvred into the position of cup-bearer at court in order to attract James's attention. After the king became sufficiently interested, it was Abbot who approached Anne to intercede on the young man's behalf and persuade James to appoint him a Gentleman of the King's Bedchamber.[26] What in the world did the Archbishop of Canterbury think he was doing? If we follow Bray's line of reasoning, Abbot must have thought that sexual relations between males constituted sodomy and yet he failed to make the connection on this occasion between the abstract concept and the actual behaviour involving James and his favourites. But if he did not see that behaviour as sodomy, how did he see it? He must have known that this behaviour amounted to something more than mere male friendship. He must have known that it involved sex. The strategy of exciting James's interest in an attractive young man, the immediate goal of placing Villiers in the Bedchamber, the long-term goal of making him the next favourite, the understanding that these favourites displaced not only one another but the king's wife – all these make it difficult to believe that the Archbishop was oblivious to the fact that James's relationships involved sex. Does it not appear, therefore, that Abbot was capable of viewing sexual relations between males, knowing that they were sexual relations, but construing them in terms other than the horrible construct of sodomy?

We cannot know for certain what Abbot thought. His behaviour is open to other interpretations, but the foregoing interpretation gains support from the statements produced by other people who criticized James. These critics were quite capable of recognizing sexual relations between males. They did not ignore or tacitly accept the phenomenon, but neither did they always couch their criticisms in the horrible terms of sodomy. James's contemporaries were quite versatile in the ways they were able to think, write and even joke about sexual relations between men without employing the monstrous construct of sodomy. Granted that sometimes the stigma of sodomy was firmly attached to James. He was accused of playing with sodomites; his favourites were called beastly companions. More often, however, he was criticized more obliquely for his darling sin, his base fellows, his merry boys, his Ganymede, his Gaveston, his Sejanus. No one applied the term 'woman-hater' to James, but it was probably another way of referring to a man who loved men. Joseph Cady has shown that 'masculine love' was yet another.[27] Sexual relations between James and his favourites are strongly implied in the polemical works of the 1650s, but the discourse of sodomy is all but missing from these works. Even the notorious muckraker Sir Edward Peyton blandly described James as a man who was 'more addicted to love males then females'.

Sodomy was the formal construct from the Church and the law to denote sex between men. It was a powerful construct that sometimes appears overtly in criticisms of James and sometimes lurks just beneath the surface. But often it is nowhere to be found. There were other ways to discourse about sex between males that reduced the subject to more prosaic dimensions. By focusing almost exclusively on sodomy, Bray sustained the impression that 'when we look at the society of England under Elizabeth I or James I its strangeness only deepens as we probe its working'.[28] That has not been our experience, however. Modern readers may not always recognize the words, terms or historical allusions used in Jacobean England to denote sexual relations between men, but the meanings of these words and the reality they described must look very familiar. When we find Francis Osborne searching for a new word that will better express this 'love, or what else posterity will please to call it', we have no trouble supplying that word. Posterity calls it homosexuality. Thus, on closer examination, the 'immense distance' alleged between the early seventeenth century and our own shrinks.

It works the other way, too. Just as we can find 'modern' ideas in the seventeenth century, so can we find 'pre-modern' ideas in the twentieth. Historians who subscribe to a model of modernization run the risk of underestimating the persistence of ideas across time. One such idea which has shown remarkable persistence is sodomy. Bray wrote that sodomy was part of 'a mental universe [that] is alien to us now'. The sodomite, he confidently asserted, 'is now an alien idea'.[29] But even a superficial awareness of current debates about the decline of the family, God and AIDS, gays in the military, homosexual marriage, the age of consent for sexual relations, or any number of issues involving sexuality reveals that the construct of sodomy is not at all an alien idea in the Anglo-American world at the end of the twentieth century. For a great many people, the sodomite is still a very real figure, still acting against nature, still disobeying God, still immersed in debauchery, still a sign and cause of the world's ills. We are still waiting for the revolution.

The argument that homosexuality is a peculiar invention of the eighteenth or nineteenth century resembles a similar argument that occurred a few years ago over the alleged invention of love and family. Lawrence Stone and others argued that heartless pre-modern concepts of marriage and family were transformed in the eighteenth century into a new ideal of warm and loving family relations. Marriages before the eighteenth century were supposed to have been dreary, loveless financial transactions arranged by parents with no regard for the parties involved. Husbands and wives did not love one another, and parents did not love their children. Then came the watershed, the turning point, the revolution in personal relations. Now arranged marriages became companionate marriages and parents stopped beating their children. The era of romantic love and 'affective individualism' had suddenly arrived.[30] Of course, all this turned out to be a gross over-simplification. Among other problems, it denied the 'common humanity' of all those men and women who lived before the eighteenth century.[31] It also ignored the unpleasant fact that abuse and violence are endemic in the *modern* family.

Bray's schematic approach to the history of homosexuality mirrored Stone's approach to the family. In fact, Bray consciously subscribed to Stone's paradigm.[32] Consequently, Bray's pioneering work and many subsequent works on the history of homosexuality suffer from the same misguided desire to discover a crucial turning point, the same tendency to exaggerate change at the expense of continuity, and the same failure to grant 'common humanity' to the males who loved one another before the eighteenth century. Indeed, Bray's book painted a surprisingly unsympathetic picture of these unfortunate pre-modern males. He alleged that homosexuality in the earlier seventeenth century was 'deep-rooted', 'ubiquitous', existing on 'a massive and ineradicable scale'. Yet, as he described it, most of this was 'institutionalized homosexuality', involving the exploitation of students by teachers or servants by masters. Even in the theatre, he described homosexuality as 'prostitution'. Sex between these males was an expression of power, not of love.[33] It is not until the paradigmatic shift at the end of the seventeenth century that Bray shows us adult men who freely and genuinely loved one another stepping onto the historical stage. Only then, Bray claims, did 'homosexuality in a recognisably modern form first appear'.[34]

It is easy to exaggerate change and underestimate the degree of continuity if you do not know much about the period preceding the one you are studying. The impression that one particular century constituted 'the' century of critical change may simply be based on inadequate knowledge of the preceding centuries.[35] Using the evidence we have unearthed regarding James, we might reasonably claim that the true turning point occurred between the 1620s and the 1650s, between the outraged sodomitical discourse of people such as D'Ewes and Scott and the secularized matter-of-fact discourse of writers such as Weldon and Osborne. We could claim there was a 'Jacobean Revolution' in sexual constructs or point to the Interregnum as the birthplace of modern homosexuality. It would be presumptuous, however, to make such claims. The case of King James brought attitudes out into the open, but it remains to be seen how radically new or perennial those attitudes were.

Another assertion often found in the history of homosexuality is that prior to the modern age, when there was no clear-cut bipolar division between heterosexual and homosexual, men enjoyed a kind of sexual polymorphism – what people today might call bisexuality. Randolph Trumbach's imposing analysis of sexuality in the eighteenth century is predicated on this view of the preceding century. It is his assumption that 'before 1700 probably most males felt desire for both males and females'. Then in the eighteenth century there was a 'revolution in gender relations', after which the 'majority of men now desired only women'.[36]

There are few examples from seventeenth-century England to support this claim, most of them drawn from fictional literature and atypical libertines. Anyone who reads widely in the history of homosexuality finds these few examples repeated incestuously from one work to another.[37] Yet the idea has passed into the realm of textbook fact. For example, in his recent book on *English Sexualities, 1700–1800*, Tim Hitchcock writes that sodomy in the seventeenth century 'was seen largely as an extension of a more pervasive libertinism'. He includes King James alongside the famous Restoration rake, the Earl of Rochester, in this class of people who were 'generally part of a pattern of bisexual behaviour'. Then Hitchcock repeats the familiar refrain that 'the classic image of the seventeenth-century libertine as having a catamite on one arm and a whore on the other expresses clearly the extent to which bisexuality was the norm'.[38] In fact, it shows precisely the opposite. Libertines do not demonstrate norms; they *violate* norms. That is what makes them libertines. In our contemporary world, pop music stars similarly try to shock their audiences by appearing bisexual. This device would have no shock value if bisexuality were the norm. What it really shows is that heterosexuality is the norm.

The multitudinous sources we have examined for the Jacobean period show the same thing. No doubt men, especially powerful men, were freer than women to indulge in sexually transgressive behaviour. But this behaviour was definitely considered transgressive, which shows that people already had the idea in their heads, if not yet the word in their vocabulary, that heterosexuality was the norm. James's contemporaries did not think it was normal for a man to go around with a whore on one arm and a catamite on the other. Libertines might do that, but not ordinary men, and especially not ordinary married men. From the observations of a bewildered Thomas Howard shortly after James arrived in England, through the scornful libels of the 1620s, to the polemics of the 1650s, James's love of other males was treated as an oddity. As Osborne expressed it, people imagined some sort of sexual activity occurring between James and his favourites, but those activities did 'exceed my expressions no less than they do my experience'.[39] Even the royalist writers of the 1650s felt constrained to explain how it was that James took a 'fancy' to his favourites. His own wife and children did not think it was normal.

Throughout his life James upset people because he did not fit the norm. The more 'boys and base fellows' there were at court, the greater the alarm, precisely because the norm was being violated. Society can tolerate a little sexual transgression in a few libertines; it may even serve a useful social function. Transgressive behaviour in kings, however, is risky behaviour because one of their very reasons for existing is to embody and enforce norms. As his high-minded writings illustrate, James understood this fact well. No one would have been more horrified than James to find his name coupled with Rochester's in a list of seventeenth-century libertines!

The more one thinks about it, the more astonishing it is that no one has explored King James's sexual relations more thoroughly. In any event, the results of such an examination contradict several popular views in the history of homosexuality. James's love of other males provoked a chorus of protest, which does not square with the thesis that people failed to recognize and tacitly accepted the existence of sodomy in Jacobean England. At the same time, James's love of other males was often described in ordinary human terms that remind us of modern views about homosexuality, which does not square with the thesis that monstrous sodomy was the only construct for sex between males prior to the eighteenth century when the invention of homosexuality is supposed to have begun. Finally, James's love of other males was treated by his contemporaries as something quite remarkable and exceptional, which does not square with the thesis that bisexuality or sexual polymorphism was commonplace among pre-modern men. Theory has been running ahead of the facts in the history of homosexuality, and James is one of the more inconvenient facts.

It must be admitted, however, that the picture looks a lot more complicated if we shift our focus away from James to the other males who entered into sexual relationships with him. There were three males who almost certainly had sexual relations with James (Lennox, Somerset and Buckingham), and a minimum of four others who probably did (Alexander Lindsey, the Earl of Huntly, Philip Herbert and James Hay). There were additional males who aspired to be favourites, the ones who were put forward by rival factions and were described as sprouting up at court like mushrooms. Some of the latter may have been naive about what would be expected of them if they succeeded in becoming favourites, but that still leaves quite a few who were willing to enter into sexual relations with James. Nor were these merely physical relationships. James and Lennox truly loved one another. James was grief-stricken at the death of Lennox, who willed that his heart should be removed and sent to the king. We do not have sufficient evidence for all of James's other relationships, but there can be no doubt that he deeply loved Somerset and Buckingham, and at least in the case of the latter his love was requited. Of course this does not prove that all males in Jacobean England experienced homoerotic feelings or were sexually polymorphous, but it does show that males in Renaissance England did not always think of themselves as needing to love or have sex exclusively with females. Favourites, potential favourites and the men who sponsored them did not act as if heterosexuality was mandatory. On the other hand, James represented an exceptional opportunity for these young men. It is noteworthy that they were willing to seize that opportunity, but it is anybody's guess whether they had any interest in sexual relations with males other than James. There is no evidence that they did. Quite the contrary, except for Lennox, the ones for whom we have more information proceeded to marry and have exclusively heterosexual sex. How, then, can we explain the seeming ease with which they contemplated and in some cases consummated a sexual relationship with James?

Age may be the key. Here at last we have a theoretical approach to the history of homosexuality that our research does appear to corroborate. Although our study of James does not support Randolph Trumbach's contention that prior to 1700 the majority of men desired both males and females, it can be used to support his contention that there was a significant change among those males who did desire other males, a change from age-structured relationships involving an older man and an adolescent to relationships involving two adult men.[40] The modern homosexual relationship involving two adult males, he asserts, 'first appeared in the early eighteenth century' or 'in the generation after 1700'.[41] Only after that date did sexual acts occur 'increasingly between two adult males rather than between an adult and an adolescent male'.[42] This view is consistent with James M. Saslow's observation that 'adult–youth sex clearly predominated' in the Renaissance and Michael Rocke's formidable study of Renaissance Florence, in which he showed that a great many Florentine males during the 1400s passed through three stages of sexual activity: as adolescents they were 'passive' or 'receptive' partners of older men, as young men they became the 'active' or 'dominant' partners in such relationships, and around the age of thirty they married and more or less stopped having sex with other males.[43] It would have been rare, therefore, for homosexual relationships to involve two adult men. Instead, relationships typically involved adults and younger males 'between puberty and the age, around eighteen to twenty, at which the growth of a beard and the appearance of other secondary sexual traits became pronounced and they began to lose what this society considered the beauty and erotic appeal of adolescence'. Relationships of this sort were ubiquitous in Florence. Rocke estimates that 'the majority of local males at least once during their lifetimes were officially incriminated for engaging in homosexual relations'; or, put another way, 'by age forty, at least two of every three men had been incriminated'.[44]

There is a growing body of opinion that the Florentine pattern of homosexual relations 'between active men and passive adolescents' was typical of all Europe until about 1700. There is no evidence of homosexual relations occurring in England on anything like the scale Rocke found in Florence, but where they did occur, scholars like Trumbach believe they followed the same age-differentiated pattern. The evidence is sparse, Trumbach admits, 'but what there is in the way of trial records, literary texts, and biographical material supports the pattern of relations between active men and passive boys'. According to Trumbach, other scholars working on England have been reluctant to acknowledge this pattern in their evidence:

> scholars who work on the literary evidence from England, whether Bruce Smith, Alan Bray, Jonathan Goldberg, or Gregory Bredbeck, do their level best to ignore the age-structured, or as they would tend to say, the pederastical nature of the behavior in their sources. They quote lines about sex between men and boys and then immediately, or within a line or two, transform this into evidence for sexual relations between two adult men.[45]

What does our evidence suggest? To a considerable degree, the relationships we have studied were age-differentiated and were perceived by contemporaries as age-differentiated. First there is James himself. It is true that he does not fit the Florentine pattern because he married earlier and continued to have male lovers after his marriage. But marriage was forced upon James by his need to produce heirs. More significant is the fact that his relationships with his major favourites were age-differentiated, and he did pass from being the boy in these relationships to being the older man. James got older of course, but the point is that his partners did not. James was 13 when Esmé Stuart arrived in Scotland at the age of approximately 37. He thus began as the junior member in a relationship with a much older man. James's other favourites in Scotland were roughly his own age, but by the time he ascended to the English throne, he was ready to enter into age-differentiated relationships again, this time as the older member. James was 37 when Philip Herbert became his favourite at the age of 18. James was 41 when he became infatuated with Robert Carr who was about 20 (Carr's exact age is unknown). James was 48 when he first went to bed with Buckingham about the time the young man turned 23. One might deny that these later relationships were, strictly speaking, pederastic because Carr and Buckingham were young adults rather than boys.[46] But Carr and Buckingham were barely adults, and James was twice their age. These were certainly age-differentiated relationships. If we take twenty years as the distance between generations, they even qualify as transgenerational relationships.

Of course, the picture is further complicated by the fact that all these men were married at some point. James and Esmé Stuart look as if they did not quite complete the passage to the third stage described by Rocke because after they became married adults they continued to have significant relationships with younger men. For Esmé Stuart the affair with James may have begun as an opportunistic exception, but blossomed into something more genuine. Likewise, James's persistent involvement with young men in later life would make him what Rocke calls a 'more dedicated sodomite'. By contrast with James and Esmé Stuart who continued to function at the second stage after marriage, Somerset and Buckingham apparently skipped over the second stage altogether, going straight from being the junior partner in an age-differentiated relationship with James to marriage. Somerset apparently made this passage all too well to suit James since he stopped going to bed with him sometime after marrying Frances Howard. These are far too few examples with too many variations to draw firm conclusions. For what it is worth, no one in the group followed the complete three-stage progression discovered by Rocke in Florence. Nevertheless, what Rocke and Trumbach do rightly call to our attention is the age-differentiated or age-graded nature of these relationships. All of the major relationships James was involved in were at the outset pederastic or near-pederastic.

Furthermore, whatever their true ages, James treated his favourites as if he thought of them as boys. One small indication of this may be the diminutive nicknames he gave them ('Sandie' for Lindsey and 'Steenie' for Buckingham). Another was the tendency to treat them as sons. Even Huntly, who was four years older than James, was referred to as 'good sonne'.[47] Another was his tendency to treat his favourites as pupils whom he set out to instruct and mould. He tried to teach Somerset Latin. In the case of Buckingham, as the Earl of Clarendon described, James 'took much delight in indoctrinating his young unexperienced favourite'.[48] In his dedication of *A Meditation Upon the Lords Prayer* to Buckingham, James combined the roles of father and teacher, describing himself as 'not onely your politike, but also your aeconomike Father' who 'dayly take[s] care to better your understanding'.[49] But the best evidence that James viewed his favourites as boys comes from the correspondence written while Buckingham and Prince Charles were in Spain in 1623. Here, as we saw in chapter 2, James addressed Buckingham as his child and son. 'My only sweet and dear child' is the salutation on several letters addressed to Buckingham, not to his true son Charles. Most revealing of the paternalistic attitude James adopted is the letter in which he referred to Buckingham as 'my sweet child and wife' and himself as 'your dear dad and husband'. While they were in Spain, Prince Charles was 22 years old and Buckingham was an even older 30, but in the addresses and the bodies of the letters James wrote to them, he regularly referred to them as 'my sweet boys'.[50]

Apart from the facts of James's relationships, they were certainly *perceived* by others as pederastic relationships. Ganymede was a boyish figure. In 'The Warre of the Gods', where Ganymede represents Buckingham, he was described as a 'white fayst boy'. The author of *Corona Regia* implied that James was a pederast. He wrote that James chose only young men who were 'fresh blooming and lovely', that Buckingham was an 'adolescent of incomparable form', and that James, imitating Christ who said the little children should be allowed to see him, invited the company of the most attractive boys. Clarendon described James's first English favourite, Herbert, as 'a young man, scarce of age'. The Earl of Southampton complained about 'boys and base fellows' in the Privy Council. Sir Fulke Greville referred to James's favourites as 'children of favor'. The French ambassador observed that James chose for his favourites males who were still in the prime of their youth with beautiful faces, preferably beardless. Sir Anthony Weldon wrote that James's favourites had 'young Faces, and smooth Chins'. Francis Osborne wrote that James was attracted to Somerset 'before he had either *Wife or Beard*'. Tiberius, to whom James was compared by implication, was noted for his sexual perversions with children. Tiberius's favourite, Sejanus, to whom Buckingham was compared, began his career as a serving boy and was described as a catamite – that is, a boy in a pederastic relationship. Buckingham, in fact, complained that his expressions toward James were interpreted as 'crude catamite words'. Sir Edward Peyton called attention to the youthfulness of James's favourites. He said Gondomar joked with James about being able to 'make privy counsellors sage at the age of twenty-one, which his master (the King of Spaine) could not till sixty'. Lucy Hutchinson wrote that Buckingham prostituted himself to James, and that Charles cleaned the court of catamites. Judging from the masque *Coelum Britannicum*, Charles himself viewed the situation this way. In the newly reformed court pictured there, '*Ganimede* is forbidden the Bedchamber, and must only minister in publique. The Gods must keepe no Pages, nor Groomes of their Chamber under the age of 25, and those provided of a competent stocke of beard.'[51] Note the cut-off age specified here. Where homosexual relations were concerned, James's contemporaries may still have considered a young man up to the age of 25 a boy. Modern historians can debate whether or not James's relationships were truly pederastic, but there is less room for debate about the public *perception* of those relationships.

Our evidence is skewed because our subject was a king who had the prerogative of choosing younger men for his lovers. Nevertheless, it may be true that people in Renaissance England tended to think of sexual relationships between males as pederastic relationships. We have run across this tendency with respect to other men in addition to James. Christopher Marlowe was accused of saying that only fools loved not 'tobacco and boys'; and Sir Anthony Weldon described Sir Anthony Ashley as a man who 'never loved any but boyes'. John Aubrey called Sir Francis Bacon a pederast; and Sir Simonds D'Ewes described Bacon's alleged partner as 'a very effeminate-faced youth' and 'catamite'.[52] This habit of viewing sexual relations between males as pederastic relationships had a long lineage, going back at least as far as ancient Greece. John Hacket made the most explicit analogy between ancient pederasty and Jacobean England when he wrote that Buckingham 'was our *English Alcibiades*' (a student and reputed lover of Socrates).[53]

Thus there does appear to have been a predilection to equate male sexual relationships with pederastic relationships. Indeed, despite Bray's concentration on sodomy, pederasty may actually have been the dominant construct for sex between males in seventeenth-century England. Pederasty did not carry the supernatural connotations of sodomy. It was still abhorrent but not quite as alien and monstrous as the 'detestable, and abominable sin, amongst Christians not to be named'. Pederasty may therefore have made the subject of sex between males easier to think and talk about. Of course, these two constructs were not mutually exclusive, and even if pederasty was the dominant construct which people employed in discoursing about sex between males, that does not prove that it was the dominant pattern in actual practice. In the final analysis, the evidence surrounding James is highly suggestive but nowhere near as definitive as the data Rocke compiled for Florence.

D'Ewes's reference to Bacon's lover as 'a very effeminate-faced youth' brings us to our final conclusion: in Jacobean England sexual relations between males were definitely linked with effeminacy. The argument that effeminacy meant something different in the seventeenth century – that it meant a man was excessively interested in women or that he was wanton like a woman – is based on a few eccentric usages of the word. As we demonstrated in chapters 4 and 5 with numerous examples, the principal meaning of effeminacy in the seventeenth century was the same as in the twentieth century. In the great majority of instances, in Renaissance England when a man was labelled effeminate, it meant that he looked and acted like a woman, which meant that he was weak, soft, tender, unmanly. King James himself warned his son to avoid being 'effeminate in your cloathes, in perfuming, preening, or such like'.[54]

Effeminate meant then what effeminate means now. And it was linked to male sexual relationships. Although Mark D. Jordan underplays the issue of effeminacy in his masterly history of sodomy in medieval Christian thought, it runs like a thread throughout his book. From St Paul to St Thomas Aquinas, one of the things that made sodomy loathsome was that it involved men who were effeminate. The Latin adjective was *mollis* (from which we get the English word mollify). We have to wait till the eighteenth century to find mollies and molly houses, but behind them lay an ancient association between homosexuality and effeminacy.[55] At the end of his book, Jordan identifies three reasons why sodomy was so disturbing to Christian theologians. The 'worst' of these three, Jordan observes, was the linkage between sodomy and misogyny. A man who had sex with another man was thought of as degrading himself, surrendering to an 'essentialized feminine' in his nature. In Jordan's own words: 'Effeminacy of one kind or another is regularly alleged as a consequence of same-sex copulation.'[56] As we showed in chapter 4, although some current scholars labour mightily to explain it away, the connection between effeminacy and sodomy is plain as day in the anti-theatrical tracts of Philip Stubbes, John Rainolds and William Prynne, written in the late sixteenth and early seventeenth centuries. The modern scholar Eve Kosofsky Sedgwick came to the correct conclusion that effeminacy was already part of a distinctive male homosexual role in seventeenth-century England. She did not know how right she was when she called this 'the King James version'.[57]

But was effeminacy linked to *both* partners? Among those scholars who acknowledge that effeminacy was associated with males who had sex with other males, some still allege that this stigma was attached to just the passive or submissive male. This distinction is problematic because it assumes that effeminacy is not an integral part of male homosexulaity, not a permanent or biological fact, but merely a happenstance product of social construction. In reality, the linkage between effeminacy and male homosexuality may not be as accidental or malleable as this view assumes. On the other hand, it is true that in relationships where one partner is clearly submissive and the other clearly dominant, effeminacy is more likely to be attributed to the former than the latter. And this is the case with respect to age-differentiated or pederastic relationships. A youth in a pederastic relationship is more likely to be considered effeminate because he appears to be the passive or submissive partner, whereas the older man can maintain an aura of masculinity by appearing to be the active or dominant partner. Indeed, Trumbach, who believes that such relationships were the norm until about 1700 when they were replaced by relationships involving two adult males, is also among those who believe the stigma of effeminacy was first attached to adult males at the same time. Prior to that time effeminacy had been limited to the junior partner; afterwards it was applied to all 'regardless of whether an individual's partner was adult or adolescent, or whether an individual was active or passive in the sexual act, penetrating or penetrated'.[58] Again the revolution is supposed to have occurred in the eighteenth century – what Trumbach confidently calls 'the first century of the modern western world's existence'.[59] Alan Sinfield agrees with Trumbach that 'the key move is the relocation of effeminacy', but he does not see this move as being fully accomplished until the trials of Oscar Wilde at the end of the nineteenth century. Before that time, he claims, 'effeminacy and same-sex passion might be aligned, but not exclusively, or even particularly'.[60]

In the case of King James, there is no doubt that effeminacy was attributed to his favourites, and with good justification. We saw ample proof of that. But the stigma of effeminacy was also attached to James himself. Thomas Scott, who complained about the 'effeminate fashions and mollifying pleasures' of the times, and more pointedly 'effaeminate Courtiers', also berated James for his lack of manliness. He taunted James with the memory of martial heroes like Sir Walter Raleigh and Queen Elizabeth, 'that deceased English *Virago*'. He said that England did not need a 'King of Schollers' but 'a man of war' (following the example set by God himself).[61] Scott was the most strident critic of James on this score, but he was far from alone. If there was a 'relocation of effeminacy' to the adult male, Sinfield would like to prolong the process, extending it into the nineteenth century. The evidence surrounding James suggests that it should also be extended backwards into the seventeenth century. Here again – if there was any change at all – it was more likely evolutionary than revolutionary.

The problem in James's case is that we cannot know how much the doubts about his manliness arose from his relations with effeminate favourites and how much from his pacific foreign policy. He appeared to be ruled by his feelings or ruled by his favourites. In both these respects, he looked like the passive or subordinate partner, but it was his passivity in foreign affairs that his critics found most irksome. Thomas Scott and John Reynolds voiced the exasperation people felt about James's lack of action. They portrayed him as a sluggard rocked to sleep by a lullaby of peace. They berated him because the King of Spain was master of the practical world, while James sat idly by and theorized. They scolded, implored and exhorted him to take action. His passivity called his manhood into question and made him more susceptible to charges of effeminacy. If he had been a more martial figure, the effeminacy of his favourites might not have rubbed off on him.

A comparison with William III (1689–1702) may be instructive. He, too, was associated with male sexual favourites. In the 1690s under William, as earlier under James, it was 'said that one of the ways to find favor with the king was to be a handsome young man appointed to wait on him in his bedchamber'.[62] Yet William managed to escape the stigma of effeminacy that was attached to James, chiefly because of 'his rather macho image as a military hero'.[63] Could James have escaped the stigma of effeminacy if he had been a macho military hero? If that had been the case, he would have better fulfilled his subjects' expectations of him. In the final analysis, however, he would not actually have been as great a king because, as Sir Anthony Weldon appreciatively remarked, James's supreme accomplishment was to give his subjects – whether they wanted it or not – two decades of peace during the age of Europe's religious wars.

Notes and References

Introduction

1. A few historians do stand out for their superior handling of James's sexuality. See Caroline Bingham, *James I of England* (London, 1981), pp. 78–80, 83–4, 134–5, 160–1. By far the best study of one of James's lovers is Roger Lockyer, *Buckingham: The Life and Political Career of George Villiers, First Duke of Buckingham 1592–1628* (London, 1981). See also David M. Bergeron, *Royal Family, Royal Lovers: King James of England and Scotland* (Columbia, MO, 1991), pp. 28–31, 165–6, 170, 183–4. Bergeron's forthcoming *King James and Letters of Homoerotic Desire* (Iowa City, 1999), an edition of the letters between James and Buckingham, should be another important contribution to the subject. There are two good recent surveys of James's life: S.J. Houston, *James I*, 2nd edn (London, 1995) and Roger Lockyer, *James VI and I* (London, 1998). In view of the forthright treatment of sexuality in his *Buckingham*, it is surprising and disappointing to see Lockyer play down this subject in his more recent study of James. Lockyer merely writes that 'James found his principal emotional – and *conceivably* sexual – fulfilment in handsome young men with fine French manners, on whom he lavished not only affection but money, places and titles' (p. 12). Italics mine.
2. David H. Willson, *King James VI and I* (New York, 1967), p. 337. Similarly, referring to an occasion when James may have arranged to meet a male lover, Willson calls it 'an immoral purpose' (p. 456 n. 6).
3. Lee also adopted at times an almost snickering tone (referring to James's lovers as 'the apple of the king's eye' and 'James's pretty favorite'). Maurice Lee Jr, *Great Britain's Solomon* (Urbana, 1990), pp. 234–6, 240–2, 247–9, 255. See also Lee's 'James I and the Historians: Not a Bad King After All?', *Albion*, 16 (Summer 1984), 157–63.
4. Jenny Wormald, 'James VI and I: Two Kings or One?', *History*, 68 (June 1983), 187–92. See also her 'Gunpowder, Treason, and Scots', *Journal of British Studies*, 24, no. 2 (April 1985), 141–68. Wormald should have much more to say on these subjects in her long-awaited biography of James. At the 1996 meeting of the North American Conference on British Studies, Wormald said that the problem for James (as opposed to Queen Elizabeth) 'was not one of gender but of nationality'. I would say that the problem for James was a combination of both gender and nationality.
5. I have in mind here Alan Bray, Randolph Trumbach, Jonathan Goldberg, Bruce R. Smith, Gregory Bredbeck and others, whose works will be cited in due course.
6. Bray, *Homosexuality in Renaissance England* (London, 1982), pp. 13, 55, 62, 70, 111, 121 n. 14, 130 n. 77. Bray was sceptical about James's alleged homosexuality. In his well-known article on male friendship, Bray cautioned readers not to assume that James's favourites crossed the line from friendship to sodomy. Alan Bray, 'Homosexuality and the Signs of Male Friendship in

Elizabethan England', *History Workshop Journal*, issue 29 (Spring 1990), 13. There are other authors who have given James more attention than Bray did. Most noteworthy are Jonathan Goldberg, *James I and the Politics of Literature: Jonson, Shakespeare, Donne, and Their Contemporaries* (London, 1983) and Bruce R. Smith, *Homosexual Desire in Shakespeare's England: A Cultural Poetics* (Chicago, 1991). A short but good essay about King James and the history of homosexuality is Ellis Hanson, 'Sodomy and Kingcraft in *Urania* and *Antony and Cleopatra*', in Claude J. Summers (ed.), *Homosexuality in Renaissance and Enlightenment England: Literary Representations in Historical Context* (New York, 1992), pp. 135–51. Less successful is Robert Shephard, 'Sexual Rumours in English Politics: The Cases of Elizabeth I and James I', in Jacqueline Murray and Konrad Eisenbichler (eds), *Desire and Discipline: Sex and Sexuality in the Premodern West* (Toronto, 1996), pp. 101–22.

7. Bray, *Homosexuality in Renaissance England*, p. 17.

8. Michael Rocke, *Forbidden Friendships: Homosexuality and Male Culture in Renaissance Florence* (Oxford, 1996), pp. 6, 9.

9. David M. Halperin makes an especially cogent argument for the recent invention of homosexuality in *One Hundred Years of Homosexuality and Other Essays on Greek Love* (New York, 1990). He writes: 'Homosexuality and heterosexuality, as we currently understand them, are modern, Western, bourgeois productions' (p. 8).

10. Alan Bray, *Homosexuality in Renaissance England*, pp. 10, 103, 104, 108, 112. After writing 'London's Sodomites: Homosexual Behavior and Western Culture in the Eighteenth Century', *Journal of Social History*, 11, no. 1 (Fall 1977), 1–33, Randolph Trumbach began to argue for a major watershed in the early eighteenth century. See his 'Sodomitical Subcultures, Sodomitical Roles, and the Gender Revolution of the Eighteenth Century: The Recent Historiography', in Robert Purks Maccubbin (ed.), *'Tis Nature's Fault: Unauthorized Sexuality During the Enlightenment* (Cambridge, 1987), pp. 109–21; 'Sodomitical Assaults, Gender Role, and Sexual Development in Eighteenth-Century London', in Kent Gerard and Gert Hekma (eds), *The Pursuit of Sodomy: Male Homosexuality in Renaissance and Enlightenment Europe* (New York, 1989), pp. 407–29; 'The Birth of the Queen: Sodomy and the Emergence of Gender Equality in Modern Culture, 1660–1750', in Martin Duberman and others (eds), *Hidden from History: Reclaiming the Gay and Lesbian Past* (New York, 1989), pp. 129–40; 'Sodomy Transformed: Aristocratic Libertinage, Public Reputation and the Gender Revolution of the 18th Century', in Michael S. Kimmel (ed.), *Love Letters Between a Certain Late Nobleman and the Famous Mr. Wilson* (New York, 1990), 105–24; 'Erotic Fantasy and Male Libertinism in Enlightenment England', in Lynn Hunt (ed.), *The Invention of Pornography: Obscenity and the Origins of Modernity, 1500–1800* (New York, 1993), pp. 253–82; 'London's Sapphists: From Three Sexes to Four Genders in the Making of Modern Culture', in Gilbert Herdt (ed.), *Third Sex, Third Gender: Beyond Sexual Dimorphism in Culture and History* (New York, 1994), pp. 111–36; and 'Are Modern Western Lesbian Women and Gay Men a Third Gender?', in Martin Duberman (ed.), *A Queer World: The Center for Lesbian and Gay Studies Reader* (New York, 1997), pp. 87–99. Trumbach's view will soon be summed up in his two-volume *Sex and the Gender Revolution*, forthcoming from the University of Chicago Press.

11. Randolph Trumbach, *Sex and the Gender Revolution*, vol. 1, *Heterosexuality and the Third Gender in Enlightenment London* (Chicago, 1998). See especially pp. 3–22.
12. 'New-inventionism' is Joseph Cady's apt term for the social or cultural constructionist position. See his '"Masculine Love", Renaissance Writing, and the "New Invention" of Homosexuality', in Summers, *Homosexuality in Renaissance and Enlightenment England*, pp. 9–40; 'Renaissance Awareness and Language for Heterosexuality: "Love" and "Feminine Love"', in Claude J. Summers and Ted-Larry Pebworth (eds), *Renaissance Discourses of Desire* (Columbia, MO, 1993), pp. 143–58; 'The "Masculine Love" of the "Princes of Sodom" "Practicing the Art of Ganymede" at Henri III's Court: The Homosexuality of Henry III and His *Mignons* in Pierre de L'Estoile's *Mémoires-Journaux*', in Murray and Eisenbichler, *Desire and Discipline*, pp. 123–54. See also Rictor Norton, *The Myth of the Modern Homosexual: Queer History and the Search for Cultural Unity* (London, 1997) and Gregory W. Bredbeck, 'Tradition and the Individual Sodomite: Barnfield, Shakespeare, and Subjective Desire', in Summers, *Homosexuality in Renaissance and Enlightenment England*, pp. 41–68. Simon Shepherd questions the social constructionist position (which he calls 'the virgin birth of the homosexual') more gingerly in 'What's So Funny About Ladies' Tailors? A Survey of Some Male (Homo)sexual Types in the Renaissance', *Textual Practice*, 6 (1992), 17–30.
13. James M. Saslow, 'Homosexuality in the Renaissance: Behavior, Identity, and Artistic Expression', in Duberman, *Hidden from History*, p. 97.
14. Alan Bray, 'Homosexuality and the Signs of Male Friendship', p. 1.
15. In their 'Introduction' to *Hidden from History*, George Chauncey Jr, Martin Bauml Duberman and Martha Vicinus note this 'reluctance of most historians to discuss the role of effeminacy in gay male cultural history' (p. 7).
16. For the distinction between adolescent effeminacy, which may have been commonplace before the eighteenth century, and adult effeminacy, which is supposed to have emerged in the eighteenth century, see the works of Randolph Trumbach cited above. See also Saslow's 'Homosexuality in the Renaissance', pp. 92–3, 98–9.
17. Alan Sinfield, *The Wilde Century: Effeminacy, Oscar Wilde and the Queer Moment* (New York, 1994). See especially pp. 4 and 27.
18. James M. Saslow, *Ganymede in the Renaissance* (New Haven, 1986), p. 243 n. 31; Carl Miller, *Stages of Desire: Gay Theatre's Hidden History* (London, 1996), p. 148; Thomas Cogswell, *The Blessed Revolution: English Politics and the Coming of War, 1621–1624* (Cambridge, 1989), p. 72. Cogswell's source was Andrew Clark, 'Dr. Plume's Notebook', *The Essex Review*, XIV (1905), 9–12, 163. Unfortunately, this notebook is a collection of gossip, anecdotes and extracts compiled later in the seventeenth century, so it falls far short of being authentic firsthand testimony.
19. David Cressy, 'Gender Trouble and Cross-Dressing in Early Modern England', *Journal of British Studies*, 35 (October 1996), 451.
20. Carole Levin, *The Heart and Stomach of a King: Elizabeth I and the Politics of Sex and Power* (Philadelphia, 1994).
21. David Underdown observed: 'Critics of James I's foreign policy and his extravagant court saw in both a decline from the – paradoxically – manly

virtues of Queen Elizabeth's days', *A Freeborn People: Politics and the Nation in Seventeenth-Century England* (Oxford, 1996), p. 27. Lord Treasurer Salisbury may have inadvertently betrayed apprehension about James's manliness when he reassuringly told Parliament in 1610, 'yt may appeare unto us that we have a man to our Kinge (and happy are we that our Kinge is a man)'. S.R. Gardiner (ed.), *Parliamentary Debates in 1610* (London, 1862), p. 25.

22. For recent appreciative studies of James, see Linda Levy Peck (ed.), *The Mental World of the Jacobean Court* (Cambridge, 1991); Jenny Wormald's 'James VI and I: Two Kings or One?'; Maurice Lee Jr's 'James I and the Historians'; Lee, *Government by Pen: Scotland under James VI and I* (London, 1980); Lee, *Great Britain's Solomon: James VI and I in His Three Kingdoms* (Urbana, 1990); Gordon Donaldson, *Scotland: James V to James VII* (Edinburgh, 1971); and R. C. Munden, 'James I and "the growth of mutual distrust": King, Commons, and Reform, 1603–1604', in Kevin Sharpe (ed.), *Faction and Parliament: Essays on Early Stuart History* (Oxford, 1978), pp. 43–72. S.J. Houston's *James I* is an unusually well-balanced survey. G.P.V. Akrigg provides a concise, perceptive and nicely balanced assessment of James's relative strengths and weaknesses in the introduction to his *Letters of King James VI and I* (Berkeley, 1984), pp. 15–20. For a pioneering reevaluation, see Marc L. Schwarz, 'James I and the Historians: Toward a Reconsideration', *Journal of British Studies*, 13, no. 2 (May 1974), 114–34. For a more recent survey of the literature, see Susanne Collier, 'Recent Studies in James VI and I', *English Literary Renaissance*, 23, no. 3 (1993), 509–19.

23. Pauline Croft, 'Libels, Popular Literacy and Public Opinion in Early Modern England', *Historical Research*, 68 (October 1995), 279; Croft, 'The Reputation of Robert Cecil: Libels, Political Opinion and Popular Awareness in the Early Seventeenth Century', *Transactions of the Royal Historical Society*, sixth series, 1 (London, 1991), pp. 43–69; Alastair Bellany, '"Raylinge Rymes and Vaunting Verse": Libellous Politics in Early Stuart England, 1603–1628', in Kevin Sharpe and Peter Lake (eds), *Culture and Politics in Early Stuart England* (Stanford, 1993), pp. 285–310; Bellany, 'Mistress Turner's Deadly Sins: Sartorial Transgression, Court Scandal, and Politics in Early Stuart England', *Huntington Library Quarterly*, 58, no. 2 (1996), 179–210; Thomas Cogswell, 'Underground Verse and the Transformation of Early Stuart Political Culture', in Susan D. Amussen and Mark Kishlansky (eds), *Political Culture and Cultural Politics in Early Modern England: Essays Presented to David Underdown* (Manchester, 1995), pp. 277–300; Lockyer, *James VI and I*, p. 173.

24. Richard Cust, 'Honour and Politics in Early Stuart England', *Past and Present*, 149 (November 1995), 58.

1 Life and Loves

1. For an extended discussion of James's life up to the age of seventeen, see Caroline Bingham, *The Making of a King: The Early Years of James VI and I* (London, 1968), especially chapters 2 and 3.

2. Maurice Lee Jr, *Great Britain's Solomon: James VI and I in His Three Kingdoms* (Urbana, IL, 1990), p. 32.
3. David Harris Willson, *King James VI and I* (New York, 1967), pp. 19–27.
4. Neil Cuddy, 'The Revival of the Entourage: The Bedchamber of James I, 1603–1625', in David Starkey and others (eds), *The English Court: from the Wars of the Roses to the Civil War* (London, 1987), pp. 180–1.
5. Joseph Cady, '"Masculine Love", Renaissance Writing, and the "New Invention" of Homosexuality', in Claude Summers (ed.), *Homosexuality in Renaissance and Enlightenment England: Literary Representations in Historical Context* (New York, 1992), pp. 17, 26, 37 n. 24; Joseph Cady, 'The "Masculine Love" of the "Princes of Sodom" "Practicing the Art of Ganymede" at Henri III's Court: The Homosexuality of Henry III and His *Mignons* in Pierre de L'Estoile's *Mémoires-Journaux*', in Jacqueline Murray and Konrad Eisenbichler (eds), *Desire and Discipline: Sex and Sexuality in the Premodern West* (Toronto, 1996), pp. 123–54.
6. David Calderwood, *History of the Kirk of Scotland*, ed. Thomas Thomson (Edinburgh, 1843), III, 480, 642, 775–7.
7. Joseph Bain (ed.), *Calendar of Letters and Papers Relating to the Affairs of the Borders of England and Scotland* (Edinburgh, 1894), I, 82.
8. For Lennox, see Leslie Stephen and Sidney Lee (eds), *The Dictionary of National Biography* (Oxford, 1917), XIX, 77–80 [hereafter *DNB*]; Bingham, *Making of a King*, chapters 5 and 6; Willson, *King James VI and I*, pp. 32–43, 58–9; Lee, *Great Britain's Solomon*, chapter 2; Gordon Donaldson, *Scotland: James V to James VII* (Edinburgh, 1971), chapter 10; *The Diary of Mr. James Melvill 1556–1601* (Edinburgh, 1829), pp. 59–96.
9. James I, *The Essayes of a Prentise, in the Divine Art of Poesie* (Edinburgh, 1585), sigs G2ᵛ, G3ʳ, G4ᵛ, H1ᵛ, H3ᵛ, H4ʳ. I have modernized spelling. It is not just a guess that the Phoenix represented Lennox. In an anagram at the outset of the poem, James spelled out his name. The modern critic Jonathan Goldberg has brilliantly analysed James's writings, but his analysis of this particular work does not quite ring true. Focusing on the image of the phoenix/Lennox crouched between the king's bleeding legs, Goldberg wrote, 'It is not difficult to imagine the self-pleasing thoughts that move the poem.' Surely the overall tone of the 'Tragedie Called Phoenix' is not self-pleasing. Jonathan Goldberg, *James I and the Politics of Literature: Jonson, Shakespeare, Donne, and Their Contemporaries* (London, 1983), pp. 23, 81. The phoenix was a common symbol in the literature of the period. Shakespeare used a female phoenix in *Henry VIII* to represent the succession from Elizabeth I to James I. Ivo Kamps, *Historiography and Ideology in Stuart Drama* (Cambridge, 1997), pp. 132–5. Sir Philip Sidney and his circle used the phoenix in their writings. Margaret P. Hannay, *Philip's Phoenix: Mary Sidney, Countess of Pembroke* (New York, 1990), pp. 67–9, 81–2.
10. William K. Boyd (ed.), *Calendar of the State Papers Relating to Scotland and Mary, Queen of Scots 1547–1603* (Edinburgh, 1910), VI, 129, 130. [Hereafter *CSPScotland*.]
11. Fontenay's report is printed in Robert Ashton (ed.), *James I by his Contemporaries* (London, 1969), pp. 1–3.
12. David Calderwood, *History of the Kirk of Scotland*, ed. Thomas Thomson (Edinburgh, 1843), III, 698. Spelling modernized. It is believable that

James's contemporaries described him as 'foul-mouthed'. On the other hand, it is hard to know how much stock to put in charges that he was slovenly or dirty. Willson, *King James VI and I*, pp. 27, 36, 191, 208, 379; Lawrence Stone, *The Causes of the English Revolution 1529–1642* (London, 1972), p. 89.

13. Ashton, *James I by his Contemporaries*, p. 3. Ashton explained in a footnote: 'Fontenay is almost certainly referring to James' affection for male favourites.' According to David H. Willson, Fontenay wrote that James's 'love for favourites is indiscreet'. This may convey Fontenay's meaning, but it is not an accurate translation. *King James VI and I*, p. 53. For the original French, which Ashton translated more accurately, see Historical Manuscripts Commission, *Salisbury MSS.* (London, 1889), III, 59–61. For James's health, see A.W. Beasley, 'The Disability of James VI & I', *The Seventeenth Century*, 10, no. 2 (1995), 151–62.

14. Lee, *Great Britain's Solomon*, pp. 238–41. Lee observed: 'From…may 1587 to the death of Robert Cecil twenty-five years later none of the handsome young men of whom the king was fond – and they were plentiful – had any political influence.' See also Willson, *King James VI & I*, pp. 98–100.

15. S.J. Houston, *James I*, 2nd edn (London, 1995), p. 110.

16. William K. Boyd and Henry W. Meikle (eds), *Calendar of the State Papers Relating to Scotland and Mary, Queen of Scots 1547–1603* (Glasgow, 1915; Edinburgh, 1936), IX, 676, 698–707; X, 1–8.

17. W.B. Patterson, *King James VI and I and the Reunion of Christendom* (Cambridge, 1997), pp. 13–21; Jenny Wormald, 'James VI and I: Two Kings or One?', *History*, 68 (June 1983), 197–8; *DNB*, VIII, 186–90.

18. Lee, *Great Britain's Solomon*, p. 241.

19. *CSPScotland*, IX, 655.

20. Akrigg, *Letters*, p. 98.

21. *CSPScotland*, X, 122, 124. I have modernized spelling in the last quotation. See also Ethel Carleton Williams, *Anne of Denmark: Wife of James VI of Scotland: James I of England* (London, 1970), p. 15.

22. Willson, *King James VI and I*, pp. 85–95. For Anne's life, see Ethel Williams's *Anne of Denmark* cited above. Williams gives only cursory attention to James's extramarital sexual relations. See, for example, pp. 51 and 56.

23. A.L. Rowse, *Homosexuals in History: A Study of Ambivalence in Society, Literature and the Arts* (New York, 1977), p. 54.

24. Lee, *Great Britain's Solomon*, p. 74.

25. Maurice Ashley, *The House of Stuart: Its Rise and Fall* (London, 1980), p. 116.

26. Willson, *King James VI and I*, p. 95.

27. Even Pearl Hogrefe fell into the trap of describing Anne as 'frivolous, without any intellectual interests'. *Tudor Women: Commoners and Queens* (Ames, IA, 1975), p. 142. Two excellent correctives to the traditional view are Leeds Barroll, 'The Court of the First Stuart Queen', in Linda Levy Peck (ed.), *The Mental World of the Jacobean Court* (Cambridge, 1991), pp. 191–208 and Barbara Kiefer Lewalski, 'Enacting Opposition: Queen Anne and the Subversions of Masquing' in Lewalski, *Writing Women in Jacobean England* (Cambridge, MA, 1993), pp. 15–43. See also David M. Bergeron, 'Masculine Interpretation of Queen Anne, Wife of James I', *Biography*, 18, no. 1 (1995), 42–54.

28. Allen B. Hinds (ed.), *Calendar of State Papers and Manuscripts, Relating to English Affairs, Existing in the Archives and Collections of Venice*, X (London, 1912), 513. [Hereafter *CSPV*.]

29. From James's *Basilikon Doron* in Johann P. Sommerville (ed.), *King James VI and I: Political Writings* (Cambridge, 1994), p. 42.

30. Anne had spent her earliest years in the care of her grandparents, but afterward was raised by her mother, who provided a strong female role model. See chapter 1 of Williams's *Anne of Denmark*.

31. David M. Bergeron, *Royal Family, Royal Lovers: King James of England and Scotland* (Columbia, MO, 1991), pp. 52–63, 72. See also his 'Francis Bacon's *Henry VII*: Commentary on King James I', *Albion*, 24 (Spring 1992), 17–26.

32. For Anne's religious position, see Peter E. McCullough, *Sermons at Court: Politics and Religion in Elizabethan and Jacobean Preaching* (Cambridge, 1998), pp. 169–82.

33. Sir Anthony Weldon, *The Court and Character of King James* (London, 1651), p. 168; Godfrey Goodman, *The Court of King James the First* (London, 1839), I, 168. See more about this below in chapter 7.

34. Goldberg, *James I and the Politics of Literature*, p. 24.

35. Allen F. Westcott (ed.), *New Poems By James I of England* (New York, 1911), pp. 19–21.

36. Frederick von Raumer, *History of the Sixteenth and Seventeenth Centuries, Illustrated by Original Sources* [trans. H.E. Lloyd] (London, 1835), II, 196. In letters he exchanged with the Duke of Buckingham later in his life, both writers sometimes referred to the women in their lives as 'the cunts'. Akrigg, *Letters*, pp. 436, 440, 441 n. 6, 442.

37. David M. Bergeron, *Shakespeare's Romances and the Royal Family* (Lawrence, KS, 1985), p. 40; Bergeron, *Royal Family*, pp. 81–2; Williams, *Anne of Denmark*, p. 112; Willson, *King James VI and I*, p. 403.

38. I am greatly condensing events in this paragraph. For more detail see Maurice Lee Jr, *Government by Pen: Scotland under James VI and I* (Urbana, IL, 1980), chapter 1; Lee, *Great Britain's Solomon*, chapter 3; Willson, *King James VI and I*, chapters 7 and 8; Donaldson, *Scotland: James V to James VII*, chapters 10–12; Rosalind Mitchison, *Lordship to Patronage: Scotland 1603–1745* (London, 1983), chapter 1; Jennifer M. Brown, 'Scottish Politics 1567–1625' in Alan G.R. Smith (ed.), *The Reign of James VI and I* (London, 1973), pp. 22–39; and Jenny Wormald, *Court, Kirk, and Community: Scotland 1470–1625* (Toronto, 1981), chapter 9. For an especially sympathetic treatment of James's relations with the Kirk, see Wormald's 'Ecclesiastical Vitriol: the Kirk, the Puritans and the Future King of England', in John Guy (ed.), *The Reign of Elizabeth I: Court and Culture in the Last Decade* (Cambridge, 1995), pp. 171–91.

39. From James's *Basilikon Doron* in Sommerville, *Political Writings*, p. 28.

40. Ibid., pp. 26–7. I have modernized spelling.

41. Willson, *King James VI and I*, p. 60.

42. James Craigie (ed.), *The Poems of James VI of Scotland* (Edinburgh, 1958); Allan F. Westcott (ed.), *New Poems By James I of England* (New York, 1911).

43. Craigie, *Poems*, II, 174–5, 192–3.

44. There are two modern editions of these works: Charles Howard McIlwain (ed.), *The Political Works of James I* (New York, 1965) and Johann

P. Sommerville (ed.), *King James VI and I: Political Writings* (Cambridge, 1994).

45. Jenny Wormald, 'James VI and I, Basilikon Doron and the True Law of Free Monarchies: The Scottish Context and the English Translation', in Peck, *Mental World*, pp. 36–54; Glenn Burgess, *The Politics of the Ancient Constitution* (University Park, PA, 1993), pp. 152–6; Burgess, *Absolute Monarchy and the Stuart Constitution* (New Haven, 1996), pp. 40–3; Conrad Russell, 'Divine Rights in the Early Seventeenth Century', in John Morrill, Paul Slack, and Daniel Woolf (eds), *Public Duty and Private Conscience in Seventeenth-Century England* (Oxford, 1993), pp. 101–20. Compare J.P. Sommerville, *Politics and Ideology in England 1603–1640* (London, 1986), pp. 47, 93, 101, 115–17, 132–4, 160, 181; Sommerville, 'James I and the Divine Right of Kings: English Politics and Continental Theory', in Peck, *Mental World*, pp. 55–70; J.H. Burns, *The True Law of Kingship: Concepts of Monarchy in Early Modern Scotland* (Oxford, 1996), chapters 7 and 8; and Sommerville's introduction to James's *Political Writings*.

46. The following quotations come from Sommerville's edition of James's *Political Writings*, pp. 62, 63, 65, 75, 76, 83.

47. Wormald, 'Basilikon Doron and the Trew Law of Free Monarchies', pp. 50–2.

48. Sommerville, *Political Writings*, p. 49. See also p. 4.

49. G.B. Harrison (ed.). *King James the First Daemonologie (1597) [and] Newes From Scotland* (New York, 1966), p. 15.

50. James Craigie (ed.), *Minor Prose Works of King James VI and I* (Edinburgh, 1982), p. 190.

51. *Daemonologie, In Forme of a Dialogue, Divided into Three Bookes* (Edinburgh, 1597), pp. 30, 43–4, 78. I have modernized spelling. Two modern editions are available in Harrison's *King James the First Daemonologie (1597) [and] Newes From Scotland* and Craigie, *Minor Prose Works*, pp. 1–58. See also Christina Larner, 'James VI and I and Witchcraft', in Smith, *The Reign of James VI and I*, pp. 74–90; Stuart Clark, 'King James's *Daemonologie*: Witchcraft and Kingship', in Sydney Anglo (ed.), *The Damned Art: Essays in the Literature of Witchcraft* (London, 1977), pp. 156–81; P.G. Maxwell-Stuart, 'The Fear of the King is Death: James VI and the Witches of East Lothian', in William G. Naphy and Penny Roberts (eds), *Fear in Early Modern Society* (Manchester, 1997), pp. 209–25. Clark credits (or blames) James for introducing two distinctly continental beliefs about witchcraft into Scotland – the idea of a pact between the witch and the Devil and the idea of the sabbat, though this appears to be an exaggeration of his personal role. James did not really say much about the sabbat, which he called convenings, and he spent more time speculating on how witches get to these meetings with the Devil than what they do after they arrive there except for the 'kissing of his hinder parts'. *Daemonologie*, pp. 35–40.

52. The *Counterblaste* is printed in Craigie's edition of James's *Minor Prose Works*, pp. 83–99. I am quoting pp. 85 and 99 and have modernized spelling.

53. William Arbuckle, 'The "Gowrie Conspiracy" – Part I' and 'The "Gowrie Conspiracy" – Part II', *Scottish Historical Review*, 36 (April and October 1957), 1–24, 89–110. Willson, *King James VI and I*, pp. 126–30; *DNB*, XVII, 502–9; Louis A. Barbé, *The Tragedy of Gowrie House: An Historical Study*

(London, 1887). A work that is very prejudiced against James but full of details and analysis is George Malcolm Thomson, *A Kind of Justice: Two Studies in Treason* (London, 1970).

54. It took some time to locate a third man who was supposed to have been in the room. When a man named Andrew Henderson did come forward claiming to be the mysterious third man, he did not fit the description James had given. Henderson's version of events differed from James's in some details, but it was generally supportive. Afterwards Henderson was well provided for by James, which casts further doubt on whether he was a bona fide witness to the events. Arbuckle, 'The "Gowrie Conspiracy" – Part II', pp. 99–102; Thomson, *A Kind of Justice*, pp. 56–9.

55. Arbuckle, 'The "Gowrie Conspiracy" – Part II', p. 89; Alexandre Teulet (ed.), *Relations Politiques de la France et de L'Espagne avec L'Ecosse au XVI Siècle* (Paris, 1862), IV, 229–35.

56. Francis Osborne, *Some Traditional Memorials on the Reign of King James* (London, 1658), in *The Works of Francis Osborn*, 7th edn (London, 1673), p. 536.

57. McCullough, *Sermons at Court*, p. 119.

58. Willson tactfully buried this speculation in a footnote: 'It is not impossible that the King retired with the Master [of Ruthven] for an immoral purpose.' *King James VI and I*, p. 452 n. 6. See also Thomson, *A Kind of Justice*, pp. 73–4.

59. Arbuckle, 'The "Gowrie Conspiracy" – Part II', p. 96. I have modernized spelling. Teulet, *Relations Politiques*, IV, 234–5.

60. See, for example, Conrad Russell, *The Causes of the English Civil War* (Oxford, 1990), pp. 43–52.

61. Patrick Collinson, 'The Jacobean Religious Settlement: The Hampton Court Conference', in Howard Tomlinson (ed.), *Before the English Civil War: Essays on Early Stuart Politics and Government* (London, 1983), pp. 27–52; Kenneth Fincham and Peter Lake, 'The Ecclesiastical Policy of King James I', *Journal of British Studies*, 24 (1985), 169–207; several of the essays in Kenneth Fincham (ed.), *The Early Stuart Church* (Stanford, CA, 1993); and Kenneth Fincham, *Prelate as Pastor: The Episcopate of James I* (Oxford, 1990).

62. Sommerville, *Political Writings*, p. 139. See also pp. 161, 193.

63. McCullough, *Sermons at Court*, p. 101.

64. J.R. Tanner (ed.), *Constitutional Documents of the Reign of James I* (Cambridge, 1960), p. 297.

65. Willson, *King James VI and I*, p. 358.

66. Maurice Lee Jr, *James I and Henry IV: An Essay in English Foreign Policy 1603–1610* (Urbana, IL, 1970), pp. 13, 16. Lee thought the early years of James's reign compared to Winston Churchill's description of England in the 1930s, wasted years of ignominious passivity. Given Lee's normally favourable view of James, it is tempting to wonder whether the passions of the Vietnam war era drove him to take this uncharacteristically negative view of the king's foreign policy.

67. W.B. Patterson, *King James VI and I and the Reunion of Christendom* (Cambridge, 1997).

68. James originally intended for his oldest son, Henry, to marry a Catholic, but this role fell to Charles when Henry died in 1612. See Roy Strong, 'England

and Italy: The Marriage of Henry Prince of Wales', in Richard Ollard and Pamela Tudor-Craig (eds), *For Veronica Wedgwood These: Studies in Seventeenth-Century History* (London, 1986), pp. 59–88.

69. Lee, *James I and Henry IV*, pp. 174–85.
70. The literature on James's abortive effort at union has been mushrooming in recent years. See, for example, B. Galloway, *The Union of England and Scotland 1603–1608* (Edinburgh, 1986); Brian Levack, *The Formation of the British State: England, Scotland, and the Union 1603–1707* (Oxford, 1987); chapter 2 in Lee, *Government By Pen*; Jenny Wormald, 'The Union of 1603' in Roger A. Mason (ed.), *Scots and Britons: Scottish Political Thought and the Union of 1603* (Cambridge, 1994), pp. 17–40; Jenny Wormald, 'James VI, James I, and the Identity of Britain' in Brendan Bradshaw and John Morrill (eds), *The British Problem, c. 1534–1707: State Formation in the Atlantic Archipelago* (New York, 1996), pp. 148–71. James made an eloquent plea on the subject in a speech to Parliament in 1607. See Sommerville, *Political Writings*, pp. 159–78.
71. On the other hand, as Keith Brown acknowledges, Scotophobia was matched across the border by Anglophobia. People on both sides of the border were wary of a union, and in light of today's devolutionary movement, it is no longer so clear that James was on the right side of this issue. See Brown's *Kingdom or Province? Scotland and the Regal Union, 1603–1715* (New York, 1992), pp. 86–8.
72. Sommerville, *Political Writings*, p. 173.
73. Lee, *Government by Pen*, p. 220.
74. Cuddy, 'The Revival of the Entourage', pp. 173–225 and 'Anglo-Scottish Union and the Court of James I, 1603–1625', *Transactions of the Royal Historical Society*, fifth series, 39 (London, 1989), 107–24.
75. Tanner, *Constitutional Documents*, p. 222. G.R. Elton tried to discount the significance of the 'Apology' and J.H. Hexter to reassert it. See Elton, 'A High Road to Civil War?' in his *Studies in Tudor and Stuart Politics and Government: Papers and Reviews 1946–1972* (Cambridge, 1974), pp. 164–82 and Hexter, 'The Apology' in Ollard, *For Veronica Wedgwood These*, pp. 13–44.
76. R.C. Munden, 'James I and "the Growth of Mutual Distrust": King, Commons, and Reform, 1603–1604', in Kevin Sharpe (ed.), *Faction and Parliament: Essays on Early Stuart History* (Oxford, 1978), pp. 43–72. Conrad Russell minimizes the transition from Elizabeth's to James's Parliaments in 'English Parliaments 1593–1606: One Epoch or Two?', in D.M. Dean and N.L. Jones (eds), *The Parliaments of Elizabethan England* (Oxford, 1990), pp. 191–213.
77. Before a Scottish Parliament met, the agenda was determined in advance by a committee known as the Lords of the Articles which James could pack with his own men, and legislation was lumped together in one large package which discouraged close scrutiny of any particular item. Wormald, *Court, Kirk, and Community*, pp. 157–8; Lee, *Government by Pen*, p. 6.
78. Linda Levy Peck, '"For a King not to be bountiful were a fault": Perspectives on Court Patronage in Early Stuart England', *Journal of British Studies*, 25 (1986), 31–61 and *Court Patronage and Corruption in Early Stuart England* (London, 1990).

79. In 1610 James similarly declared 'that Christmas and open tide is ended'. Sommerville, *Political Writings*, pp. 166, 197.
80. Eric Lindquist, 'The Failure of the Great Contract', *Journal of Modern History*, 57 (December 1985), 617–51.
81. S.R. Gardiner, *History of England from the Accession of James I to the Outbreak of the Civil War 1603–1642* (London, 1883–4, 1894–6), III, 197–8.
82. For James's view of this course of events in 1621, see his 'Declaration' printed in Sommerville, *Political Writings*, pp. 250–67. For the Commons' petition on foreign policy and their 'Protestation', see J.P. Kenyon (ed.), *The Stuart Constitution 1603–1688: Documents and Commentary*, 2nd edn (Cambridge, 1986), pp. 39–43.
83. Sommerville, *Political Writings*, p. 181.
84. *Journals of the House of Lords*, III, 283.
85. Sommerville, *Political Writings*, pp. 23, 33–7.
86. Raumer, *History*, II, 200.
87. Ibid., II, 210.
88. The writer was Sir John Harington. See Thomas Park (ed.), *Nugae Antiquae* (London, 1804), I, 348–54; Norman McClure (ed.), *The Letters and Epigrams of Sir John Harington* (New York, 1977; reprint of 1930 edition), pp. 118–21.
89. Raumer, *History*, II, 266.
90. Sommerville, *Political Writings*, p. 51. It may not be fair to call James a 'drunkard', as Kevin Sharpe has done, but it is reasonable to wonder if he was an alcoholic. Sharpe, 'Private Conscience and Public Duty in the Writings of James VI and I', in Morrill, *Public Duty*, p. 100.
91. See especially Wormald's 'Two Kings or One?'.
92. Cuddy, 'Anglo-Scottish Union and the Court of James I', pp. 107–24.
93. S.R. Gardiner (ed.), *Parliamentary Debates in 1610* (London, 1862), pp. xiii–xiv.
94. Cuddy, 'Anglo-Scottish Union and the Court of James I', pp. 116–17; Pauline Croft, 'Libels, Popular Literacy and Public Opinion in Early Modern England', *Historical Research*, 68 (October 1995), 278 n. 57; Gardiner, *History*, II, 111; Norman E. McClure (ed.), *The Letters of John Chamberlain* (Philadelphia, 1939), I, 238, 241.
95. Gardiner, *Parliamentary Debates in 1610*, p. 11.
96. Gordon Williams (ed.), *A Dictionary of Sexual Language and Imagery in Shakespearean and Stuart Literature* (London, 1994), I, 258–61.
97. Ibid., pp. 13, 144. Wentworth actually said that he would be glad to hear that the King of Spain spent all his money on favourites and wanton courtiers, but this was obviously an indirect way of commenting upon James's behaviour. Judging from James's reportedly angry reaction, he knew that he was the real target of Wentworth's criticism. Mary Anne Everett Green (ed.), *Calendar of State Papers, Domestic Series, of the Reign of James I* (London, 1857), I, 646–7, 649–50.
98. Thomas L. Moir, *The Addled Parliament of 1614* (Oxford, 1958), pp. 137–9, 142–8; Maija Jansson, *Proceedings in Parliament 1614 (House of Commons)* (Philadelphia, 1988), pp. xxxiv–xxxv, 415, 420, 423.
99. W. Dunn Macray (ed.), *The History of the Rebellion and Civil Wars in England Begun in the Year 1641, by Edward, Earl of Clarendon* (Oxford, 1888), I, 74. For Herbert see *DNB*, IX, 659–63.

100. Willson, *King James VI and I*, p. 403.
101. Park, *Nugae Antiquae*, I, 390–7; McClure, *Letters and Epigrams of Sir John Harington*, pp. 32–4.
102. For Carr, see Willson, *King James VI and I*, pp. 336–56; G.P.V. Akrigg, *Jacobean Pageant or the Court of King James I* (New York, 1967), pp. 177–204; and *DNB*, III, 1081–5.
103. Gardiner, *History of England*, II, 166–87. Thomas Birch (ed.), *The Court and Times of James I* (London, 1849), I, 254, 261, 269, 273, 276, 284–8.
104. Historical Manuscripts Commission, *Report on the Manuscripts of the Marquess of Downshire Preserved at Easthampstead Park Berks* (London, 1940), IV, 385.
105. McClure, *Chamberlain Letters*, I, 548; Birch, *Court and Times*, I, 336.
106. Gardiner, *History*, II, 331–63.
107. David Lindley, *The Trials of Frances Howard: Fact and Fiction at the Court of King James* (London, 1993).
108. Arthur Wilson, *The History of Great Britain, Being the Life and Reign of King James The First* (London, 1653), p. 71.
109. Houston, *James I*, p. 111. Roger Lockyer also referred to 'the aura of sleaze which hung around James's court'. *James VI and I* (London, 1998), p. 173. Alastair Bellany, '"Rayling Rymes and Vaunting Verse": Libellous Politics in Early Stuart England, 1603–1628', in Kevin Sharpe and Peter Lake (eds), *Culture and Politics in Early Stuart England* (London, 1993), pp. 285–310; Alastair Bellany, 'Mistress Turner's Deadly Sins: Sartorial Transgression, Court Scandal, and Politics in Early Stuart England', *Huntington Library Quarterly*, 58, no. 2 (1996), 179–210.
110. Roger Lockyer, *Buckingham: The Life and Political Career of George Villiers, First Duke of Buckingham 1592–1628* (London, 1981), pp. 12–18.
111. Akrigg, *Letters*, p. 336.
112. John Nichols, *The Progresses, Processions, and Magnificent Festivities of King James the First* (London, 1828), III, 80–1; Lockyer, *Buckingham*, pp. 19–20. Queen Anne tried to warn Abbot, 'I know your Master better than you all; for if this young man be once brought in, the first persons that he will plague must be you that labour for him.' When Abbot recounted this episode years later, he had been sequestered from his office and could only belatedly agree: 'Noble Queen! how like a prophetess or oracle did you speak!'
113. For Buckingham's career see Roger Lockyer's *Buckingham* cited above. For balance see Michael B. Young, 'Buckingham, War, and Parliament: Revisionism Gone Too Far', *Parliamentary History* , 4 (1985), 45–69. For a concise life of Buckingham see the *DNB*, XX, 327–37.
114. Francis Bamford (ed.), *A Royalist's Notebook: The Commonplace Book of Sir John Oglander* (New York, 1971), p. 41.
115. Philip Yorke, second Earl of Hardwicke (ed.), *Miscellaneous State Papers from 1501 to 1726* (London, 1778), I, 455, 471.
116. Historical Manuscripts Commission, *Supplementary Report on the Manuscripts of the Earl of Mar & Kellie* (London, 1930), p. 65.
117. State papers, domestic, reign of James the First, Public Record Office, London. [Hereafter SP 14.] SP 14/88/14. Italics mine.
118. SP 14/88/57.

119. SP 14/90/135.
120. *CSPV*, XVII, 439.
121. Lockyer, *Buckingham*, p. 120. See also pp. 55–60, 119, 152–4 and Bingham, *James I*, p. 195.
122. Akrigg, *Letters*, p. 374. On a visit to Buckingham's home, James similarly implored, 'God send a smilinge boy within a while'. Craigie, *Poems*, II, 177.
123. Sir Anthony Weldon's description of this phenomenon is well known and sometimes treated as caricature. He did write with a mocking tone, but the bare facts were largely as he described them. Weldon, *Court and Character*, p. 125. The Venetian ambassador, writing in 1622, used language remarkably similar to Weldon's. *CSPV*, XVII, 442.
124. The standard authorities on Cranfield are R.H. Tawney, *Business and Politics under James I: Lionel Cranfield as Merchant and Minister* (Cambridge, 1958) and Menna Prestwich, *Cranfield: Politics and Profits under the Early Stuarts: the Career of Lionel Cranfield, Earl of Middlesex* (Oxford, 1966). It is easy to overestimate Cranfield's accomplishments and his motives, however. For a corrective, see Michael B. Young, 'Illusions of Grandeur and Reform at the Jacobean Court: Cranfield and the Ordnance', *Historical Journal*, 22, no. 1 (1979), 53–73.
125. For James's renewed push to bring the Kirk in Scotland into greater conformity with England, see chapter 5 of Lee's *Government by Pen*.
126. Kevin Sharpe, *The Personal Rule of Charles I* (New Haven, 1992). See especially pp. 179–235.

2   Sodomy

1. *Criminal Trials and Other Proceedings Before the High Court of Justiciary in Scotland*, Publications of the Bannatyne Club (n.p., 1830), vol. 19, pt. 4, pp. 332–5. I have modernized spelling.
2. For example, one would love to know the contents of the books, ballads, pasquils, rhymes and libels regarding the Duke of Lennox that James suppressed and destroyed. See William K. Boyd (ed.), *Calendar of the State Papers Relating to Scotland and Mary, Queen of Scots 1547–1603* (Edinburgh, 1907, 1910), VI, 59, 563. Hereafter *CSPScotland*.
3. [Thomas Scott], *Sir Walter Rawleighs Ghost or Englands Forewarner* (Utrecht, 1626), p. 2.
4. Sir Edward Coke, *The Third Part of the Institutes of the Laws of England* (London, 1797), pp. 57–8.
5. Bray, *Homosexuality in Renaissance England* (London, 1982), pp. 46–80, quoting pp. 57, 76, 79. There never has been any evidence for Bray's contention that homosexuality in Renaissance England was 'deep-rooted', 'ubiquitous' and existed 'on a massive and ineradicable scale' (pp. 52, 79). B.R. Burg made the same argument that 'homosexuality was greeted with little hostility or opprobrium in the early seventeenth century'. There was, he writes, 'no abiding concern with restricting homosexual acts in the age of James I and Charles I', and 'there was little alarm over sexual relations between adults of the same sex'. See his 'Ho Hum, Another Work of the Devil: Buggery and Sodomy in Early Stuart England', in Salvatore J. Licata

Notes and References 169

and Robert P. Peterson (eds), *The Gay Past: A Collection of Historical Essays* (New York, 1985), pp. 69–78.

6. Mark D. Jordan, *The Invention of Sodomy in Christian Theology* (Chicago, 1997), p. 7.
7. CSPScotland, V, 355, 423, 431, 514, 521, 610, 619, 634, 637, 650, 693–4; VI, 149, 162, 167, 172–4.
8. Joseph Bain (ed.), *Calendar of Letters and Papers Relating to the Affairs of the Borders of England and Scotland* (Edinburgh, 1894), I, 82. Spelling modernized.
9. David Moysie, *Memoirs of the Affairs of Scotland* (Edinburgh, 1830), pp. xiii, 26. Spelling modernized..
10. David Harris Willson, *King James VI and I* (New York, 1956), p. 36.
11. Moysie, *Memoirs of the Affairs of Scotland*, p. 26.
12. *Calendar of Letters and Papers Relating to the Affairs of the Borders*, I, 77, 80, 81, 86.
13. David Calderwood, *History of the Kirk of Scotland*, ed. Thomas Thomson (Edinburgh, 1843), III, 642. Here and elsewhere I have modernized Calderwood's spelling.
14. Calderwood, *History of the Kirk*, III, 641.
15. CSPScotland, VI, 171–4.
16. Calderwood, *History of the Kirk*, III, 649.
17. CSPScotland, VI, 149. See also Robert Pitcairn (ed.), *The Autobiography and Diary of Mr James Melvill* (Edinburgh, 1842), p. 174.
18. CSPScotland, VI, 51–2.
19. Calderwood, *History of the Kirk*, III, 653, 658.
20. CSPScotland, VI, 130.
21. Pitcairn, *Autobiography and Diary of Mr James Melvill*, p. 76. I have modernized spelling.
22. Joseph Cady, 'The "Masculine Love" of the "Princes of Sodom" "Practicing the Art of Ganymede" at Henri III's Court: The Homosexuality of Henry III and His *Mignons* in Pierre de L'Estoile's *Mémoires-Journaux*', in Jacqueline Murray and Konrad Eisenbichler (eds), *Desire and Discipline: Sex and Sexuality in the Premodern West* (Toronto, 1996), pp. 123–54.
23. One woman was associated with the debauchery of the court – the Countess of Arran. The clergy viewed her as a scandalous and sinful woman because she divorced her second husband on grounds of impotence to marry the Earl of Arran by whom she was already pregnant. The child was born out of wedlock. But there is nothing to link the Countess with James, and her appearance as a demonic female figure late in the day in the declaration issued by the lords who staged the coup against Lennox looks as if it could actually have been an effort to avoid implying that the sins of the court were homosexual. Calderwood, *History of the Kirk*, III, 654, 658.
24. John Hacket, *Scrinia Reserata: A Memorial Offer'd to the Great Deservings of John Williams* (London, 1693), p. 39.
25. Willson, *King James VI and I*, p. 36. G.P.V. Akrigg wrote that Lennox introduced James 'to poetry and possibly to homosexuality'. *Letters of King James VI and I* (Berkeley, 1984), p. 5.
26. Willson, *King James VI and I*, pp. 32–6, 47.

27. Antonia Fraser, *King James* (London, 1974), pp. 36–7.
28. Maurice Lee Jr, *Great Britain's Solomon: James VI and I in His Three Kingdoms* (Urbana, 1990), p. 236; Houston, *James I*, p. 5.
29. *CSPScotland*, IX, 701. Spelling modernized.
30. Ibid., X, 17.
31. Ibid., IX, 558.
32. Sir James Melville, *Memoirs of His Own Life* (London, 1922), p. 220.
33. *CSPScotland*, IX, 701.
34. Ibid., IX, 706. See also X, 1, 3, 6.
35. Ibid., X, 3.
36. Ibid., X, 6.
37. Ibid., X, 8.
38. Harington, *Nugae Antiquae*, I, 390–7; McClure, *Letters and Epigrams of Sir John Harington*, pp. 32–4.
39. Akrigg, *Letters of King James VI and I*, pp. 336–7.
40. Lee, *Great Britain's Solomon*, p. 249. Lee makes the same assertion in 'James I and the Historians: Not a Bad King After All?', *Albion*, 16, no. 2 (Summer 1984), 158. Roger Lockyer appears to share my interpretation of James's words. See his *Buckingham: The Life and Political Career of George Villiers, First Duke of Buckingham 1592–1628* (London, 1981), p. 22.
41. M.C. Hippeau (ed.), *Mémoires Inédits du Comte Leveneur de Tillières* (Paris, 1862), p. 4.
42. Elisabeth Bourcier (ed.), *The Diary of Sir Simonds D'Ewes (1622–1624)* (Paris, 1974), pp. 57, 87. Sir Edward Peyton described Buckingham as a man whom James 'would tumble and kiss as a mistress'. *Divine Catastrophe of the House of Stuarts*, in Sir Walter Scott (ed.), *Secret History of the Court of James the First* (Edinburgh, 1811), II, 348.
43. The classic work on the boundary between friendship and sodomy is Alan Bray, 'Homosexuality and the Signs of Male Friendship in Elizabethan England', *History Workshop Journal*, issue 29 (Spring 1990), pp. 1–19.
44. *Documentos inéditos para la historia de Espana* (Madrid, 1936), I, 101–2. I am grateful to Carolyn Nadeau for assistance in translating this letter. Compare S.R. Gardiner, *History of England from the Accession of James I to the Outbreak of the Civil War 1603–1642* (London, 1883–4, 1894–6), III, 98.
45. Johann P. Sommerville (ed.), *King James VI and I: Political Writings* (Cambridge, 1994), p. 181.
46. Lee, *Great Britain's Solomon*, p. 248
47. Bray, *Homosexuality in Renaissance England*, pp. 63–4; Jonathan Goldberg, 'Sodomy and Society: the Case of Christopher Marlowe', in David Scott Kastan and Peter Stallybrass (eds), *Staging the Renaissance: Reinterpretations of Elizabethan and Jacobean Drama* (New York, 1991), pp. 75–83. For Marlowe, see also chapter 8 of Carl Miller, *Stages of Desire: Gay Theatre's Hidden History* (London, 1996).
48. Rictor Norton, *The Myth of the Modern Homosexual: Queer History and the Search for Cultural Unity* (London, 1997), p. 221.
49. Akrigg, *Letters*, pp. 431–2. This letter is undated but apparently written between late 1622 and late 1624.
50. Jonathan Goldberg, *James I and the Politics of Literature: Jonson, Shakespeare, Donne, and Their Contemporaries* (London, 1983), p. 142.

51. Akrigg, *Letters*, pp. 387, 437, 439, 440, 442.
52. Most of these letters are among the Harleian MSS. in the British Library. Many can be found in print in Akrigg's previously cited *Letters of King James VI and I*; Philip Yorke, second Earl of Hardwicke (ed.), *Miscellaneous State Papers from 1501 to 1726* (London, 1778), volume I; James Orchard Halliwell (ed.), *Letters of the Kings of England* (London, 1848), volume II; and an appendix in Hugh Ross Williamson, *George Villiers, First Duke of Buckingham, Study for a Biography* (London, 1940). David M. Bergeron's *King James and Letters of Homoerotic Desire* (Iowa City, 1999) will finally give us a modern and complete edition of these letters.
53. Goldberg, *James I and the Politics of Literature*, p. 144.
54. Akrigg, *Letters*, p. 387.
55. Lockyer, *Buckingham*, p. 153; Akrigg, *Letters*, p. 392.
56. Akrigg, *Letters*, pp. 416, 421.
57. Halliwell, *Letters*, II, 171–2; James Craigie (ed.), *The Poems of James VI of Scotland* (Edinburgh, 1958), II, 192–3.
58. *Oxford English Dictionary*, 2nd edn (Oxford, 1989), XVII, 340.
59. Lockyer, *Buckingham*, p. 28.
60. Hardwicke, *State Papers*, I, 410, 449, 451.
61. This letter is printed in Williamson, *George Villiers, First Duke of Buckingham*, pp. 235–6.
62. Lockyer, *Buckingham*, p. 22. Compare Lee, *Great Britain's Solomon*, p. 248. Jonathan Goldberg notes the existence of stained glass windows depicting James and Buckingham at Wroxton. The inscription beneath James indicates that he slept there in 1619. Goldberg infers that Buckingham slept with him. Goldberg, *James I and the Politics of Literature*, pp. 145–6.
63. What Rictor Norton has written about Oscar Wilde relates to a much later period in time but might be said to describe James: 'Oscar Wilde was married and had two children. That does not mean he was bisexual.' If we wish to put it in modern terms, 'it is obviously more accurate to call him a married homosexual than a bisexual'. Norton, *The Myth of the Modern Homosexual*, p. 55.
64. Bruce Smith emphasizes James's homosexuality as a function of his power, a kind of sexual politics comparable to Queen Elizabeth's use of her virginity for political purposes. 'James's homosexuality may be the equivalent of Elizabeth's virginity: the erotic seal of men's political transactions with one another.' *Homosexual Desire*, p. 75.
65. Akrigg, *Letters*, pp. 338–9.
66. Sommerville, *Political Writings*, p. 76.
67. Sir Henry Wotton, 'A Short View of the Life and Death of George Villiers, Duke of Buckingham', in William Oldys (ed.), *The Harleian Miscellany* (London, 1808–13), VIII, 614.
68. W. Dunn Macray (ed.), *The History of the Rebellion and Civil Wars in England Begun in the Year 1641, by Edward, Earl of Clarendon* (Oxford, 1888), I, 38. Though he would be considered a less reputable source, Arthur Wilson wrote that James 'cast his eye upon a young Gentleman, so rarely *moulded*, that he meant to make him a *Masterpiece*'. *The History of Great Britain, Being the Life and Reign of King James The First* (London, 1653), p. 79.
69. Hardwicke, *State Papers*, I, 471, 454.

70. Sommerville, *Political Writings*, p. 23; C.H. McIlwain, (ed.), *The Political Works of James I* (New York, 1965), p. 20. The other crimes were witchcraft, murder, incest, poisoning and false coin (counterfeiting). James also made a point of excluding sodomy from a general pardon issued after the Parliament of 1610. Akrigg, *Letters*, pp. 314–15.

71. Bray is oddly noncommittal on the subject of James. In *Homosexuality in Renaissance England* he does not even discuss James's alleged homosexuality (except in a footnote), and in 'Homosexuality and the Signs of Male Friendship in Elizabethan England' (p. 13) he cautions against assuming its existence.

72. Hardwicke, *State Papers*, I, 454. Buckingham continued in slightly less suggestive language, 'therefore give me leave to stop, with mine, that hand which hath been but too ready to execute the motions and affections of that kind obliging heart to me'.

73. Coke, *The Third Part of the Institutes*, pp. 58–9. See also Coke, *The Reports of Sir Edward Coke, Knt., in Thirteen Parts* (London, 1826), VI, 243. Coke's thinking is really quite muddled when it comes to specific sex acts. He states that sodomy can be committed 'by mankind with mankind, or with brute beast, or by womankind with brute beast'. This language omitted the possibility of a woman with another woman or, more surprisingly, a man with a woman having anal intercourse. Although Coke said that penetration was required, this qualification did not help the Earl of Castlehaven in 1631. One of the servants Castlehaven was accused of sodomizing testified: 'My Lord made me lie with him … and once spent his seed, but did not penetrate my body, and I understand he had often done the like with others.' Castlehaven accordingly declared his innocence on the grounds that he had not penetrated. The Lord Chief Justice declared, however, 'It is buggery by the law; for the law of this land makes no distinction of buggery, if there is *emissio seminis*.' A majority of the jurors agreed and convicted Castlehaven on a vote of 15–12. The chief servant Castlehaven was allegedly involved with was referred to as his 'favourite'. Caroline Bingham, 'Seventeenth-Century Attitudes Toward Deviant Sex', *Journal of Interdisciplinary History*, 1, no. 3 (Spring 1971), 447–68; T.B. Howell (ed.), *Cobbett's Complete Collection of State Trials* (London, 1809–26), III, 410, 412. For anyone who does not have access to Howell's record of the trial, a substantial excerpt is printed in Ian McCormick (ed.), *Secret Sexualities: A Sourcebook of 17th and 18th Century Writing* (London, 1997), pp. 53–62. See also Cynthia Herrup, ' "To Pluck Bright Honour from the Pale-faced Moon": Gender and Honour in the Castlehaven Story', *Transactions of the Royal Historical Society*, 6th series, volume 6 (Cambridge, 1996), 137–59 and 'The Patriarch at Home: The Trial of the Second Earl of Castlehaven for Rape and Sodomy', *History Workshop Journal*, issue 41 (Spring 1996), 1–18.

74. Elisabeth Bourcier, *The Diary of Sir Simonds D'Ewes (1622–1624)* (Paris, 1974), pp. 92–3.

3   Base Fellows

1. D'Ewes expressed more violent disapproval of Sir Francis Bacon, as we shall see at the conclusion of this chapter.

2. Gregory W. Bredbeck, *Sodomy and Interpretation: Marlowe to Milton* (Ithaca, 1991), pp. 3–23.

3. Elisabeth Bourcier (ed.), *The Diary of Sir Simonds D'Ewes (1622– 1624)* (Paris, 1974), pp. 92–3.

4. John Harington, *Nugae Antique* (London, 1804), I, 394.

5. Bourcier, *Diary of Sir Simonds D'Ewes*, p. 101. Three months later a 'Dr. White' was imprisoned, but he may not be the same person. Norman E. McClure (ed.), *The Letters of John Chamberlain* (Philadelphia, 1939), II, 473.

6. Thomas Scott, *The Belgicke Pismire: Stinging the slothfull Sleeper, and Awaking the Diligent to Fast, Watch, Pray; and Worke out Theire Owne Temporall and Eternall Salvation with Feare and Trembling* (London, 1622), p. 40. For Scott, see Peter Lake, 'Constitutional Consensus and Puritan Opposition in the 1620s: Thomas Scott and the Spanish Match', *Historical Journal*, 25, no. 4 (1982), 805–25 and Markku Peltonen, *Classical Humanism and Republicanism in English Political Thought 1570–1640* (Cambridge, 1995), chapter 5.

7. Thomas Scott, *The Projector. Teaching A Direct, Sure, and ready way to restore the decayes of the Church and State both in Honour and Revenue* (London, 1623), pp. 20, 33–4.

8. Gordon Williams (ed.), *A Dictionary of Sexual Language and Imagery in Shakespearean and Stuart Literature* (London, 1994), II, 577–9; Alan Bray, *Homosexuality in Renaissance England* (London, 1982), p. 65; James M. Saslow, *Ganymede in the Renaissance* (New Haven, 1986), pp. 1–3. For Ganymede in the Middle Ages, see chapter 9, 'The Triumph of Ganymede: Gay Literature of the High Middle Ages', in John Boswell, *Christianity, Social Tolerance, and Homosexuality: Gay People in Western Europe from the Beginning of the Christian Era to the Fourteenth Century* (Chicago, 1980), pp. 243–68. For artistic representations of the Ganymede myth, see Gerda Kempter, *Ganymed: Studien zur Typologie, Ikonographie und Ikonologie* (Cologne, 1980).

9. Carl Miller, *Stages of Desire: Gay Theatre's Hidden History* (London, 1996), p. 177.

10. Bruce R. Smith, *Homosexual Desire in Shakespeare's England* (Chicago, 1991), pp. 191–2, 195–6.

11. Smith (ibid., pp. 206–8) discusses one major example, Christopher Marlowe's *Dido Queen of Carthage*. See also Jonathan Goldberg, *Sodometries. Renaissance Texts, Modern Sexualities* (Stanford, 1992), pp. 126–35. For other examples, see Bray, *Homosexuality*, pp. 16, 33, 52, 54, 60.

12. John Mason, *The Turke. A Worthie Tragedie* (London, 1610), sig. C3^r.

13. Smith, *Homosexual Desire*, p. 203.

14. Francis Fairholt (ed.), 'Poems and Songs on the Assassination of the Duke of Buckingham', in *Early English Poetry, Ballads, and Popular Literature of the Middle Ages* 29 (London, 1850), p. 49; W. Douglas Hamilton (ed.), *Original Papers Illustrative of the Life and Writings of John Milton* (London, 1859), p. 67. 'The Warre of the Gods' was brought to my attention by Bruce Smith in *Homosexual Desire*, pp. 202–3 and 307 n. 19. I have subsequently read the original in the commonplace book of Tobias Alston, among the Osborne manuscripts (b197) in the Beinecke Library of Yale University. Quotations are from pages 112–13 of Alston's book. There appears to be sexual innuendo about Buckingham and James in another poem in Alston's collection: 'A Proper New Song made of those that Comenst [Commenced] the King being at Cambridge, December 1624' on pages 48–54.

15. The French ambassador's dispatches have been published in German and translated from the German, into English. For the German, see Friedrich von Raumer, *Briefe aus Paris zur Erlauterung der Geschichte des sechzehnten und siebzehnten Jahrhunderts* (Leipzig, 1831), II, 276–7. For the English translation, see Frederick von Raumer, *History of the Sixteenth and Seventeenth Centuries, Illustrated by Original Sources*, [trans. H.E. Lloyd] (London, 1835), II, 219–20.

16. Robert Shepard, 'Sexual Rumours in English Politics: The Cases of Elizabeth I and James I', in Jacqueline Murray and Konrad Eisenbichler (eds), *Desire and Discipline: Sex and Sexuality in the Premodern West* (Toronto, 1996), p. 112.

17. George Wither, *Wither's Motto* (London, 1621), sigs D5^r, D5^v; Thomas Birch (ed.), *The Court and Times of James I* (London, 1849), II, 266; Dale B. Randall, *Jonson's Gypsies Unmasked* (Durham, NC, 1975), pp. 177–8.

18. George Wither, *Abuses Stript and Whipt* (London, 1613), p. 177.

19. The pamphlet was *Tom Tell Troath*, discussed below. James Orchard Halliwell (ed.), *The Autobiography and Correspondence of Sir Simonds D'Ewes* (London, 1845), I, 191–2.

20. *Corona Regia* (1615), pp. 68, 89, 90–2, 104–5. Winfried Schleiner, 'Sciopius' Pen against the English King's Sword: The Political Function of Ambiguity and Anonymity in Early Seventeenth-Century Literature', *Renaissance and Reformation*, 26 (1990), 271–84 and ' "That Matter Which Ought Not To Be Heard Of": Homophobic Slurs in Renaissance Cultural Politics', *Journal of Homosexuality*, 26, no. 4 (1994), 62–5. I am grateful for correspondence on this subject with Professor Schleiner who, most recently, was inclining to doubt that Schoppe was the author of *Corona Regia*. See also David Harris Willson, *King James VI and I* (Oxford, 1956), pp. 238–9; Logan Pearsall Smith (ed.), *The Life and Letters of Sir Henry Wotton* (Oxford, 1966), II, 88, 91–3, 280–1; J.P. Sommerville, 'James I and the Divine Right of Kings', in Linda Levy Peck (ed.), *The Mental World of the Jacobean Court* (Cambridge, 1991), pp. 59–60.

21. Historical Manuscripts Commission, *Report on the Manuscripts of the Marquess of Downshire Preserved at Easthampstead Park Berks* (London, 1940), IV, 443, 503.

22. *Documentos inéditos para la historia de Espana* (Madrid, 1936), I, 101–2. I am grateful to Benjamin Nelson for assistance in translating this letter.

23. Bourcier, *Diary of Sir Simonds D'Ewes*, p. 100.

24. Boswell, *Christianity, Social Tolerance, and Homosexuality*, p. 298.

25. Joseph Cady, 'The "Masculine Love" of the "Princes of Sodom" "Practicing the Art of Ganymede" at Henri III's Court: The Homosexuality of Henry III and His *Mignons* in Pierre de L'Estoile's *Mémoires-Journaux*', in Murray and Konrad, *Desire and Discipline*, pp. 140–1. I am grateful to the author for this reference and other assistance. See also Keith Cameron, *Henry III: A Maligned or Malignant King?* (Exeter, 1978), pp. 17–19, 81–4.

26. Marlowe's *Edward the Second* in Havelock Ellis (ed.), *Christopher Marlowe: Five Plays* (New York, 1956), pp. 270, 276, 279, 282, 300.

27. Modern scholars disagree about the sodomitical or homosexual content of Marlowe's *Edward II*. John M. Berdan, 'Marlowe's *Edward II*', *Philological Quarterly* 3 (1924), 197–207; Bredbeck, *Sodomy and Interpretation*, pp. 48–77,

56–7 n. 46; Stephen Orgel, 'Nobody's Perfect: Or Why Did the English Stage Take Boys for Women?', in Ronald R. Butters and others (eds), *Displacing Homophobia: Gay Male Perspectives in Literature and Culture* (Durham, NC, 1989), p. 25; Joseph A. Porter, 'Marlowe, Shakespeare, and the Canonization of Heterosexuality', in the same anthology, pp. 127–48; Alan Bray, 'Homosexuality and the Signs of Male Friendship in Elizabethan England', *History Workshop Journal*, issue 29 (Spring 1990), 9–10; Miller, *Stages of Desire*, pp. 171–90. Two recent and complex analyses of the subject can be found in Goldberg, *Sodometries*, pp. 114–26 and Smith, *Homosexual Desire in Shakespeare's England*, pp. 209–23. Compare also chapter 4 of Mario Digangi's *The Homoerotics of Early Modern Drama* (Cambridge, 1997). Digangi's book came to my attention after I had completed my own manuscript. We discuss several of the same themes but interpret them very differently.

28. Richard F. Hardin, *Michael Drayton and the Passing of Elizabethan England* (Lawrence, KS, 1973), pp. 15–16, 44–5.

29. Bredbeck, *Sodomy and Interpretation*, p. 49.

30. [Elizabeth Cary, Lady Falkland], 'The History of the Most Unfortunate Prince, King Edward the Second', in William Oldys (ed.), *The Harleian Miscellany: A Collection of Scarce, Curious, and Entertaining Pamphlets and Tracts, as Well in Manuscript as in Print* (London, 1809), I, 67–95. Barbara Kiefer Lewalski, 'Elizabeth, Lady Falkland, and the Authorship of *Edward II*', in *Writing Women in Jacobean England* (Cambridge, MA, 1993), pp. 317–20; Leslie Stephen and Sidney Lee (eds), *The Dictionary of National Biography* (Oxford, 1917), III, 1150–1.

31. W.J. Smith (ed.), *Herbert Correspondence: The Sixteenth and Seventeenth Century Letters of the Herberts of Chirbury, Powis Castle and Dolguog, formerly at Powis Castle in Montgomeryshire* (Cardiff, 1963), I, 74. Sir Simonds D'Ewes wrote that Yelverton 'laid open ... so many of the Marquis's inordinate actions, comparing him to the Spencers, that misled King Edward the Second'. James Orchard Halliwell (ed.), *The Autobiography and Correspondence of Sir Simonds D'Ewes* (London, 1845), I, 186.

32. McClure, *Chamberlain Letters*, II, 369.

33. S.R. Gardiner (ed.), *Parliamentary Debates in 1610* (London, 1862), p. 121.

34. Moses Hadas (ed.), *The Complete Works of Tacitus*, trans. Alfred John Church and William Jackson Brodribb (New York, 1942), pp. 144–227, especially pp. 144–5, 168–9, 178, 183, 189–90.

35. Joseph Gavorse (ed.), *The Lives of the Twelve Caesars by Suetonius* (New York, 1959), pp. 145–6.

36. Ben Jonson, *Sejanus His Fall*, ed. Philip J. Ayres (Manchester, 1990), pp. 16–22.

37. Philip J. Finkelpearl, '"The Comedians' Liberty": Censorship of the Jacobean Stage Reconsidered', *English Literary Renaissance*, 16 (Winter 1986), 128.

38. Dale B. Randall convincingly argues that Jonson got away with writing a masque 'paid for by Buckingham, starring Buckingham, and, with wonderful wit, satirizing Buckingham'. *Jonson's Gypsies Unmasked*, p. 128. See also pp. 10, 37–47, 165.

39. Jonson, *Sejanus*, p. 49.

40. Anne Barton, *Ben Jonson, Dramatist* (Cambridge, 1984), pp. 92–111; Annabel Patterson, *Censorship and Interpretation: The Conditions of Writing and Reading in Early Modern England* (Madison, WI, 1984), pp. 49–57; Jonathan Goldberg, *James I and the Politics of Literature: Jonson, Shakespeare, Donne, and Their Contemporaries* (London, 1983), pp. 68–70, 142, 176–7; Smith, *Homosexual Desire*, pp. 203–4; Rebecca W. Bushnell, *Tragedies of Tyrants: Political Thought and Theater in the English Renaissance* (Ithaca, NY, 1990), pp. 131–7; Martin Butler, 'Ben Jonson and the Limits of Courtly Panegyric', in Kevin Sharpe and Peter Lake (eds), *Culture and Politics in Early Stuart England* (Stanford, 1993), pp. 91–115.

41. Goldberg, *James I and the Politics of Literature*, p. 177.

42. Patterson, *Censorship and Interpretation*, p. 18.

43. Jonson, *Sejanus*, pp. 91, 198–200.

44. Goldberg, *James I and the Politics of Literature*, p. 144. This letter is printed in Philip Yorke, second Earl of Hardwicke (ed.), *Miscellaneous State Papers from 1501 to 1726* (London, 1778), I, 460, where 'catamite' is incorrectly transcribed as 'Catonic'.

45. Raumer, *History*, II, 219.

46. Ibid., II, 234.

47. Ibid., II, 259–78.

48. Lockyer, *Buckingham*, p.120. See also pp. 55–60, 119 and 152–4.

49. Raumer, *History*, II, 269.

50. The French ambassador Beaumont reported near the beginning of James's reign that 'the King's reputation suffers much by base and feeble actions, which are remarked in his private conduct and life'. Ibid., II, 210.

51. H.E. Lloyd, Raumer's English translator, found this story so offensive that he omitted it from his translation. Raumer, *History*, II, 261. Raumer himself took no chances with this story. Instead of translating it into the German, he gave his readers the *Urtext*, that is the original French of Tillières's dispatch, and I have translated this into English. Raumer, *Briefe*, II, 317.

52. Raumer, *History*, II, 261.

53. Raumer, *History*, II, 246.

54. S.R. Gardiner, *History of England from the Accession of James I to the Outbreak of the Civil War 1603–1642* (London, 1883–84, 1894–96), IV, 296.

55. Deuteronomy 23:18 states that one should not bring the 'price' (Authorized Version) or the 'wages' (Revised Standard Version) of a dog into the house of the Lord for payment. See also Stephen Orgel, *Impersonations: The Performance of Gender in Shakespeare's England* (Cambridge, 1996), pp. 28, 158–9 n. 30.

56. The author was probably Thomas Scott, whose works we will discuss at greater length in chapter 5. *Tom Tell Troath: Or, A free Discourse touching the Manners of the Time. Directed to his Majestie by Waye of humble Advertisement*, in *Harleian Miscellany*, II, 419–38, especially pp. 424, 434–7; *Tom Tell Troath* (1630), pp. 8, 14, 25–6, 28.

57. Alexander Leighton, *Speculum belli sacri; or the looking–glasse of the holy war* (n.p., 1624), pp. 24, 90, 95–7.

58. Norman Macdougall, *James III: A Political Study* (Edinburgh, 1982), pp. 126–8, 162–5, 269–95. See especially p. 285. David Calderwood, *History of the Kirk of Scotland*, ed. Thomas Thomson (Edinburgh, 1843), IV, 8.

59. Halliwell, *Autobiography and Correspondence of Sir Simonds D'Ewes*, I, 264.
60. Richard Cust, 'News and Politics in Early Seventeenth–Century England', *Past and Present*, 112 (1986), p. 66.
61. Allen B. Hinds and others (eds), *Calendar of State Papers and Manuscripts Relating to English Affairs Existing in the Archives and Collections of Venice* (London, 1864–1940), XVII, 438. Hereafter cited as *CSPV*.
62. Jennifer Brady, 'Fear and Loathing in Marlowe's *Edward II*', in Carol Levin and Karen Robertson (eds), *Sexuality and Politics in Renaissance Drama* (Lewiston, NY, 1991), p. 179.
63. I follow the common practice here of referring to the process used against Bacon as an impeachment. Technically it was one stage in the evolution of that process which had not yet been fully developed or named as such. See Colin G.C. Tite, *Impeachment and Parliamentary Judicature in Early Stuart England* (London, 1974). See also Jonathan Marwil, *The Trials of Counsel: Francis Bacon in 1621* (Detroit, MI, 1976). For this Parliament in general, see Robert Zaller, *The Parliament of 1621: A Study in Constitutional Conflict* (Berkeley, 1971).
64. Conrad Russell, *Parliaments and English Politics 1621–1629* (Oxford, 1979), pp. 112–13.
65. Oliver Lawson Dick (ed.), *Aubrey's Brief Lives* (London, 1950), p. 11.
66. The Victorian editor of D'Ewes's autobiography omitted much of this language on the grounds that it was 'too gross for publication'. Halliwell, *Autobiography*, I, 191–2. Alan Bray recovered the excised portion from the original manuscript in the British Museum and printed it in his 'Homosexuality and the Signs of Male Friendship', p. 14. The full text taken from an obscure eighteenth-century printing is now more handily available in Ian McCormick (ed.), *Secret Sexualities: A Sourcebook of 17th and 18th Century Writing* (London, 1997), pp. 52–3.
67. Nieves Mathews, *Francis Bacon: The History of a Character Assassination* (New Haven, 1996), p. 309.
68. Perez Zagorin, *Francis Bacon* (Princeton, NJ, 1998), pp. 12–14.
69. Gardiner, *History*, IV, 102.
70. Neil Cuddy, 'The Conflicting Loyalties of a "vulger counselor": The Third Earl of Southampton, 1597–1624', in John Morrill, Paul Slack and Daniel Woolf (eds), *Public Duty and Private Conscience in Seventeenth–Century England* (Oxford, 1993), pp. 121–50; Gardiner, *History*, IV, 126, 133, 137.
71. Mary Anne Everett Green (ed.), *Calendar of State Papers, Domestic Series, of the Reign of James I* (London, 1858), III, 269. One 'boy' Southampton may have had in mind was Philip Herbert, Earl of Montgomery, with whom he had quarrelled in 1610. *DNB*, IX, 659.
72. Pauline Croft, 'Libels, Popular Literacy and Public Opinion in Early Modern England', *Historical Research*, 68 (October 1995), 276 and 'The Reputation of Robert Cecil: Libels, Political Opinion and Popular Awareness in the Early Seventeenth Century', *Transactions of the Royal Historical Society*, sixth series, vol. 1 (1991), 46; Roger Lockyer, 'An English *Valido*? Buckingham and James I', in Richard Ollard and Pamela Tudor-Craig (eds), *For Veronica Wedgwood These: Studies in Seventeenth-Century History* (London, 1986), p. 51.
73. Lisa Jardine, 'Boy Actors, Female Roles, and Elizabethan Eroticism', in David Scott Kastan and Peter Stallybrass (eds), *Staging the*

Renaissance: Reinterpretations of Elizabethan and Jacobean Drama (New York, 1991), pp. 62–3.

74. In his satirical description of the Scottish nobility, Sir Anthony Weldon likewise alleged that 'their followers are their fellows'. *A Perfect Description of the People and Country of Scotland* in Sir Walter Scott (ed.) *The Secret History of the Court of James the First* (Edinburgh, 1811), II, 86.

75. Lawrence Stone, *The Crisis of the Aristocracy 1558–1641* (Oxford, 1965), p. 666.

76. In this respect, Southampton succeeded in staying on the safe side of that fine line between male friendship and sodomy delineated in Alan Bray's essay on 'Homosexuality and the Signs of Male Friendship'.

77. In addition to Neil Cuddy's 'Conflicting Loyalties', cited above, see also Richard C. McCoy, 'Old English Honour in an Evil Time: Aristocratic Principle in the 1620s', in R. Malcolm Smuts (ed.), *The Stuart Court and Europe: Essays in Politics and Political Culture* (Cambridge, 1996), pp. 133–55.

78. *CSPV*, XVII, 75–6.

79. David Underdown, *A Freeborn People: Politics and the Nation in Seventeenth-Century England* (Oxford, 1996), p. 27, quoting William Trumbull.

4 Effeminacy and Peace

1. There is a strong body of scholarly opinion that homosexuality simply was not linked to effeminacy until long after James's reign. In addition to the works about to be cited, see also Stephen Orgel, 'Nobody's Perfect: Or Why Did the English Stage Take Boys for Women?', in Ronald R. Butters and others (eds), *Displacing Homophobia: Gay Male Perspectives in Literature and Culture*, (Durham, 1989), pp. 7–29; and Jean E. Howard, 'Crossdressing, The Theatre, and Gender Struggle in Early Modern England', *Shakespeare Quarterly*, 3, no. 3 (Winter 1988) 418–40.

2. Alan Bray, *Homosexuality in Renaissance England* (London, 1982), pp. 130–1 n. 77; Richard Davenport-Hines, *Sex, Death and Punishment: Attitudes to Sex and Sexuality in Britain since the Renaissance* (London, 1990), p. 57; Bruce R. Smith, *Homosexual Desire in Shakespeare's England* (Chicago, 1991), p. 196.

3. Jonathan Goldberg, *Sodometries: Renaissance Texts, Modern Sexualities* (Stanford, 1992), p. 111.

4. Smith, *Homosexual Desire in Shakespeare's England*, pp. 171, 180, 196.

5. Alan Sinfield, *The Wilde Century: Effeminacy, Oscar Wilde and the Queer Moment* (New York, 1994), p. 27.

6. See the Early Modern English Dictionaries Database which is available on the internet at www.chass.utoronto.ca:8080/english/emed/emedd.html.

7. Thomas Scott, *The Projector. Teaching A Direct, Sure, and ready way to restore the decayes of the Church and State both in Honour and Revenue* (London, 1623), p. 31.

8. Anthony Fletcher, *Gender, Sex & Subordination in England 1500–1800* (New Haven, 1995), pp. 87, 96.

9. Mark D. Jordan, *The Invention of Sodomy in Christian Theology* (Chicago, 1997), pp. 13, 15, 100, 122, 125, 169.

10. Randolph Trumbach, 'Are Modern Western Lesbian Women and Gay Men a Third Gender?', in Martin Duberman (ed.), *A Queer World: The Center for Lesbian and Gay Studies Reader* (New York, 1997), pp. 87–99 and 'Erotic Fantasy and Male Libertinism in Enlightenment England', in Lynn Hunt (ed.), *The Invention of Pornography: Obscenity and the Origins of Modernity, 1500–1800* (New York, 1993), pp. 254–5.

11. Phillip Stubbes, *The Anatomie of Abuses* (London, 1583; Da Capo facsimile edition, New York 1972), sigs. G1^{r-v}, L8^{r-v}. See also F5^v.

12. Marjorie Garber, *Vested Interests: Cross-Dressing and Cultural Anxiety* (New York, 1992), p. 29. See also Goldberg, *Sodometries*, p. 112.

13. William Prynne, *Histriomastix* (London, 1633; Garland facsimile edition, New York, 1974), pp. 208–9, 213.

14. Stubbes published many puritan pamphlets. Rainolds was the leading representative of the puritan position at the Hampton Court Conference. Prynne was a leading antagonist of Archbishop Laud in Charles I's reign. Leslie Stephen and Sidney Lee (eds), *Dictionary of National Biography* (London, 1921–2), XVI, 432–7, 623–5; XIX, 118–20. Hereafter *DNB*.

15. Compare Laura Levine, *Men in Women's Clothing: Anti-Theatricality and Effeminization 1579–1642* (Cambridge, 1994), pp. 24, 140–1 n. 4 and Laura Levine, 'Men in Women's Clothing: Anti-Theatricality and Effeminization from 1579 to 1642', *Criticism*, 28, no. 2 (Spring 1986), 136, 138–9 n. 4. Levine thought there was a steady increase in the fear of effeminization, but she rejected any 'Regiocentric' explanation for this fear on the assumption that James's subjects revered him too much to associate him with either effeminization or sodomy. For a view closer to my own, see Linda Woodbridge, *Women and the English Renaissance: Literature and the Nature of Womankind, 1540–1620* (Urbana, 1984), pp. 144, 161, 168, 181.

16. Baldesar Castiglione, *The Book of the Courtier*, translated by Charles S. Singleton (New York, 1959), pp. 32–6. I am grateful to Barbara Harris for suggesting these comparisons with Castiglione.

17. Randolph Trumbach, 'London's Sodomites: Homosexual Behavior and Western Culture in the Eighteenth Century', *Journal of Social History*, 11, no. 1 (Fall 1977), 1–33.

18. C. H. McIlwain (ed.), *The Political Works of James I* (New York, 1965), p. 46 and Johann P. Sommerville (ed.), *King James VI and I: Political Writings* (Cambridge, 1994), p. 53.

19. John Harington, *Nugae Antique* (London, 1804), I, 390–6.

20. Ibid., I, 395.

21. M.C. Hippeau (ed.), *Mémoires Inédits du Comte Leveneur de Tillières* (Paris, 1862), pp. 1–4, 16.

22. Francis Osborne, *Traditional Memorials on the Reign of King James*, in *The Works of Francis Osborn*, 7th edn (London, 1673), p. 534.

23. Here again the Early Modern English Dictionaries Database is a handy corrective.

24. Sir James Melville, *Memoirs of His Own Life* (London, 1922), p. 53.

25. James Orchard Halliwell (ed.), *The Autobiography and Correspondence of Sir Simonds D'Ewes* (London, 1845), I, 166–7, 175, 186, 191.

26. Godfrey Goodman, *The Court of King James the First* (London, 1839), I, 225–6.

27. John Hacket, *Scrinia Reserata: A Memorial Offer'd to the Great Deservings of John Williams* (London, 1693), p. 120.
28. Francis Bamford (ed.), *A Royalist's Notebook: The Commonplace Book of Sir John Oglander* (New York, 1971), p. 41.
29. W. Dunn Macray (ed.), *The History of the Rebellion and Civil Wars in England Begun in the Year 1641, by Edward, Earl of Clarendon* (Oxford, 1888), I, 10–11.
30. Edward Hyde, Earl of Clarendon, *The Characters of Robert Earl of Essex, Favourite to Queen Elizabeth, and George D. of Buckingham, Favourite to K. James and K. Ch. I* (London, 1706), p. 19. I am grateful to David M. Bergeron for bringing this work to my attention.
31. Caroline Bingham, *James I of England* (London, 1981), p. 159.
32. R. Malcolm Smuts, *Court Culture and the Origins of a Royalist Tradition in Early Stuart England* (Philadelphia, 1987), p. 104. In 1625 Marshal Bassompierre was struck by Buckingham's beauty, both in his person and in the precious gems and clothing he wore. Maréchal de Bassompierre, *Journal de Ma Vie: Mémoires du Maréchal de Bassompierre* (Paris, 1875), p. 204.
33. Norman E. McClure (ed.), *The Letters of John Chamberlain* (Philadelphia, 1939), II, 442, 479, 553, 560, 571, 580; SP 14/162/13; Hacket, *Scrinia Reserata*, p. 189; Historical Manuscripts Commission, *Supplementary Report on the Manuscripts of the Earl of Mar and Kellie* (London, 1930), pp. 133, 140, 145; Roger Lockyer, *Buckingham: The Life and Political Career of George Villiers, First Duke of Buckingham 1592–1628* (London, 1981), pp. 121–2; Allen B. Hinds and others (eds), *Calendar of State Papers and Manuscripts Relating to English Affairs Existing in the Archives and Collections of Venice*, (London, 1864–1940), XVIII, 268, 279, 343, 401. Hereafter cited as *CSPV*.
34. McClure, *Chamberlain Letters*, II, 144.
35. Thomas Beard, *The Theatre of Gods Judgements* (Islip, 1612), p. 419. This section is essentially the same in the 1597 edition. Among the sodomites of history, Beard included 'Pope *Julius* the third, whose custome was to promote none to Ecclesiasticall livings, save onely his buggerers' (p. 421).
36. Barnaby Rich, *Opinion Diefied, discovering the ingins, traps, and traynes that are set to catch opinion* (London, 1613), pp. 37, 53.
37. Smuts, *Court Culture*, p. 104; Kevin Sharpe, *Criticism and Compliment: The Politics of Literature in the England of Charles I* (Cambridge, 1987), p. 18; Kevin Sharpe, *Politics and Ideas in Early Stuart England: Essays and Studies* (London, 1989), p. 203; Anne Barton, *Ben Jonson, Dramatist* (Cambridge, 1984), pp. 300–4; Malcolm Smuts, 'Cultural Diversity and Cultural Change at the Court of James I', in Linda Levy Peck (ed.), *The Mental World of the Jacobean Court* (Cambridge, 1991), p. 109; William Cavendish, Earl of Newcastle, *The Country Captaine and The Variety, Two Comedies* (London, 1649). The character Manley appeared in *The Variety*, which was first performed in 1641.
38. David H. Willson, *King James VI and I* (New York, 1956), pp. 271–2.
39. Bamford, *A Royalist's Notebook*, p. 193.
40. Frederick von Raumer, *History of the Sixteenth and Seventeenth Centuries, Illustrated by Original Documents* [trans. H.E. Lloyd] (London, 1835), II, 204, 208.
41. *CSPV*, X, 513.
42. Raumer, *History*, II, 282.

43. Nowell Smith (ed.), *Sir Fulke Greville's Life of Sir Philip Sidney* (Oxford, 1907), pp. 9–10, 176, 178–9, 182, 214, 218–19. After Salisbury's death, Greville became a major office holder at James's court. His life of Sidney was published posthumously in 1652. For Greville, see Ronald Rebholz, *The Life of Fulke Greville, First Lord Brooke* (Oxford, 1971). For Greville and the general nostalgia for Elizabeth's reign, see Barton, *Ben Jonson*, pp. 305–12 and Mervyn James, *Society, Politics and Culture: Studies in Early Modern England* (Cambridge, 1986), pp. 396–400.

44. Gregory W. Bredbeck, *Sodomy and Interpretation: Marlowe to Milton* (Ithaca, 1991), pp. 14–15.

45. *CSPV*, XV, 114.

46. John Everard, *The Arriereban: a Sermon* (London, 1618), pp. 27, 29, 74, 87–96.

47. William B. Hunter (ed.), *The Complete Poetry of Ben Jonson* (New York, 1968), pp. 151, 147 n. 2. This poem was written about 1620.

48. Margot Heinemann, *Puritanism and Theatre: Thomas Middleton and Opposition Drama under the Early Stuarts* (Cambridge, 1980), epecially chapters 10 and 12; Jonathan Goldberg, *James I and the Politics of Literature: Johnson, Shakespeare, Donne, and Their Contemporaries* (Baltimore, 1983); Annabel Patterson, *Censorship and Interpretation: The Conditions of Writing and Reading in Early Modern England* (Madison, 1984); Barton, *Ben Jonson*; Albert H. Tricomi, *Anticourt Drama in England 1603–1642* (Charlottesville, VA, 1989), especially chapters 14–16; Philip J. Finkelpearl, *Court and Country Politics in the Plays of Beaumont and Fletcher* (Princeton, NJ, 1990); Margot Heinemann, 'Drama and Opinion in the 1620s: Middleton and Massinger', in J.R. Mulryne and Margaret Shewring (eds), *Theatre and Government Under the Early Stuarts* (Cambridge, 1993), pp. 237–65; Jean Howard, *The Stage and Social Struggle in Early Modern England* (London, 1994); Gordon McMullan, *The Politics of Unease in the Plays of John Fletcher* (Amherst, 1994). For a study of Jacobean drama with an interpretation nearly opposite my own, see chapter 5 of Mario Degangi's *The Homoerotics of Early Modern Drama* (Cambridge, 1997).

49. Tricomi, *Anitcourt Drama*, p. 33. Jonson apparently trod this fine line with amazing success in *The Gypsies Metamorphosed* (1621), which amused James although it came dangerously close to suggesting that Buckingham was the rapacious leader of a pack of thieves. Dale B.J. Randall, *Jonson's Gypsies Unmasked* (Durham, NC, 1975) and Goldberg, *James I and the Politics of Literature*, pp. 128–41.

50. A.R. Waller (ed.), *The Works of Beaumont and Fletcher* (Cambridge, 1912), p. 81.

51. Raumer, *History*, II, 219–20.

52. Especially good on this subject is Tricomi, *Anticourt Drama*, chapters 1–4. See also Philip J. Finkelpearl, '"The Comedians' Liberty": Censorship of the Jacobean Stage Reconsidered', *English Literary Renaissance*, 16, no. 1 (Winter 1986), 123–38.

53. Heinemann, *Puritanism and Theatre*, p. 217.

54. Howard, *The Stage and Social Struggle*, p. 52.

55. Patterson, *Censorship and Interpretation*, pp. 75–7.

56. For the these last years of James's reign see especially Heinemann, 'Drama and Opinion in the 1620s'; Heinemann, *Puritanism and Theatre*, chapters 10

and 12; Tricomi, *Anticourt Drama*, chapters 14–16; A.A. Bromham and Zara Bruzzi, *The Changeling and the Years of Crisis, 1619–1624: A Hieroglyph of Britain* (London, 1990); and Jerzy Limon, *Dangerous Matter: English Drama and Politics in 1623/4* (Cambridge, 1986).

57. Raumer, *History*, II, 206–7.
58. Barbara Kiefer Lewalski, 'Enacting Opposition: Queen Anne and the Subversions of Masquing' in Lewalski, *Writing Women in Jacobean England* (Cambridge, MA, 1993), pp. 15–43 and 'Anne of Denmark and the Subversions of Masquing', *Criticism*, 35 (Summer 1993), 341–55. See also Stephen Orgel, *The Illusion of Power: Political Theatre in the English Renaissance* (Berkeley, 1975), pp. 60–1; Simon Shepherd, *Amazons and Warrior Women: Varieties of Feminism in Seventeenth-Century Drama* (New York, 1981), p. 138; Leeds Barroll, 'The Court of the First Stuart Queen', in Linda Levy Peck (ed.), *The Mental World of the Jacobean Court* (Cambridge, 1991), pp. 191–208; and Marion Wynne-Davies, 'The Queen's Masque: Renaissance Women and the Seventeenth-Century Court Masque', in S.P. Cerasno and Marion Wynne-Davies (eds), *Gloriana's Face: Women, Public and Private, in the English Renaissance* (New York, 1992), pp. 79–104.
59. Raumer, *History*, II, 206.
60. Shakespeare's *Henry V* was entered in the Stationers' Register in 1600. The poet Michael Drayton published the 'Ballad of Agincourt', commemorating Henry V's most famous victory, in 1606 and 1619. Richard F. Hardin, *Michael Drayton and the Passing of Elizabethan England* (Lawrence, KS, 1973), pp. 6–7. Malcom Smuts makes the interesting observation that Prince Henry 'patronized Drayton's epic on the reign of Henry V'. Smuts, 'Cultural Diversity and Cultural Change at the Court of James I', p. 110.
61. David M. Bergeron, *Royal Family, Royal Lovers: King James of England and Scotland* (Columbia, MO, 1991), pp. 52–63, 72.
62. *CSPV*, XI, 10.
63. Raumer, *History*, II, 210.
64. The best single work on Prince Henry is Roy Strong, *Henry, Prince of Wales and England's Lost Renaissance* (London, 1986). For Henry's fervent militarism, see pp. 57–72. See also Bergeron, *Royal Family*, pp. 92–107; Bergeron, *Shakespeare's Romances and the Royal Family* (Lawrence, KS, 1985), pp. 51–9; Shepherd, *Amazons and Warrior Women*, pp. 120–4; and William Hunt, 'Spectral Origins of the English Revolution: Legitimation Crisis in Early Stuart England', in Geoff Eley and William Hunt (eds), *Reviving the English Revolution: Reflections and Elaborations on the Work of Christopher Hill* (London, 1988), pp. 305–32.
65. Orgel, *Illusion of Power*, pp. 66–70.
66. Caroline Bingham, *James I of England* (London, 1981), p. 101.
67. Strong, *Henry, Prince of Wales*, pp. 12, 221. See also Peter E. McCullough, *Sermons at Court: Politics and Religion in Elizabethan and Jacobean Preaching* (Cambridge, 1998), pp. 169–82.
68. *CSPV*, X, 513–14.
69. *CSPV*, XI, 507.
70. *CSPV*, X, 513.
71. Raumer, *History*, II, 209.
72. *CSPV*, XV, 420, quoted in David M. Bergeron, 'Francis Bacon's *Henry VII*: Commentary on King James I', *Albion*, 24 (Spring 1992), 24. Kevin Sharpe,

'The Image of Virtue: The Court and Household of Charles I, 1625–1642', in his *Politics and Ideas*, pp. 147–73. Sharpe observes that 'Charles I was in many respects a complete contrast to his father' (p. 147).

73. Charles Carlton, *Charles I: The Personal Monarch*, 2nd edn (London, 1995), p. 26.

5 Manliness and War

1. Susan Dwyer Amussen ' "The Part of a Christian Man": the Cultural Politics of Manhood in Early Modern England', in Susan D. Amussen and Mark A. Kishlansky (eds), *Political Culture and Cultural Politics in Early Modern England* (Manchester, 1995), p. 220.
2. Anthony Fletcher, *Gender, Sex & Subordination in England 1500–1800* (New Haven, 1995), p. 129.
3. Jenny Wormald, 'James VI and I: Two Kings or One?', *History*, 68 (June 1983), 191.
4. For James's own thoughts on hunting, see his *Basilikon Doron* in Johann P. Sommerville (ed.), *King James VI and I: Political Writings* (Cambridge, 1994), p. 56. See also David H. Willson, *King James VI and I* (New York, 1956), pp. 179–83. William Brenchley Rye (ed.), *England as Seen by Foreigners* (London, 1865), p. 154.
5. George Calvert, Lord Baltimore, *The Answer to Tom-Tell-Troth* (London, 1642), p. 2. This pamphlet was written a few years after James's death, probably in 1630. Calvert may not have been the true author.
6. [John Reynolds], *Vox Coeli, or Newes from Heaven* (Elisium [Utrecht?], 1624), preface.
7. Rhodes Dunlap, 'James I, Bacon, Middleton, and the Making of the Peace-Maker', in Josephine W. Bennett and others (eds), *Studies in the English Renaissance Drama* (New York, 1959), pp. 82–94; W.W. Greg, *A Companion to Arber* (Oxford, 1967), pp. 56–7; W.B. Patterson, *King James VI and I and the Reunion of Christendom* (Cambridge, 1997), p. 296 n. 9. See also Susan Dwyer Amussen, 'The Peacemaker: A Critical Introduction', in Gary Taylor (ed.), *The Complete Works of Thomas Middleton* (Oxford, forthcoming). I am grateful to Professor Amussen for sharing her work in advance with me.
8. Willson, *King James VI and I*, pp. 306–8; Mary Anne Everett Green (ed.), *Calendar of State Papers, Domestic Series, of the Reign of James I* (London, 1858), II, 434. Fletcher, *Gender*, p. 131. I am grateful to James Robertson for this point.
9. *The Peace-Maker: or Great Brittaines Blessing* (London, 1618), sigs. A4^r, C3^r–D1^r, D4^r, D4^v, E3^v.
10. King James, *A Meditation Upon the Lords Prayer, Written by the Kings Majestie, For the benefit of all his subjects, especially of such as follow the Court* (London, 1619), preface and pp. 71, 78–81, 91, 93–4.
11. See the differing views expressed in J.R. Hale, 'Incitement to Violence? English Divines on the Theme of War, 1578 to 1631', in *Renaissance War Studies* (London, 1983), chapter 18, and Ben Lowe, 'Religious Wars and the "Common Peace": Anglican Anti-War Sentiment in Elizabethan England', *Albion*, 28, no. 3 (Fall 1996), 415–35. Even during the war-fever of the

1620s, James had his defenders. See, for example, Robert Tisdale, *Pax Vobis, or, Wits Changes: Tuned in a Latine Hexameter of Peace* (London, 1623). Tisdale criticized the advocates of war as 'brain-sick wits, with whispering charmes' and 'envious Criticks full of Spight, and Splene' (pp. 9, 14).

12. Amussen, 'Cultural Politics of Manhood', pp. 213–33.
13. Mervyn James, *Society, Politics and Culture: Studies in Early Modern England* (Cambridge, 1986), chapter 8.
14. Steven Marx, 'Shakespeare's Pacifism', *Renaissance Quarterly*, 45 (Spring 1992), 79.
15. For commentary on this controversy see Sandra Clark, '*Hic Mulier, Haec Vir*, and the Controversy over Masculine Women', *Studies in Philology*, 82 (Spring 1985), 157–83; Simon Shepherd, *Amazons and Warrior Women: Varieties of Feminism in Seventeenth-Century Drama* (New York, 1981), pp. 68, 84–7; Garber, *Vested Interests*, pp. 31–2; David Underdown, *A Freeborn People: Politics and the Nation in Seventeenth-Century England* (Oxford, 1996), pp. 64–67.
16. *Hic Mulier: or, The Man-Woman* (n.p., 1620), sig. A3^r. Abridged versions of *Hic Mulier* and *Haec Vir* are printed in Katherine Usher Henderson and Barbara F. McManus (eds), *Half Humankind: Contexts and Texts of the Controversy about Women in England, 1540–1640* (Urbana, 1985), pp. 264–89. Gender confusion is represented in the Latin titles of these works by the combination of the masculine word for 'this' with 'woman' and the feminine 'this' with 'man'. The correct Latin would be *haec mulier* and *hic vir*. See also the anonymous *Muld Sacke: or The Apologie of Hic Mulier* (London, 1620).
17. *Haec Vir: or The Womanish-Man* (n.p., 1620), sigs. C2^r, C3^v.
18. John Everard, *The Arriereban: a Sermon* (1618), pp. 91–3, 101. I have modernized punctuation for clarity here. See also Barnaby Rich, *The Irish Hubbub, or the English Hue and Crie* (London, 1618). Rich wrote, 'they are not worthy to carry the name of men, that are so farre in love with their owne deformities' (p. 8) and 'Let men shew themselves to be like men, that doe now shew themselves like women' (p. 22).
19. Laura Levine, *Men in Women's Clothing: Anti-Theatricality and Effeminization 1579–1642* (Cambridge, 1994), pp. 8–9. But compare David Cressy, 'Gender Trouble and Cross-Dressing in Early Modern England', *Journal of British Studies*, 35, no. 4 (October 1996), 438–65. See also Fletcher, *Gender*, p. 130, and Stephen Orgel, 'Nobody's Perfect: Or Why Did the English Stage Take Boys for Women?', in Ronald R. Butters and others (eds), *Displacing Homophobia: Gay Male Perspectives in Literature and Culture* (Durham, NC, 1989), pp. 14–15. In Orgel's words, 'The fear of effeminization is a central theme in all discussions of what constitutes a 'real man' in the period'. For example, Romeo complains about Juliet: "Thy beauty hath made me effeminate,/And in my temper softened valor's steel!"
20. For Everard, see the *DNB*, VI, 948–9.
21. For the stage as an arena of subversion in the 1620s, see especially Margot Heinemann, 'Drama and Opinion in the 1620s: Middleton and Massinger', in J.R. Mulryne and Margaret Shewring (eds), *Theatre and Government under the Early Stuarts* (Cambridge, 1993), pp. 237–65; Margot Heinemann, *Puritanism and Theatre: Thomas Middleton and Opposition Drama under the*

Early Stuarts (Cambridge, 1980), chapters 10 and 12; Tricomi, *Anticourt Drama*, chapters 14–16; A.A. Bromham and Zara Bruzzi, *The Changeling and the Years of Crisis, 1619–1624: A Hieroglyph of Britain* (London, 1990); and Jerzy Limon, *Dangerous Matter: English Drama and Politics in 1623/4* (Cambridge, 1986).

22. *Tom Tell-Troath: Or, A free Discourse touching the Manners of the Time. Directed to his Majestie by Waye of Humble Advertisement* in William Oldys (ed.), *The Harleian Miscellany: A Collection of Scarce, Curious, and Entertaining Pamphlets and Tracts, as Well in Manuscript as in Print* (London, 1809), II, 419, 423, 424, 426, 434, 436; *Tom Tell Troath* ([London?], 1630), pp. 2, 6–8, 24, 27.

23. Sabrina A. Baron, 'From Manuscript to Print: Recycling Political Rhetoric in Seventeenth-Century England', *Gutenberg Yearbook* (1997), pp. 1–7.

24. For Scott see Markku Peltonen, *Classical Humanism and Republicanism in English Political Thought 1570–1640* (Cambridge, 1995), chapter 5; Thomas Cogswell, *The Blessed Revolution: English Politics and the Coming of War, 1621–1624* (Cambridge, 1989), pp. 24–7, 283–95; Peter Lake, 'Constitutional Consensus and Puritan Opposition in the 1620s: Thomas Scott and the Spanish Match', *Historical Journal*, 25, no. 4 (1982), 805–25; Louis B. Wright, 'Propaganda Against James I's "Appeasement" of Spain', *The Huntington Library Quarterly*, 6, no. 2 (February 1943), 149–72. There is some attention to Scott's sexual metaphors in A.A. Bromham and Zara Bruzzi, *The Changeling and the Years of Crisis, 1619–1624: A Hieroglyph of Britain* (London, 1990), pp. 42–3, 45, 56, 72, 62–3.

25. Thomas Scott, *Vox Populi, Or Newes from Spayne* ([London], 1620), sigs. B1ᵛ, C1ʳ⁻ᵛ, D1ᵛ.

26. Greg, *A Companion to Arber*, pp. 63–4, 176–7, 228–9.

27. Thomas Scott, *The Belgicke Pismire* (London, 1622), pp. 13, 31.

28. Thomas Scott, *A Tongue-Combate* (n.p., 1623), p. 62.

29. D.R. Woolf, 'Two Elizabeths: James I and the Late Queen's Famous Memory', *Canadian Journal of History*, 20 (August 1985), 184. Elsewhere Woolf refers to 'Scott's comparatively mild philippics' (p. 187). See also Bromham and Bruzzi, *The Changeling and the Years of Crisis*, p. 57.

30. See Proverbs, chapters 6 and 26.

31. Thomas Scott, *The Belgicke Pismire*, pp. 10–12, 37–40.

32. Thomas Scott, *The Belgick Souldier: Dedicated to the Parliament. Or, Warre was a Blessing* (Dort, 1624), pp. 4–5, 14, 34–5, 38, 39.

33. [Thomas Scott], *Robert, Earl of Essex His Ghost Sent from Elizian, to the Nobility, Gentry, and Communaltie of England* (Paradise [London], 1624), pp. 4, 13, 16–17.

34. Alexander Leighton, *Speculum Belli Sacra; or the Looking-Glasse of the Holy War* (n.p., 1624), p. 32.

35. Hale, 'Incitement to Violence?', pp. 494–6.

36. Greg, *A Companion to Arber*, pp. 68, 225–6. The title-pages of both works declared that they were written by S. R. N. I.

37. Reynolds, *Vox Coeli*, pp. 54, 65, 88. In the preface to this work, Reynolds claimed that he originally composed it in 1621.

38. John Harrington, *The Commonwealth of Oceana*, in *The Political Writings of James Harrington*, ed. Charles Blitzer (Indianapolis, IN, 1955), p. 40. In Harrington's words, under Morpheus the two kingdoms representing

Scotland and England were 'not only to be joined under one head, but to be cast, as it were, by a charm into that profound sleep which [was] broken at length by the trumpet of civil war'.

39. [John Reynolds], *Votivae Angliae: or the desires and wishes of England to per-swade his majestie to drawe his sword for the restoring of the Pallatynate to prince Fredericke* (Utrecht, 1624), sigs. A4^v, B1^v, B2^r, E1^r. For both these pamphlets by Reynolds, see Cogswell, *Blessed Revolution*, pp. 289–91.

40. Allen B. Hinds and others (eds), *Calendar of State Papers and Manuscripts Relating to English Affairs Existing in the Archives and Collections of Venice* (London, 1864–1940), XVII, 429. Hereafter cited as *CSPV*.

41. *The French Herauld Sent to the Princes of Christendome* (London, 1622), pp. 12, 20. *CSPV*, XVII, 319, 320 n.

42. *A Courtly Masque: The Device Called the World Tost at Tennis, As it hath beene divers times Presented to the Contentment of many Noble and Worthy Spectators, By the Prince his Servants* (London, 1620). For modernized spelling, I have quoted from the version printed in A.H. Bullen (ed.), *The Works of Thomas Middleton* (New York, 1964 reprint of 1885 edition), VII, 160, 166, 178, 182, 187–8, 190–1. For the political context of another play by Middleton and Rowley, see Bromham and Bruzzi, *The Changeling and the Years of Crisis*, cited above.

43. Bullen, *The Works of Thomas Middleton*, VII, 147, 190–1. Gerald Eades Bentley, *The Jacobean and Caroline Stage: Plays and Playwrights* (Oxford, 1956), IV, 907–11. I am grateful to Ted McGee of the University of Waterloo who has generously shared his knowledge of the masque with me. The masque was first brought to my attention by his paper, 'Patronage, Performance, and Self-Promotion', presented at the 1993 meeting of the North American Conference on British Studies. McGee writes that this masque 'is, in a sense, the first Caroline masque, for it promoted the aggressive, Protestant, militaristic policy of Prince Charles'.

44. J. William Hebel (ed.), *The Works of Michael Drayton* (Oxford, 1961), III, 170–4. For Drayton see Richard F. Hardin, *Michael Drayton and the Passing of Elizabethan England* (Lawrence, KS, 1973), especially pp. 6, 8, 88–92.

45. Wallace Notestein, Frances Helen Relf, and Hartley Simpson (eds.), *Commons Debates 1621* (New Haven, 1935), II, 85–6, 450, 496; III, 449, 455.

46. The current authority on the subject is Conrad Russell, *Parliaments and English Politics 1621–1629* (Oxford, 1979), pp. 85–144. Russell concludes (p. 142): 'Early in November 1621, it was beginning to look as if James might be under irresistible pressure for war. The effect of the intervention in the House of Commons was to make this pressure not merely resistible, but negligible.'

47. For the tumultuous greeting they received on their return, see Thomas Cogswell, 'England and the Spanish Match', in Richard Cust and Ann Hughes (eds), *Conflict in Early Stuart England: Studies in Religion and Politics 1603–1642* (London, 1989), pp. 107–33. For the determination of Charles and Buckingham to exact revenge, see my 'Why Did Prince Charles and the Duke of Buckingham Want War?' in *Selected Papers from the West Virginia Shakespeare and Renaissance Association*, 11 (Spring 1986), 62–71.

48. The standard accounts now are Russell's *Parliaments and English Politics 1621–1629* and Cogswell's *Blessed Revolution*, both cited above. Russell

found no great war-fever in Parliament; Cogswell did. In either case, at least a tentative commitment to war was made. Anyone interested in pursuing the question further should also consult Simon Adams, 'Spain or the Netherlands? Dilemmas of Early Stuart Foreign Policy', in Howard Tomlinson (ed.), *Before the English Civil War: Essays in Early Stuart Politics and Government* (London, 1983); Simon Adams, 'Foreign Policy and the Parliaments of 1621 and 1624', in Kevin Sharpe (ed.), *Faction and Parliament: Essays on Early Stuart History* (Oxford, 1978); and Roger Lockyer, *Buckingham: The Life and Political Career of George Villiers, First Duke of Buckingham 1592–1628* (London, 1981).

49. James's deteriorating health and strength may have been a factor, as the French ambassador Tillières seemed to imply. Friedrich von Raumer, *Briefe aus Paris zur Erlauterung der Geschichte des sechzehnten und siebzehnten Jahrhunderts* (Leipzig, 1831), II, 323.

50. Caroline Bingham, *James I of England* (London, 1981), p. 161.

51. Thomas Scott, *Vox Dei* (n.p., 1624), pp. 58, 63, 76, 77, 81. *Vox Regis* (Utrecht, 1624), Scott's description of the frontispiece. For similar effusive praise and jubilation, see Scott's *The Second Part of Vox Populi* (Goricom [London], 1624) and *Symmachia: Or, A True-Loves Knot Tyed Betwixt Great Britaine and the United Provinces by the Wisedome of King James* (Utrecht, 1624).

52. These emotional devices are evident in the letter from Buckingham to James printed in Philip Yorke, second Earl of Hardwicke (ed.), *Miscellaneous State Papers from 1501 to 1726* (London, 1778), I, 460, 466–7.

53. *CSPV*, XVIII, 174.

54. Unless otherwise noted, citations to the 1624 parliamentary diaries of Sir Simonds D'Ewes, Sir Walter Earle, Sir William Spring, Edward Nicholas, John Pym and John Holles are based on the transcripts at the Yale Center for Parliamentary History. I am deeply indebted to Maija Jansson for her assistance at Yale. D'Ewes diary, fol. 86; Spring diary, p. 135; *Journals of the House of Commons* (London, 1742–1826), I, 742.

55. *Journals of the House of Commons*, I, 722; Christopher Thompson, *Sir Nathaniel Rich's Diary of Proceedings in the House of Commons in 1624* (Wivenhoe, Essex, 1985), p. 25; Earle diary, fol. 34.

56. George L. Mosse, *Nationalism and Sexuality: Respectability and Abnormal Sexuality in Modern Europe* (New York, 1985), p. 115. For the controversial linkage between homosexuality and effeminacy, see pp. 41–7.

57. Mark Girouard, *The Return to Camelot: Chivalry and the English Gentleman* (New Haven, 1981).

58. Spring diary, p. 42.

59 *Journals of the House of Lords* (London, 1767–77), III, 282.

60. Henry Ellis (ed.), *Original Letters, Illustrative of English History* (London, 1824), III, 118.

61. *Tom Tell Troath* (1630), pp. 3, 8; *Harleian Miscellany*, II, 420, 425.

62. Earle's diary, fol. 43^v. In the words of the *Commons Journal* (I, 725), Charles 'bid him [James] think no more of him (for he lost) but desire him to reflect his Royal Thoughts on his Sister, and her Children'.

63. SP 14/160/33.

64. Charles Carlton, *Charles I: The Personal Monarch*, 2nd edn (London, 1995), p. 50.

65. Spring diary, p. 43; Nicholas diary, fol. 33^v; *Commons Journal*, I, 734. The Black Prince was the oldest son of Edward III. Many MPs in 1624 cited precedents from the reign of Edward III when chivalry was strong (he founded the Order of the Garter) and England was winning victories in the Hundred Years War. The Black Prince's expedition into Spain in 1367 has not always been viewed as favourably as it was by Phelips.
66. Earle's diary, fol. 33^v.
67. Nicholas diary, fol. 72^v.
68. Nicholas diary, fol. 33^v. In Spring's version of this speech, Phelips said, 'it is now time like Englishmen to do'. Spring diary, p. 43.
69. Nicholas diary, fol. 38^v.
70. Spring diary, p. 134.
71. Pym diary, fol. 7.
72. Thompson, *Rich's Diary*, p. 43.
73. Pym diary, fol. 34^v.
74. Thompson, *Rich's Diary*, p. 33.
75. Spring diary, p. 105; Holles diary, fol. 97; SP 14/160/63.
76. *CSPV*, XVIII, 265.
77. This passage comes from James's speech on 5 March 1624. *Journals of the House of Lords*, III, 250–1. It is printed in J.R. Tanner (ed.), *Constitutional Documents of the Reign of James I* (Cambridge, 1960), pp. 296–9, where it is erroneously attributed to 8 March.

6   Legacy

1. [Thomas Scott], *Sir Walter Rawleighs Ghost or Englands forewarner* (Utrecht, 1626), pp. 4, 20. Scott's charge of effeminacy and utilization of an Elizabethan ghost was mirrored in Philip Nichols, *Sir Francis Drake Revived: Calling Upon this Dull or Effeminate Age to Followe His Noble Steps for Golde and Silver* (London, 1626).
2. Leslie Stephen and Sidney Lee (eds), *The Dictionary of National Biography* (Oxford, 1917), XVII, 1006; *A Briefe and True Relation of the Murther of Mr. Thomas Scott Preacher of Gods Word and Batchelor of Divinitie, Committed by John Lambert Souldier of the Garrison of Utricke* (London, 1628).
3. For the political narrative of these years, see Conrad Russell, *Parliaments and English Politics 1621–1629* (Oxford, 1979). For the death toll, see Michael B. Young, 'Buckingham, War, and Parliament: Revisionism Gone Too Far', *Parliamentary History Yearbook*, 4 (1985), 62, 69 n. 120.
4. Francis Bamford (ed.), *A Royalist's Notebook: The Commonplace Book of Sir John Oglander* (New York, 1971), p. 197.
5. John Hacket, *Scrinia Reserata: A Memorial Offer'd to the Great Deservings of John Williams* (London, 1693), p. 190.
6. Compare Roger Lockyer's *Buckingham: The Life and Political Career of George Villiers, First Duke of Buckingham 1592–1628* (London, 1981) with my own 'Buckingham, War, and Parliament', cited above.
7. James Holstun, ' "God Bless Thee, Little David!": John Felton and his Allies,' *ELH*, 59 (1992), 513–52.

8. Thomas Middleton, *A Game at Chess*, ed. J.W. Harper (New York, 1966), p. 92. For the context of this play, see Thomas Cogswell, 'Thomas Middleton and the Court, 1624: *A Game at Chess* in Context', *Huntington Library Quarterly*, 47 (1984), 273–88; Jerzy Limon, *Dangerous Matter: English Drama and Politics in 1623/4* (Cambridge, 1986), chapter 4.

9. Many of the poems about Buckingham were gathered together and published in Francis Fairholt (ed.), 'Poems and Songs on the Assassination of the Duke of Buckingham', in *Early English Poetry, Ballads, and Popular Literature of the Middle Ages*, 29 (London, 1850). Here I am citing p. 49. References to Buckingham's sexuality did not always involve men; they sometimes involved women. What the poets wanted to create was an impression of overall debauchery, which, however, fits nicely with Alan Bray's description of sodomy. One poem implied sex with men by referring to Buckingham's 'curious fare' and 'vices fowle'. Several poems include 'lust' in a list of Buckingham's sins. One styles him 'the peere of lust'. Another accuses him of spending England's treasure on 'pandors, minions, pimpes, and whores'. When Buckingham went to France, one poet asked, 'Is there noe whore at court to stay thee?' Another poet observed that English ladies mourned his absence because 'they'l have noe babies / Untill hee doth retourne'. Fairholt, 'Poems', pp. 10, 14, 48, 52, 58, 64, 65, 67, 69. These poems and other varieties of 'underground' writing have attracted renewed attention in recent years. See, for example, Thomas Cogswell, 'Underground Verse and the Transformation of Early Stuart Political Culture', in Susan D. Amussen and Mark Kishlansky (eds), *Political Culture and Cultural Politics in Early Modern England: Essays Presented to David Underdown* (Manchester, 1995), pp. 277–300; Alastair Bellany, '"Raylinge Rymes and Vaunting Verse": Libellous Politics in Early Stuart England, 1603–1628', in Kevin Sharpe and Peter Lake (eds), *Culture and Politics in Early Stuart England* (Stanford, 1993), pp. 285–310; Gerald Hammond, *Fleeting Things: English Poets and Poems 1616–1660* (Cambridge, MA, 1990), pp. 49–66; and Holstun's 'God Bless Thee, Little David!', cited above.

10. Fairholt, 'Poems', pp. 14, 19, 24, 37–8.

11. Commonplace book of Tobias Alston, pp. 136–8, Beinecke Library, Yale University. The key to understanding that Buckingham was the target of this poem is the fact that he was Lord Admiral of England, a fact alluded to at the outset of the poem. As the anonymous author of this poem explains, a capon is 'a carved cocke', a 'creature so honest that a Queene may leye with it all night in her bosome; reddy booted & spurred the King may take it on huntinge'. Whereas the Earl of Essex brought honour to England, and Sir Francis Drake brought gold, says this poet, Buckingham, after spending all of his own estate as well as the king's and queen's, merely produced a capon.

12. Bellany, 'Raylinge Rymes', p. 305.

13. S. R. Gardiner, *History of England from the Accession of James I to the Outbreak of the Civil War 1603–1642* (London, 1883–4, 1894–6), VI, 106–8; Thomas Birch (ed.), *The Court and Times of Charles I* (London, 1849), I, 101; James Orchard Halliwell (ed.), *The Autobiography and Correspondence of Sir Simonds D'Ewes* (London, 1845), II, 186.

14. Roger Lockyer, 'An English Valido? Buckingham and James I', in Richard Ollard and Pamela Tudor-Craig (eds), *For Veronica Wedgwood These: Studies in*

Seventeenth-Century History (London, 1986), p. 58. Lockyer tries to distinguish between the role Buckingham played under James and the role he played under Charles, arguing that it was only under the latter that Buckingham obtained too much power and undermined royal authority.

15. Pierre Matthieu, *The Powerful Favorite, Or, The Life of Aelius Sejanus* (Paris, 1628), pp. 1, 5, 46, 114, 154. For the use of Matthieu's works as political propaganda, see David Underdown, *A Freeborn People: Politics and the Nation in Seventeenth-Century England* (Oxford, 1996), pp. 32, 36.

16. [Elizabeth Cary, Lady Falkland], 'The History of the Most Unfortunate Prince, King Edward the Second', in William Oldys (ed.), *The Harleian Miscellany: A Collection of Scarce, Curious, and Entertaining Pamphlets and Tracts, as Well in Manuscript as in Print* (London, 1809), I, 95.

17. Fairholt, 'Poems', pp. 5, 37–9.

18. W. Douglas Hamilton (ed.), *Original Papers Illustrative of the Life and Writings of John Milton* (London, 1859), p. 67. Gill was a friend of John Milton. See Christopher Hill, *Milton and the English Revolution* (Harmondsworth, 1979), pp. 27–9.

19. J.A. Taylor, 'Two Unpublished Poems on the Duke of Buckingham', *Review of English Studies*, new series 40, no. 158 (May 1989), 240. See also V.L. Pearl and M.L. Pearl, 'Richard Corbett's "Against the Opposing of the Duke in Parliament, 1628" and the Anonymous Rejoinder, "An Answere to the Same, Lyne for Lyne": The Earliest Dated Manuscript Copies', *Review of English Studies*, new series 42, no. 165 (February 1991), 32–9.

20. Fairholt, 'Poems', pp. 30, 34–5, 52. The equation of the king's sceptre with his penis was a common device in the poetry of Charles II's reign, too. See Rachel Weil, 'Sometimes a Scepter is Only a Scepter: Pornography and Politics in Restoration England', in Lynn Hunt (ed.), *The Invention of Pornography: Obscenity and the Origins of Modernity, 1500–1800* (New York, 1993), pp. 125–53.

21. Allen B. Hinds and others (eds), *Calendar of State Papers and Manuscripts Relating to English Affairs Existing in the Archives and Collections of Venice* (London, 1864–1940), XVII, 439.

22. Fairholt, 'Poems', pp. 37, 41, 50.

23. Ibid., p. 31.

24. Ibid., p. 54.

25. Alan Bray, 'Homosexuality and the Signs of Male Friendship in Elizabethan England', *History Workshop Journal*, issue 29 (Spring 1990), 11.

26. James himself had been much more fortunate, of course, having inherited Robert Cecil, Earl of Salisbury from Queen Elizabeth.

27. Kevin Sharpe, *Criticism and Compliment: The Politics of Literature in the England of Charles I* (Cambridge, 1987), p. 13; 'The Image of Virtue: the Court and Household of Charles I, 1625–42', in his *Politics and Ideas in Early Stuart England: Essays and Studies* (London, 1989), pp. 147, 154; and *The Personal Rule of Charles I* (New Haven, 1992), pp. 183, 188, 190, 210, 212, 217. See also Sharpe's shorter early essay on 'The Personal Rule of Charles I' in *Politics and Ideas*, pp. 101–22.

28. John Bruce (ed.), *Calendar of State Paper, Domestic Series, of the Reign of Charles I* (London, 1859), III (1628–1629), 412. See also pp. 343, 393, and 413.

29. Roy Strong, *Van Dyck: Charles I on Horseback* (New York, 1972), p. 70.
30. Sharpe, *Politics and Ideas*, p. 172.
31. I am using the version of *Coelum Britannicum* printed in Thomas Carew, *Poems* (London, 1640), pp. 207–20.
32. One person who interpreted the masque correctly was James M. Saslow. See his *Ganymede in the Renaissance: Homosexuality in Art and History* (New Haven, 1986), p. 195. Kevin Sharpe mentions *Coelum Britannicum* in many places. For his most extended discussion, see *Criticism and Compliment*, pp. 232–43. Annabel Patterson (mistakenly, I think) wrote that 'Charles is both the old, decadent Jupiter and the new deity who will replace him.' *Censorship and Interpretation: The Conditions of Writing and Reading in Early Modern England* (Madison, WI, 1984), p. 109.
33. Albert H. Tricomi, *Anticourt Drama in England 1603–1642* (Charlottesville, VA, 1989), p. 171; Sir Robert Naunton, *Fragmenta Regalia or Observations on Queen Elizabeth, Her Times and Favorites*, ed. John S. Cerovski (London, 1985), p. 40.
34. Charles Howard McIlwain (ed.), *The Political Works of James I* (New York, 1965), pp. 5, 27, 43; Johann P. Sommerville (ed.), *King James VI and I: Political Writings* (Cambridge, 1994), pp. 4, 31, 49.
35. Jonathan Goldberg in his *James I and the Politics of Literature: Jonson, Shakespeare, Donne, and Their Contemporaries* (London, 1983), pp. 113–15, 139–41.
36. Sharpe, *Personal Rule*, p. 181. Judging James by what he practiced rather than what he preached, Sharpe writes that 'unlike his father, Charles I had an acute sense of the importance of the court as an example' (p. 210).
37. T.B. Howell (ed.), *Cobbett's Complete Collection of State Trials* (London, 1809–26), III, 409. For Castlehaven's trial, see also Caroline Bingham, Seventeenth-Century Attitudes Toward Deviant Sex', *Journal of Interdisciplinary History*, 1, no. 3 (Spring 1971), 447–68; Cynthia Herrup, ' "To Pluck Bright Honour from the Pale-faced Moon": Gender and Honour in the Castlehaven Story', *Transactions of the Royal Historical Society*, 6th series, volume 6 (Cambridge, 1996), 137–59, and 'The Patriarch at Home: The Trial of the Second Earl of Castlehaven for Rape and Sodomy', *History Workshop Journal*, issue 41 (Spring 1996), 1–18.
38. Perez Zagorin, *The Court and the Country: The Beginnings of the English Revolution* (New York, 1971).
39. For a review of the controversy, see Dwight D. Brautigam, 'The Court and the Country Revisited', in Bonnelyn Young Kunze and Dwight D. Brautigam (eds), *Court, Country and Culture: Essays on Early Modern British History in Honor of Perez Zagorin* (Rochester, 1992), pp. 55–64. See also Sharpe, *Criticism and Compliment*, pp. 11–22; R. Malcolm Smuts, *Court Culture and the Origins of a Royalist Tradition in Early Stuart England* (Philadelphia, 1987); R. Malcolm Smuts, 'Cultural Diversity and Cultural Change at the Court of James I', in Linda Levy Peck (ed.), *The Mental World of the Jacobean Court* (Cambridge, 1991), pp. 99–112; Derek Hirst, 'Court, Country, and Politics before 1629', in Kevin Sharpe (ed.), *Faction and Parliament: Essays on Early Stuart History* (Oxford, 1978), pp. 105–38.
40. Smuts, *Court Culture*, p. 74.

41. Sharpe, *Criticism and Compliment*, p. 16. See also Leah S. Marcus, 'Politics and Pastoral: Writing the Court on the Countryside', in Kevin Sharpe and Peter Lake (eds), *Culture and Politics in Early Stuart England* (Stanford, 1993), pp. 139–59.
42. Lawrence Stone, *The Causes of the English Revolution 1529–1642* (New York, 1972), p. 105. Italics mine.
43. Smuts, *Court Culture*, p. 28.
44. For the general tendency to link homosexuality with the court, see Alan Bray, *Homosexuality in Renaissance England* (London, 1982), pp. 33–7.
45. Lawrence Stone, *The Crisis of the Aristocracy 1558–1641* (Oxford, 1965), p. 666.
46. Stone, *Causes*, p. 90.
47. Conrad Russell, *The Fall of the British Monarchies 1637–1642* (Oxford, 1991), pp. vii–viii.
48. Conrad Russell, *The Causes of the English Civil War* (Oxford, 1990), p. 211.
49. Conrad Russell, 'The British Problem and the English Civil War', *History*, 72 (1987), 412–14.
50. A flood of new books is now reaffirming this view of King Charles that S.R. Gardiner took one hundred years ago. Notable contributions in addition to the works of Conrad Russell cited above include Richard Cust, *The Forced Loan and English Politics 1626–1628* (Oxford, 1987); L.J. Reeve, *Charles I and the Road to Personal Rule* (Cambridge, 1989); Peter Donald, *An Uncounselled King: Charles I and the Scottish Troubles, 1637–1641* (Cambridge, 1990); and Allan MacInnes, *Charles I and the Making of the Covenanting Movement, 1625–1641* (Edinburgh, 1991).
51. Strong, *Van Dyck*, pp. 70–4, 88.
52. Godfrey Goodman, *The Court of King James the First* (London, 1839), I, 382.
53. Vernon F. Snow, *Essex the Rebel: The Life of Robert Devereux, the Third Earl of Essex 1591–1646* (Lincoln, NE, 1970), p. 70. For the campaign of 1644, culminating in the defeat at Lostwithiel, see chapter 17.

7　Memory

1. Leslie Stephen and Sidney Lee (eds), *The Dictionary of National Biography* (Oxford, 1917), XX, 1073–4. Hereafter cited as *DNB*. Weldon's *A Perfect Description of the People and Country of Scotland* is printed in Sir Walter Scott (ed.), *The Secret History of the Court of James the First* (Edinburgh, 1811), II, 75–89.
2. Robert Ashton (ed.), *James I By His Contemporaries* (London, 1969), pp. 11, 17.
3. Maurice Lee Jr, 'James I and the Historians: Not a Bad King After All?', *Albion*, 16 (Summer 1984), 151.
4. Neil Cuddy, 'The Revival of the Entourage: the Bedchamber of James I, 1603–1625', in David Starkey (ed.), *The English Court from the Wars of the Roses to the Civil War* (London, 1987), p. 198.
5. Jenny Wormald, 'James VI and I: Two Kings or One?', *History*, 68 (June 1983), 191–2.
6. Christopher Durston, *James I* (London, 1993), pp. 2–3.

7. Sir Anthony Weldon, *The Court and Character of King James* (London, 1651), pp. 25–6. Since this work was published posthumously, about a year after Weldon's death, there is a very remote possibility that he was not the author or that his original work was subjected to editorial change by someone else. For our purposes, it does not ultimately matter. We are interested in the language of the text, no matter who 'Weldon' turns out to have been. Quotations are taken from the 1651 edition which was handily available to me on microfilm. I have checked all of these against the original 1650 edition and found that there are only a few quite minor differences, usually involving only spelling or punctuation.

8. Maurice Lee Jr, *Great Britain's Solomon* (Urbana, 1990), pp. xi–xii, 309–10, 318.

9. S.J. Houston, *James I*, 2nd edn (London, 1995), pp. 101, 115.

10. Weldon, *Court and Character*, p. 175. As noted above, this work was printed about a year after Weldon's death, and there is a remote possibility that he was not the author. For our purposes, for the most part, it does not matter who the true author was. We are interested in the language of the text, no matter who 'Weldon' turns out to have been.

11. Ashton, *James I by His Contemporaries*, pp. xx–xi.

12. Weldon, *Court and Character*, pp. 7, 16–17, 59, 83–4, 87, 139.

13. Ibid., p. 125. The Venetian ambassador's description was close to Weldon's. *CSPV*, XVII, 442.

14. Weldon, *Court and Character*, pp. 164–75.

15. Ibid., pp. 125–6.

16. Ibid., pp. 94–5.

17. On this subject, see also Jonathan Goldberg, *James I and the Politics of Literature: Jonson, Shakespeare, Donne, and Their Contemporaries* (London, 1983), pp. 68–9.

18. Richard C. McCoy, 'Old English Honour in an Evil Time: Aristocratic Principle in the 1620s', in R. Malcolm Smuts (ed.), *The Stuart Court and Europe: Essays in Politics and Political Culture* (Cambridge, 1996), p. 135.

19. Arthur Wilson, *The History of Great Britain, Being the Life and Reign of King James The First* (London, 1653), pp. 289–90. Like Weldon's *Court and Character*, Wilson's history was published shortly after the author's death and may have been subjected to some editorial revision. *DNB*, XXI, 552–3.

20. Kenneth C. Schellhase, *Tacitus in Renaissance Political Thought* (Chicago, 1976), pp. 147, 157–63. See also J.H.M. Salmon, 'Seneca and Tacitus in Jacobean England', in Linda Levy Peck (ed.), *The Mental World of the Jacobean Court* (Cambridge, 1991), pp. 169–88.

21. Hugh G. Dick (ed.), *Selected Writings of Francis Bacon* (New York, 1955), p. 18.

22. Wilson, *The History of Great Britain*, pp. 54, 79–80, 147, 192, 285, 289–90.

23. *A Cat May Look Upon a King* (London, 1652), pp. 50, 58–9, 63, 78, 96. Compare Weldon, *Court and Character*, pp. 106–9. Blair Worden attributes *A Cat* to Marchamont Nedham. See Worden's '"Wit in a Roundhead": the Dilemma of Marchamont Nedham', in Susan D. Amussen and Mark Kishlansky (eds), *Political Culture and Cultural Politics in Early Modern England: Essays Presented to David Underdown* (Manchester, 1995), p. 331 n. 73 and 'Milton and Marchamont Nedham', in David Armitage and

others (eds), *Milton and Republicanism* (Cambridge, 1995), pp. 158 n. 8, 160 n. 21. I am very grateful to Alastair Bellany for providing me with a copy of this work, sharing his opinion of the authorship, and directing me to Worden's essays.

24. *A Cat May Look Upon a King*, pp. 91–2.
25. Francis Osborne, *Traditional Memorials* in the *The Works of Francis Osborn* (London, 1673), pp. 496, 505, 511, 534–5. See also Ellis Hanson, 'Sodomy and Kingcraft in *Urania* and *Antony and Cleopatra*', in Claude J. Summers (ed.), *Homosexuality in Renaissance and Enlightenment England: Literary Representations in Historical Context* (New York, 1992), pp. 142–4.
26. For Ashley, see *DNB*, I, 642–3.
27. The commonplace book of Tobias Alston, Osborne MS. b197, p. 188. Beinecke Library of Yale University.
28. Michael B. Young, *Servility and Service: The Life and Work of Sir John Coke* (London, 1985), p. 75.
29. Sir Edward Peyton, *The Divine Catastrophe of the Kingly Family of the House of Stuarts*, in Scott, *Secret History*, II, 334–9, 346, 352–3. See also Catherine Drinker Bowen, *The Lion and the Throne: The Life and Times of Sir Edward Coke* (Boston, 1957), p. 417.
30. *Aulicus Coquinariae* in Scott, *Secret History*, II, 271. For Sanderson, see *DNB*, XVII, 757.
31. John S. Brewer (ed.), *The Court of King James the First; By Dr. Godfrey Goodman, Bishop of Gloucester* (London, 1839), I, 39–40, 168, 225, 393–4. For Goodman, see *DNB*, VIII, 131–4.
32. *Aulicus Coquinariae* in Scott, *Secret History*, II, 160, 188–9, 199, 223–4, 271.
33. Wormald, 'James VI and I: Two Kings or One?, p. 191 n. 16.
34. Francis Bamford (ed.), *A Royalist's Notebook: The Commonplace Book of Sir John Oglander* (New York, 1971), pp. 41, 194, 196.
35. Lucy Hutchinson, *Memoirs of the Life of Colonel Hutchinson*, ed. James Sutherland (London, 1973), pp. 42–6. For Hutchinson, see *DNB*, X, 340–1.
36. Hutchinson, *Memoirs*, pp. 42, 44.
37. Alan Bray, *Homosexuality in Renaissance England* (London, 1982), p. 10.
38. Stephen O. Murray, 'Homosexual Acts and Selves in Early Modern Europe', in Kent Gerard and Gert Hekma (eds), *Pursuit of Sodomy: Male Homosexuality in Renaissance and Enlightenment Europe* (New York, 1989), p. 458.
39. Alan Bray, 'Homosexuality and the Signs of Male Friendship in Elizabethan England', *History Workshop Journal*, issue 29 (Spring 1990), 1–19.

Conclusion: James and the History of Homosexuality

1. Maurice Lee Jr, 'James I and the Historians: Not a Bad King After All?', *Albion*, 16 (Summer 1984), 158; *Great Britain's Solomon* (Urbana, 1990), p. 249.
2. The speaker was Sir Edward Coke. Robert C. Johnson, Maija Jansson Cole, Mary Frear Keeler, and William B. Bidwell (eds), *Commons Debates 1628* (New Haven, CT, 1977), IV, 115, 119, 124, 130, 132.

3. Roger Lockyer, *Buckingham: The Life and Political Career of George Villiers, First Duke of Buckingham 1592–1628* (London, 1981); Lee, 'James I and the Historians', p. 161.

4. S.J. Houston, *James I*, 2nd edn (London, 1995), p. 110. Compare Roger Lockyer, *James VI and I* (London, 1998), p. 205.

5. Wormald made this statement at the 1996 meeting of the North American Conference on British Studies in Chicago.

6. David Cressy, 'Gender Trouble and Cross-Dressing in Early Modern England', *Journal of British Studies*, 35 (October 1996), 451.

7. Allen B. Hinds (ed.), *Calendar of State Paper and Manuscripts, Relating to English Affairs, Existing in the Archives and Collections of Venice* (London, 1911), XVII, 75–6.

8. Lawrence Stone, *The Causes of the English Revolution 1529–1642* (London, 1972), p. 89.

9. Thomas Scott, *The Belgicke Pismire: Stinging the slothfull Sleeper, and Awaking the Diligent to Fast, Watch, Pray; and Worke out Theire Owne Temporall and Eternall Salvation with Feare and Trembling* (London, 1622), p. 40.

10. Two principal proponents of this view are Conrad Russell and Kevin Sharpe. See Russell's *Parliaments and English Politics 1621–1629* (Oxford, 1979) and the essays collected in *Unrevolutionary England, 1603–1642* (London, 1990). See Sharpe's ' "Revisionism" Revisited' in *Faction and Parliament: Essays on Early Stuart History*, 2nd edn (London, 1985), pp. 9–17; 'Crown, Parliament and Locality: Government and Communication in Early Stuart England', *English Historical Review*, 101 (April 1986), 321–50; and *The Personal Rule of Charles I* (New Haven, 1992).

11. See pp. 112–13 of the commonplace book of Tobias Alston, among the Osborne manuscripts (b197) in the Beinecke Library of Yale University.

12. Frederick von Raumer, *History of the Sixteenth and Seventeenth Centuries, Illustrated by Original Sources* [trans. H.E. Lloyd] (London, 1835), II, 210, 246.

13. Edward Hyde, Earl of Clarendon, *The Characters of Robert Earl of Essex, Favourite to Queen Elizabeth, and George D. of Buckingham, Favourite to K. James and K. Ch. I* (London, 1706), pp. 21–2. I am grateful to David M. Bergeron for bringing this work to my attention.

14. George Calvert, Lord Baltimore, *The Answer to Tom-Tell-Troth* (London, 1642), pp. 1–2, 23. Baltimore may not have been the true author of this pamphlet, but his name appeared on the title-page.

15. Marlowe's *Edward the Second* in Havelock Ellis (ed.), *Christopher Marlowe: Five Plays* (New York, 1956), pp. 282, 300.

16. Francis Bamford (ed.), *A Royalist's Notebook: The Commonplace Book of Sir John Oglander* (New York, 1971), pp. 194, 196.

17. John Nichols, *The Progresses, Processions, and Magnificent Festivities of King James the First* (London, 1828), III, 80–1.

18. Raumer, *History*, II, 234.

19. Barbara Kiefer Lewalski, 'Enacting Opposition: Queen Anne and the Subversions of Masquing' in Lewalski, *Writing Women in Jacobean England* (Cambridge, MA, 1993), pp. 15, 26. See also Simon Shepherd, *Amazons and Warrior Women: Varieties of Feminism in Seventeenth-Century Drama* (New York, 1981), p. 138 and Leeds Barroll, 'The Court of the First Stuart Queen',

in Linda Levy Peck (ed.), *The Mental World of the Jacobean Court* (Cambridge, 1991), pp. 191–208.

20. Thomas Carew, *Coelum Britannicum*, printed in his *Poems* (London, 1640), pp. 212, 217.
21. Lee, *Great Britain's Solomon*, p. 255.
22. Jenny Wormald, 'James VI and I: Two Kings or One?', *History*, 68 (June 1983), 190.
23. Alan Bray, *Homosexuality in Renaissance England*, 2nd edn (New York, 1995), p. 10.
24. Stephen Orgel, *Impersonations: The Performance of Gender in Shakespeare's England* (Cambridge, 1996), p. 41.
25. I would add here all the authors who paraded the example of Edward II before the public, but Orgel is aware of this, though he seems to think that the authors and their audiences were unaware that sodomy was involved. Orgel, *Impersonations*, pp. 48–9.
26. These events are described above in chapter 1 and can also be followed in Lockyer, *Buckingham*, pp. 16–20.
27. Joseph Cady, '"Masculine Love", Renaissance Writing, and the "New Invention" of Homosexuality', in Claude J. Summers (ed.), *Homosexuality in Renaissance and Enlightenment England: Literary Representations in Historical Context* (New York, 1992), pp. 9–40; 'Renaissance Awareness and Language for Heterosexuality: "Love" and "Feminine Love"', in Claude J. Summers and Ted-Larry Pebworth (eds), *Renaissance Discourses of Desire* (Columbia, MO, 1993), pp. 143–58; 'The "Masculine Love" of the "Princes of Sodom" "Practicing the Art of Ganymede" at Henri III's Court: The Homosexuality of Henry III and His *Mignons* in Pierre de L'Estoile's *Mémoires-Journaux*', in Jacqueline Murray and Konrad Eisenbichler (eds), *Desire and Discipline: Sex and Sexuality in the Premodern West* (Toronto, 1996), pp. 123–54. Cady derides the whole idea that homosexuality was not 'invented' until the eighteenth century or later, as does Rictor Norton in *The Myth of the Modern Homosexual: Queer History and the Search for Cultural Unity* (London, 1997).
28. Bray, *Homosexuality in Renaissance England*, p. 111.
29. Ibid., pp. 26, 112.
30. Lawrence Stone, *The Family, Sex and Marriage in England 1500–1800* (New York, 1977).
31. The phrase comes from Keith Thomas's review of Stone's book in the *Times Literary Supplement*, Oct. 21, 1977.
32. Bray, *Homosexuality in Renaissance England*, pp. 112–13.
33. Ibid., pp. 51–6, 79.
34. Ibid., p. 112.
35. This point is made especially well by David Aers, 'A Whisper in the Ear of Early Modernists; or, Reflections on Literary Critics Writing the "History of the Subject"', in David Aers (ed.), *Culture and History 1350–1600: Essays on English Communities, Identities and Writing* (Detroit, MI, 1992), pp. 177–202. Rictor Norton has made this argument forcefully with respect to any alleged revolution in sexuality. 'Assertions that the modern homosexual and modern gay subculture are significantly different from the past are', in his words, 'based primarily on ignorance of the past.' Norton, *Myth of the Modern Homosexual*, p. 61.

36. Randolph Trumbach, *Sex and the Gender Revolution*, vol. 1, *Heterosexuality and the Third Gender in Enlightenment London* (Chicago, 1998), pp. 3–9.
37. Norton makes this point in *Myth of the Modern Homosexual*, pp. 59–60.
38. Tim Hitchcock, *English Sexualities, 1700–1800* (London, 1997), p. 65.
39. Francis Osborne, *Traditional Memorials* in the *The Works of Francis Osborn* (London, 1673), p. 535.
40. Randolph Trumbach, 'Sodomitical Subcultures, Sodomitical Roles, and the Gender Revolution of the Eighteenth Century: The Recent Historiography', in Robert Purks Maccubbin (ed.), *'Tis Nature's Fault: Unauthorized Sexuality During the Enlightenment* (Cambridge, 1987), pp. 109–21; 'Sodomitical Assaults, Gender Role, and Sexual Development in Eighteenth-Century London', in Kent Gerard and Gert Hekma (eds), *The Pursuit of Sodomy: Male Homosexuality in Renaissance and Enlightenment Europe* (New York, 1989), pp. 407–29; 'The Birth of the Queen: Sodomy and the Emergence of Gender Equality in Modern Culture, 1660–1750', in Martin Duberman and others (eds), *Hidden from History: Reclaiming the Gay and Lesbian Past* (New York, 1989), pp. 129–40; 'Sodomy Transformed: Aristocratic Libertinage, Public Reputation and the Gender Revolution of the 18th Century', in Michael S. Kimmel (ed.), *Love Letters Between a Certain Late Nobleman and the Famous Mr. Wilson* (New York, 1990), 105–24; 'Erotic Fantasy and Male Libertinism in Enlightenment England', in Lynn Hunt (ed.), *The Invention of Pornography: Obscenity and the Origins of Modernity, 1500–1800* (New York, 1993), pp. 253–82; 'London's Sapphists: From Three Sexes to Four Genders in the Making of Modern Culture', in Gilbert Herdt (ed.), *Third Sex, Third Gender: Beyond Sexual Dimorphism in Culture and History* (New York, 1994), pp. 111–36; 'Are Modern Western Lesbian Women and Gay Men a Third Gender?', in Martin Duberman (ed.), *A Queer World: The Center for Lesbian and Gay Studies Reader* (New York, 1997), pp. 87–99; and *Sex and the Gender Revolution*, pp. 3–22. Trumbach acknowledges his indebtedness to the early work of Mary McIntosh. Her seminal essay 'The Homosexual Role', which was first published in 1968 has been reprinted in Edward Stein (ed.), *Forms of Desire: Sexual Orientation and the Social Constructionist Controversy* (New York, 1990), pp. 25–42.
41. Trumbach, 'A Third Gender?', pp. 88–9.
42. Trumbach, 'Sodomitical Assaults', p. 408.
43. James M. Saslow, 'Homosexuality in the Renaissance: Behavior, Identity, and Artistic Expression', in Duberman, *Hidden from History*, pp. 91–3. Michael Rocke, *Forbidden Friendships: Homosexuality and Male Culture in Renaissance Florence* (Oxford, 1996).
44. Rocke, *Forbidden Friendships*, pp. 4–5, 115–17. The figures fall if we move from incriminations to convictions. In Rocke's sample there were roughly 17,000 incriminated, of whom roughly 3,000 were convicted. These figures are still astonishingly high in a city with a population of only about 40,000 inhabitants.
45. Trumbach, 'A Third Gender', p. 90.
46. Norton, *Myth of the Modern Homosexual*, pp. 87–8.
47. Lee, *Great Britain's Solomon*, p. 241; Wormald, 'Two Kings or One?, p. 197.
48. W. Dunn Macray (ed.), *The History of the Rebellion and Civil Wars in England Begun in the Year 1641, by Edward, Earl of Clarendon* (Oxford, 1888), I, 38.

49. King James, *A Meditation Upon the Lords Prayer, Written by the Kings Majestie, For the benefit of all his subjects, especially of such as follow the Court* (London, 1619), preface.

50. The letters written by James are printed in G.P.V. Akrigg, *Letters of King James VI and I* (Berkeley, 1984), pp. 388–441. For more about these letters, see chapter 2 above and David M. Bergeron's *King James and Letters of Homoerotic Desire* (Iowa City, 1999).

51. The quotations and paraphrases in this paragraph represent a summary of the evidence laid out in greater detail above in chapters 3, 4, 6, and 7, where readers can find the full context and specific sources. The only new references are Nowell Smith (ed.), *Sir Fulke Greville's Life of Sir Philip Sidney* (Oxford, 1907), p. 10; Clarendon, *History of the Rebellion and Civil Wars*, I, 74; and Sir Edward Peyton, *The Divine Catastrophe of the Kingly Family of the House of Stuarts*, in Sir Walter Scott (ed.) *The Secret History of the Court of James the First* (Edinburgh, 1811), II, 364.

52. Oliver Lawson Dick (ed.), *Aubrey's Brief Lives* (London, 1950), p. 11; Ian McCormick (ed.), *Secret Sexualities: A Sourcebook of 17th and 18th Century Writing* (London, 1997), pp. 52–3.

53. John Hacket, *Scrinia Reserata: A Memorial Offer'd to the Great Deservings of John Williams* (London, 1693), p. 39. For Alcibiades and *amor socraticus*, see Norton, *Myth of the Modern Homosexual*, pp. 144–5.

54. C.H. McIlwain (ed.), *The Political Works of James I* (New York, 1965), p. 46 and Johann P. Sommerville (ed.), *King James VI and I: Political Writings* (Cambridge, 1994), p. 53.

55. For a quite different view, see David M. Halperin, *One Hundred Years of Homosexuality and Other Essays on Greek Love* (New York, 1990), pp. 22–4, where the author manages to discuss the subject without ever using the word 'effeminacy'. Compare Norton, *Myth of the Modern Homosexual*, pp. 27–31.

56. Mark D. Jordan, *The Invention of Sodomy in Christian Theology* (Chicago, 1997), pp. 39, 100, 102, 112, 122, 125, 169. But compare page 57. Karma Lochrie noted the uneven attention Jordan gave to issues of gender in her commentary at the International Congress on Medieval Studies in May 1998.

57. Eve Kosofsky Sedgwick, *Between Men: English Literature and Male Homosexual Desire* (New York, 1985), p. 93.

58. Trumbach, 'Erotic Fantasy', p. 255.

59. Trumbach, 'Sodomitical Assaults', pp. 408, 425–6; 'Sodomitical Subcultures', p. 118; *Sex and the Gender Revolution*, p. 430.

60. Alan Sinfield, *The Wilde Century: Effeminacy, Oscar Wilde and the Queer Moment* (New York, 1994), pp. 25–47, 118–22.

61. See above, chapter 5.

62. Trumbach, 'Sodomy Transformed', p. 111.

63. Hitchcock, *English Sexualities*, pp. 66–7.

Bibliography

Unpublished primary sources

Yale University, Beinecke Library.
Commonplace book of Tobias Alston, Osborne manuscript b197
Yale University, Yale Center for Parliamentary History
Typescript of Sir Simonds D'Ewes diary for 1624
Typescript of Sir Walter Earle diary for 1624
Typescript of Sir William Spring diary for 1624
Typescript of Edward Nicholas diary for 1624
Typescript of John Pym diary for 1624
Typescript of John Holles diary for 1624
Public Record Office, London
State papers, domestic, reign of James I (SP 14)

Published primary sources

Akrigg, G.P.V. (ed.). *Letters of King James VI and I*. Berkeley, CA, 1984.
Ashton, Robert (ed.). *James I By His Contemporaries*. London, 1969.
Baltimore, George Calvert, Lord. *The Answer to Tom-Tell-Troath*. London, 1642.
Bamford, Francis (ed.). *A Royalist's Notebook: The Commonplace Book of Sir John Oglander*. New York, 1971.
Bassompierre, Maréchal de. *Journal de Ma Vie: Mémoires du Marechal de Bassompierre*. Paris, 1875.
Beard, Thomas. *The Theatre of Gods Judgements*. Islip, 1612.
Birch, Thomas (ed.). *The Court and Times of Charles I*. 2 vols. London, 1849.
—— (ed.). *The Court and Times of James I*. 2 vols. London, 1849.
Blitzer, Charles (ed.). *The Political Writings of James Harrington*. Indianapolis, IN, 1955.
Bourcier, Elisabeth (ed.). *The Diary of Sir Simonds D'Ewes (1622–1624)*. Paris, 1974.
A Briefe and True Relation of the Murther of Mr. Thomas Scott Preacher of Gods Word and Batchelor of Divinitie, Committed by John Lambert Souldier of the Garrison of Utricke. London, 1628.
Bullen, A.H. (ed.). *The Works of Thomas Middleton*. 8 vols. New York, 1964.
Calderwood, David. *History of the Kirk of Scotland*. Ed. Thomas Thomson. 8 vols. Edinburgh, 1842–9.
Calendar of Letters and Papers Relating to the Affairs of the Borders of England and Scotland. Ed. Joseph Bain. 2 vols. Edinburgh, 1894–5.
Calendar of State Papers, Domestic Series, of the Reign of Charles I. Ed. John Bruce and W.D. Hamilton. 23 vols. London, 1858–97.
Calendar of State Papers, Domestic Series, of the Reign of James I. Ed. Mary Anne Everett Green. 4 vols. London, 1857–9.

Calendar of State Papers and Manuscripts Relating to English Affairs Existing in the Archives and Collections of Venice. Ed. Allen B. Hinds and others. 38 vols. London, 1864–1940.

Calendar of the State Papers Relating to Scotland and Mary, Queen of Scots 1547–1603. Ed. William K. Boyd and Henry W. Meikle. Vols 5–10. Edinburgh and Glasgow, 1907–36.

Carew, Thomas. *Coelum Britannicum.* In *Poems,* 207–63. London, 1640.

Castiglione, Baldesar. *The Book of the Courtier.* Trans. Charles S. Singleton. New York, 1959.

A Cat May Look Upon a King. London, 1652.

Clarendon, Edward Hyde, Earl of. *The Characters of Robert Earl of Essex, Favourite to Queen Elizabeth, and George D. of Buckingham, Favourite to K. James and K. Ch. I.* London, 1706.

——. *The History of the Rebellion and Civil Wars in England Begun in the Year 1641, by Edward, Earl of Clarendon.* Ed. W. Dunn Macray. 6 vols. Oxford, 1888.

Coke, Sir Edward. *The Reports of Sir Edward Coke, Knt., in Thirteen Parts.* 6 vols. London, 1826.

——. *The Third Part of the Institutes of the Laws of England.* London, 1797.

Craigie, James (ed.). *The Poems of James VI of Scotland.* Edinburgh, 1958.

—— (ed.). *Minor Prose Works of King James VI and I.* Edinburgh, 1982.

Criminal Trials and Other Proceedings Before the High Court of Justiciary in Scotland. Publications of the Bannatyne Club, vol. 19, pt. 4. N.p., 1830.

Diary of Mr. James Melvill 1556–1601. Edinburgh, 1829.

Dick, Hugh D. (ed.). *Selected Writings of Francis Bacon.* New York, 1955.

Dick, Oliver Lawson (ed.). *Aubrey's Brief Lives.* London, 1950.

Documentos inéditos para la historia de Espana. 4 vols. Madrid, 1936–45.

Ellis, Havelock (ed.). *Christopher Marlowe: Five Plays.* New York, 1956.

Ellis, Henry (ed.). *Original Letters, Illustrative of English History.* 3 vols. London, 1824.

Everard, John. *The Arriereban: a Sermon.* London, 1618.

Fairholt, Francis (ed.). 'Poems and Songs on the Assassination of the Duke of Buckingham.' In *Early English Poetry, Ballads, and Popular Literature of the Middle Ages,* Percy Society, vol. 29. London, 1850.

[Falkland, Elizabeth Cary, Lady]. 'The History of the Most Unfortunate Prince, King Edward the Second.' In *The Harleian Miscellany,* ed. William Oldys, I, 67–95. 10 vols. London, 1808–13.

The French Herauld Sent to the Princes of Christendome. London, 1622.

Gardiner, S.R., (ed.). *Parliamentary Debates in 1610.* London, 1862.

Gavorse, Joseph, (ed.). *The Lives of the Twelve Caesars by Suetonius.* New York, 1959.

Goodman, Godfrey. *The Court of King James the First.* Ed. John S. Brewer. 2 vols. London, 1839.

Hacket, John. *Scrinia Reserata: A Memorial Offer'd to the Great Deservings of John Williams.* London, 1693.

Hadas, Moses (ed.). *The Complete Works of Tacitus.* Trans. Alfred John Church and William Jackson Brodribb. New York, 1942.

Haec Vir: or The Womanish-Man. N.p., 1620.

Halliwell, James Orchard, (ed.). *The Autobiography and Correspondence of Sir Simonds D'Ewes.* 2 vols. London, 1845.

Hamilton, W. Douglas (ed.). *Original Papers Illustrative of the Life and Writings of John Milton*. London, 1859.

Hardwicke, Philip Yorke, second Earl of (ed.). *Miscellaneous State Papers from 1501 to 1726*. 2 vols. London, 1778.

Harington, John. *Nugae Antique*. 2 vols. London, 1804.

The Harleian Miscellany: A Collection of Scarce, Curious, and Entertaining Pamphlets and Tracts, as Well in Manuscript as in Print. Ed. William Oldys. 10 vols. London, 1808–13.

Harrison, G.B. (ed.). *King James the First Daemonologie (1597) [and] Newes From Scotland*. New York, 1966.

Hebel, J. William (ed.). *The Works of Michael Drayton*. 5 vols. Oxford, 1961.

Henderson, Katherine Usher and Barbara F. McManus (eds). *Half Humankind: Contexts and Texts of the Controversy about Women in England, 1540–1640*. Urbana, IL, 1985.

Hic Mulier: or, The Man-Woman. N.p., 1620.

Hippeau, M.C. (ed.). *Mémoires Inédits du Comte Leveneur de Tillières*. Paris, 1862.

Historical Manuscripts Commission. *Report on the Manuscripts of the Marquess of Downshire Preserved at Easthampstead Park Berks*. Vol. 4. London, 1940.

——. *Salisbury MSS*. Vol. 3. London, 1889.

——. *Supplementary Report on the Manuscripts of the Earl of Mar & Kellie*. London, 1930.

Howell, T.B. (ed.). *Cobbett's Complete Collection of State Trials*. 33 vols. London, 1809–26.

Hunter, William B. (ed.). *The Complete Poetry of Ben Jonson*. New York, 1968.

Hutchinson, Lucy. *Memoirs of the Life of Colonel Hutchinson*. Ed. James Sutherland. London, 1973.

James VI & I. *Daemonologie, In Forme of a Dialogue, Divided into Three Bookes*. Edinburgh, 1597.

——. *The Essayes of a Prentise, in the Divine Art of Poesie*. Edinburgh, 1585.

——. *A Meditation Upon the Lords Prayer, Written by the Kings Majestie, For the benefit of all his subjects, especially of such as follow the Court*. London, 1619.

Jansson, Maija (ed.). *Proceedings in Parliament 1614 (House of Commons)*. Philadelphia, PA, 1988.

Johnson, Robert C., Maija Jansson Cole, Mary Frear Keeler, and William B. Bidwell (eds). *Commons Debates 1628*. 6 vols. New Haven, CT, 1977.

Jonson, Ben. *Sejanus His Fall*. Ed. Philip J. Ayres. Manchester, 1990.

Journals of the House of Commons. 81 vols. London, 1742–1826.

Journals of the House of Lords. 31 vols. London, 1767–77.

Kenyon, J.P. (ed.). *The Stuart Constitution 1603–1688: Documents and Commentary*. 2nd edn. Cambridge, 1986.

Leighton, Alexander. *Speculum belli sacri; or the looking-glasse of the holy war*. N.p., 1624.

Matthieu, Pierre. *The Powerful Favorite, Or, The Life of Aelius Sejanus*. Paris, 1628.

McClure, Norman E. (ed.). *The Letters and Epigrams of Sir John Harington*. Philadelphia, 1930; reprint New York, 1977.

—— (ed.). *The Letters of John Chamberlain*. 2 vols. Philadelphia, 1939; reprint Westport, CT, 1979.

McCormick, Ian (ed.). *Secret Sexualities: A Sourcebook of 17th and 18th Century Writing*. London, 1997.

McIlwain, C.H. (ed.). *The Political Works of James I*. New York, 1965.

Melville, Sir James. *Memoirs of His Own Life*. London, 1922.

Middleton, Thomas and William Rowley. *A Courtly Masque: The Device Called the World Tost at Tennis, As it hath beene divers times Presented to the Contentment of many Noble and Worthy Spectators, By the Prince his Servants*. London, 1620.

Middleton, Thomas. *A Game at Chess*. Ed. J.W. Harper. New York, 1966.

[Middleton, Thomas.] *The Peace-Maker: or Great Brittaines Blessing*. London, 1618.

Moysie, David. *Memoirs of the Affairs of Scotland*. Edinburgh, 1830.

Muld Sacke: or The Apologie of Hic Mulier. London, 1620.

Naunton, Sir Robert. *Fragmenta Regalia or Observations on Queen Elizabeth, Her Times and Favorites*. Ed. John S. Cerovski. London, 1985.

Newcastle, William Cavendish, Earl of. *The Country Captaine and The Variety, Two Comedies*. London, 1649.

Nichols, John. *The Progresses, Processions, and Magnificent Festivities of King James the First*. 4 vols. London, 1828.

Nichols, Philip. *Sir Francis Drake Revived: Calling Upon this Dull or Effeminate Age to Followe His Noble Steps for Golde and Silver*. London, 1626.

Notestein, Wallace, Frances Helen Relf, and Hartley Simpson (eds). *Commons Debates 1621*. 7 vols. New Haven, 1935.

Osborne, Francis. *Traditional Memorials on the Reign of King James*. In *The Works of Francis Osborn*, 467–547. 7th edition. London, 1673.

Park, Thomas (ed.). *Nugae Antiquae*. 2 vols. London, 1804.

Peyton, Edward. *The Divine Catastrophe of the Kingly Family of the House of Stuarts*. In *Secret History of the Court of James the First*, ed. Sir Walter Scott, II, 301–466. 2 vols. Edinburgh, 1811.

Pitcairn, Robert (ed.). *The Autobiography and Diary of Mr James Melvill*. Edinburgh, 1842.

Prynne, William. *Histriomastix*. London, 1633; facsimile reprint, New York, 1974.

Raumer, Frederick von. *History of the Sixteenth and Seventeenth Centuries, Illustrated by Original Sources*. Trans. [H.E. Lloyd]. 2 vols. London, 1835.

——. *Briefe aus Paris zur Erlauterung der Geschichte des sechzehnten und siebzehnten Jahrhunderts*. 2 vols. Leipzig, 1831.

[Reynolds, John]. *Votivae Angliae: or the desires and wishes of England to perswade his majestie to drawe his sword for the restoring of the Pallatynate to prince Fredericke*. Utrecht, 1624.

[Reynolds, John]. *Vox Coeli, or Newes from Heaven*. Elisium [Utrecht?], 1624.

Rich, Barnaby. *The Irish Hubbub, or the English Hue and Crie*. London, 1618.

——. *Opinion Diefied, discovering the ingins, traps, and traynes that are set to catch opinion*. London, 1613.

Rye, William Brenchley (ed.). *England as Seen by Foreigners*. London, 1865.

Sanderson, William. *Aulicus Coquinariae*. In *Secret History of the Court of James the First*, ed. Sir Walter Scott, II, 91–300. 2 vols. Edinburgh, 1811.

Scioppius [Schoppe], G. *Corona Regia*. N.p., 1615.

Scott, Thomas. *The Belgick Souldier: Dedicated to the Parliament. Or, Warre was a Blessing*. Dort, 1624.

——. *The Belgicke Pismire: Stinging the slothfull Sleeper, and Awaking the Diligent to Fast, Watch, Pray; and Worke out Theire Owne Temporall and Eternall Salvation with Feare and Trembling*. London, 1622.

———. *The Projector. Teaching A Direct, Sure, and ready way to restore the decayes of the Church and State both in Honour and Revenue.* London, 1623.

[Scott, Thomas]. *Robert, Earl of Essex His Ghost Sent from Elizian, to the Nobility, Gentry, and Communaltie of England.* Paradise [London], 1624.

———. *The Second Part of Vox Populi: Or Gondomar Appearing in the Likenes of Matchiavell in a Spanish Parliament.* Goricom [London], 1624.

[Scott, Thomas]. *Sir Walter Rawleighs Ghost or Englands Forewarner.* Utrecht, 1626.

———. *Symmachia: Or, A True-Loves Knot Tyed Betwixt Great Britaine and the United Provinces by the Wisedome of King James.* Utrecht, 1624.

———. *A Tongue-Combate.* N.p., 1623.

———. *Vox Dei.* N.p., 1624.

———. *Vox Populi, Or Newes from Spayne.* [London], 1620.

———. *Vox Regis.* Utrecht, 1624.

———. *The Workes of the Most Famous and Reverend Divine Mr. Thomas Scot, Batcheler in Divinitie.* Utrecht, 1624.

Scott, Sir Walter (ed.). *Secret History of the Court of James the First.* 2 vols. Edinburgh, 1811.

Smith, Logan Pearsall (ed.). *The Life and Letters of Sir Henry Wotton.* 2 vols. Oxford, 1966.

Smith, Nowell (ed.). *Sir Fulke Greville's Life of Sir Philip Sidney.* Oxford, 1907.

Smith, W.J. (ed.). *Herbert Correspondence: The Sixteenth and Seventeenth Century Letters of the Herberts of Chirbury, Powis Castle and Dolguog, formerly at Powis Castle in Montgomeryshire.* 2 vols. Cardiff, 1963.

Sommerville, Johann P. (ed.). *King James VI and I: Political Writings.* Cambridge, 1994.

Stubbes, Phillip. *The Anatomie of Abuses.* London, 1583; facsimile reprint New York, 1972.

Tanner, J.R. (ed.). *Constitutional Documents of the Reign of James I.* Cambridge, 1960.

Teulet, Alexandre (ed.). *Relations Politiques de la France et de L'Espagne avec L'Ecosse au XVI Siècle.* Vol. 4. Paris, 1862.

Thompson, Christopher (ed.). *Sir Nathaniel Rich's Diary of Proceedings in the House of Commons in 1624.* Wivenhoe, Essex, 1985.

Tisdale, Robert. *Pax Vobis, or, Wits Changes: Tuned in a Latine Hexameter of Peace.* London, 1623.

Tom Tell Troath: Or, A free discourse touching the manners of the Tyme. Directed to his Majestie by way of humble Advertisement. [London?], 1630.

Waller, A.R. (ed.). *The Works of Beaumont and Fletcher.* 10 vols. Cambridge, 1912.

Weldon, Sir Anthony. *The Court and Character of King James.* London, 1651.

———. *A Perfect Description of the People and Country of Scotland.* In *Secret History of the Court of James the First,* ed. Sir Walter Scott, II, 75–89. 2 vols. Edinburgh, 1811.

Westcott, Allen F. (ed.). *New Poems By James I of England.* New York, 1911.

Wilson, Arthur. *The History of Great Britain, Being the Life and Reign of King James The First.* London, 1653.

Wither, George. *Abuses Stript and Whipt.* London, 1613.

———. *Wither's Motto.* London, 1621.

Wotton, Sir Henry. 'A Short View of the Life and Death of George Villiers, Duke of Buckingham.' In *The Harleian Miscellany*, ed. William Oldys, VIII, 613–24. 10 vols. London, 1808–13.

Secondary sources

Adams, Simon. 'Foreign Policy and the Parliaments of 1621 and 1624.' In *Faction and Parliament: Essays on Early Stuart History*, ed. Kevin Sharpe, 139–72. Oxford, 1978.

——. 'Spain or the Netherlands? Dilemmas of Early Stuart Foreign Policy.' In *Before the English Civil War: Essays in Early Stuart Politics and Government*, ed. Howard Tomlinson, 79–102. London, 1983.

Aers, David. 'A Whisper in the Ear of Early Modernists; or, Reflections on Literary Critics Writing the "History of the Subject".' In *Culture and History 1350–1600: Essays on English Communities, Identities and Writing*, ed. David Aers, 177–202. Detroit, MI, 1992.

Akrigg, G.P.V. *Jacobean Pageant or the Court of King James I*. New York, 1967.

Amussen, Susan Dwyer. '"The Part of a Christian Man": the Cultural Politics of Manhood in Early Modern England.' In *Political Culture and Cultural Politics in Early Modern England*, ed. Susan D. Amussen and Mark A. Kishlansky, 213–33. Manchester, 1995.

——. '*The Peacemaker*: A Critical Introduction.' In *The Complete Works of Thomas Middleton*, ed. Gary Taylor. Oxford, forthcoming.

Arbuckle, William. 'The "Gowrie Conspiracy" – Part I' and 'The "Gowrie Conspiracy"—Part II.' *Scottish Historical Review*, 36 (April and October 1957), 1–24, 89–110.

Ashley, Maurice. *The House of Stuart: Its Rise and Fall*. London, 1980.

Barbé, Louis A. *The Tragedy of Gowrie House: An Historical Study*. London, 1887.

Baron, Sabrina A. 'From Manuscript to Print: Recycling Political Rhetoric in Seventeenth-Century England.' *Gutenberg Yearbook* (1997), 1–7.

Barroll, Leeds. 'The Court of the First Stuart Queen.' In *The Mental World of the Jacobean Court*, ed. Linda Levy Peck, 191–208. Cambridge, 1991.

Barton, Anne. *Ben Jonson, Dramatist*. Cambridge, 1984.

Beasley, A.W. 'The Disability of James VI & I.' *The Seventeenth Century*, 10, no. 2 (1995), 151–62.

Bellany, Alastair. '"Raylinge Rymes and Vaunting Verse": Libellous Politics in Early Stuart England, 1603–1628.' In *Culture and Politics in Early Stuart England*, ed. Kevin Sharpe and Peter Lake, 285–310. Stanford, CA, 1993.

——. 'Mistress Turner's Deadly Sins: Sartorial Transgression, Court Scandal, and Politics in Early Stuart England.' *Huntington Library Quarterly*, 58, no. 2 (1996), 179–210.

Bentley, Gerald Eades. *The Jacobean and Caroline Stage: Plays and Playwrights*. 7 vols. Oxford, 1956.

Berdan, John M. 'Marlowe's *Edward II*.' *Philological Quarterly*, 3 (1924), 197–207.

Bergeron, David M. 'Francis Bacon's *Henry VII*: Commentary on King James I.' *Albion*, 24 (Spring 1992), 17–26.

——. *King James and Letters of Homoerotic Desire*. Iowa City, 1999.

——. 'Masculine Interpretation of Queen Anne, Wife of James, I'. *Biography*, 18, no. 1 (1995), 42–54.

——. *Royal Family, Royal Lovers: King James of England and Scotland*. Columbia, MO, 1991.

——. *Shakespeare's Romances and the Royal Family*. Lawrence, KS, 1985.

Bingham, Caroline. *James I of England*. London, 1981.

——. *The Making of a King: The Early Years of James VI and I*. London, 1968.

——. 'Seventeenth-Century Attitudes Toward Deviant Sex.' *Journal of Interdisciplinary History*, 1, no. 3 (Spring 1971), 447–68.

Boswell, John. *Christianity, Social Tolerance, and Homosexuality: Gay People in Western Europe from the Beginning of the Christian Era to the Fourteenth Century*. Chicago, 1980.

Bowen, Catherine Drinker. *The Lion and the Throne: The Life and Times of Sir Edward Coke*. Boston, 1957.

Brady, Jennifer. 'Fear and Loathing in Marlowe's *Edward II*.' In *Sexuality and Politics in Renaissance Drama*, ed. Carol Levin and Karen Robertson, 175–91. Lewiston, NY, 1991.

Brautigam, Dwight D. 'The Court and the Country Revisited.' In *Court, Country and Culture: Essays on Early Modern British History in Honor of Perez Zagorin*, ed. Bonnelyn Young Kunze and Dwight D. Brautigam, 55–64. Rochester, 1992.

Bray, Alan. *Homosexuality in Renaissance England*. London, 1982; 2nd edn, New York, 1995.

——. 'Homosexuality and the Signs of Male Friendship in Elizabethan England.' *History Workshop Journal*, issue 29 (Spring 1990), 1–19.

Bredbeck, Gregory W. *Sodomy and Interpretation: Marlowe to Milton*. Ithaca, NY, 1991.

——. 'Tradition and the Individual Sodomite: Barnfield, Shakespeare, and Subjective Desire.' In *Homosexuality in Renaissance and Enlightenment England: Literary Representations in Historical Context*, ed. Claude Summers, 41–68. New York, 1992.

Bromham, A.A. and Zara Bruzzi. *The Changeling and the Years of Crisis, 1619–1624: A Hieroglyph of Britain*. London, 1990.

Brown, Jennifer M. 'Scottish Politics 1567–1625.' In *The Reign of James VI and I*, ed. Alan G.R. Smith, 22–39. London, 1973.

Brown, Keith M. *Kingdom or Province? Scotland and the Regal Union, 1603–1715*. New York, 1992.

Burg, B.R. 'Ho Hum, Another Work of the Devil: Buggery and Sodomy in Early Stuart England.' In *The Gay Past: A Collection of Historical Essays*, ed. Salvatore J. Licata and Robert P. Peterson, 69–78. New York, 1985.

Burgess, Glenn. *Absolute Monarchy and the Stuart Constitution*. New Haven, 1996.

——. *The Politics of the Ancient Constitution*. University Park, PA, 1993.

Burns, J.H. *The True Law of Kingship: Concepts of Monarchy in Early Modern Scotland*. Oxford, 1996.

Bushnell, Rebecca W. *Tragedies of Tyrants: Political Thought and Theater in the English Renaissance*. Ithaca, NY, 1990.

Butler, Martin. 'Ben Jonson and the Limits of Courtly Panegyric.' In *Culture and Politics in Early Stuart England*, ed. Kevin Sharpe and Peter Lake, 91–115. Stanford, CA, 1993.

Butters, Ronald R. and others (eds). *Displacing Homophobia: Gay Male Perspectives in Literature and Culture*. Durham, NC, 1989.

Cady, Joseph. 'The "Masculine Love" of the "Princes of Sodom" "Practicing the Art of Ganymede" at Henri III's Court: The Homosexuality of Henry III and His *Mignons* in Pierre de L'Estoile's *Mémoires-Journaux.*' In *Desire and Discipline: Sex and Sexuality in the Premodern West*, ed. Jacqueline Murray and Konrad Eisenbichler, 123–54. Toronto, 1996.

——. '"Masculine Love", Renaissance Writing, and the "New Invention" of Homosexuality.' In *Homosexuality in Renaissance and Enlightenment England: Literary Representations in Historical Context*, ed. Claude J. Summers, 9–40. New York, 1992.

——. 'Renaissance Awareness and Language for Heterosexuality: "Love" and "Feminine Love".' In *Renaissance Discourses of Desire*, ed. Claude J. Summers and Ted-Larry Pebworth, 143–58. Columbia, MO, 1993.

Cameron, Keith. *Henry III: A Maligned or Malignant King?*. Exeter, 1978.

Carlton, Charles. *Charles I: The Personal Monarch*. 2nd edn. London, 1995.

Clark, Sandra. '*Hic Mulier, Haec Vir*, and the Controversy over Masculine Women.' *Studies in Philology*, 82 (Spring 1985), 157–83.

Clark, Stuart. 'King James's *Daemonologie*: Witchcraft and Kingship.' In *The Damned Art: Essays in the Literature of Witchcraft*, ed. Sydney Anglo, 156–81. London, 1977.

Cogswell, Thomas. *The Blessed Revolution: English Politics and the Coming of War, 1621–1624.* Cambridge, 1989.

——. 'England and the Spanish Match.' In *Conflict in Early Stuart England: Studies in Religion and Politics 1603–1642*, ed. Richard Cust and Ann Hughes, 107–33. London, 1989.

——. 'Thomas Middleton and the Court, 1624: *A Game at Chess* in Context.' *Huntington Library Quarterly*, 47 (1984), 273–88.

——. 'Underground Verse and the Transformation of Early Stuart Political Culture.' In *Political Culture and Cultural Politics in Early Modern England: Essays Presented to David Underdown*, ed. Susan D. Amussen and Mark Kishlansky, 277–300. Manchester, 1995.

Collier, Susanne. 'Recent Studies in James VI and I.' *English Literary Renaissance*, 23, no. 3 (1993), 509–19.

Collins, Stephen L. *From Divine Cosmos to Sovereign State: An Intellectual History of Consciousness and the Idea of Order in Renaissance England*. Oxford, 1989.

Collinson, Patrick. 'The Jacobean Religious Settlement: The Hampton Court Conference.' In *Before the English Civil War: Essays on Early Stuart Politics and Government*, ed. Howard Tomlinson, 27–52. London, 1983.

Cressy, David. 'Gender Trouble and Cross-Dressing in Early Modern England.' *Journal of British Studies*, 35 (October 1996), 438–65.

Croft, Pauline. 'Libels, Popular Literacy and Public Opinion in Early Modern England.' *Historical Research*, 68 (October 1995), 266–85.

——. 'The Reputation of Robert Cecil: Libels, Political Opinion and Popular Awareness in the Early Seventeenth Century.' *Transactions of the Royal Historical Society*, sixth series, 1 (London, 1991), 43–69.

Cuddy, Neil. 'Anglo-Scottish Union and the Court of James I, 1603–1625.' *Transactions of the Royal Historical Society*, fifth series, 39 (London, 1989), 107–24.

——. 'The Conflicting Loyalties of a "vulger counselor": The Third Earl of Southampton, 1597–1624.' In *Public Duty and Private Conscience in*

Seventeenth-Century England, ed. John Morrill, Paul Slack, and Daniel Woolf, 121–50. Oxford, 1993.

——. 'The Revival of the Entourage: the Bedchamber of James I, 1603–1625.' In *The English Court from the Wars of the Roses to the Civil War,* ed. David Starkey, 173–225. London, 1987.

Cust, Richard. *The Forced Loan and English Politics 1626–1628.* Oxford, 1987.

——. 'News and Politics in Early Seventeenth-Century England.' *Past and Present,* 112 (1986), 60–90.

Davenport-Hines, Richard. *Sex, Death and Punishment: Attitudes to Sex and Sexuality in Britain since the Renaissance.* London, 1990.

Digangi, Mario. *The Homoerotics of Early Modern Drama.* Cambridge, 1997.

Donald, Peter. *An Uncounselled King: Charles I and the Scottish Troubles, 1637–1641.* Cambridge, 1990.

Donaldson, Gordon. *Scotland: James V to James VII.* Edinburgh, 1971.

Duberman, Martin and others (eds). *Hidden from History: Reclaiming the Gay and Lesbian Past.* New York, 1989.

Duberman, Martin (ed.). *A Queer World: The Center for Lesbian and Gay Studies Reader.* New York, 1997.

Dunlap, Rhodes. 'James I, Bacon, Middleton, and the Making of the Peace Maker.' In *Studies in the English Renaissance Drama,* ed. Josephine W. Bennett and others, 82–94. New York, 1959.

Durston, Christopher. *James I.* London, 1993.

Elton, G.R. 'A High Road to Civil War?' In *Studies in Tudor and Stuart Politics and Government: Papers and Reviews 1946–1972,* 164–82. Cambridge, 1974.

Fincham, Kenneth (ed.). *The Early Stuart Church.* Stanford, CA, 1993.

Fincham, Kenneth and Peter Lake, 'The Ecclesiastical Policy of King James I.' *Journal of British Studies,* 24 (1985), 169–207.

Fincham, Kenneth. *Prelate as Pastor: The Episcopate of James I.* Oxford, 1990.

Finkelpearl, Philip J. '"The Comedians' Liberty": Censorship of the Jacobean Stage Reconsidered.' *English Literary Renaissance,* 16 (Winter 1986), 123–38.

——. *Court and Country Politics in the Plays of Beaumont and Fletcher.* Princeton, 1990.

Fletcher, Anthony. *Gender, Sex & Subordination in England 1500–1800.* New Haven, 1995.

Fraser, Lady Antonia. *King James.* London, 1974.

Galloway, B. *The Union of England and Scotland 1603–1608.* Edinburgh, 1986.

Garber, Marjorie. *Vested Interests: Cross-Dressing and Cultural Anxiety.* New York, 1992.

Gardiner, S.R. *History of England from the Accession of James I to the Outbreak of the Civil War 1603–1642.* 10 vols. London, 1883–84, 1894–96.

Gerard, Kent and Gert Hekma (eds). *The Pursuit of Sodomy: Male Homosexuality in Renaissance and Enlightenment Europe.* New York, 1989.

Girouard, Mark. *The Return to Camelot: Chivalry and the English Gentleman.* New Haven, CT, 1981.

Goldberg, Jonathan. *James I and the Politics of Literature: Jonson, Shakespeare, Donne, and Their Contemporaries.* London, 1983.

——. *Sodometries: Renaissance Texts, Modern Sexualities.* Stanford, CA, 1992.

Goldberg, Jonathan. 'Sodomy and Society: The Case of Christopher Marlowe.' In *Staging the Renaissance: Reinterpretations of Elizabethan and Jacobean Drama*, ed. David Scott Kastan and Peter Stallybrass, 75–82. New York, 1991.

Greg, W.W. *A Companion to Arber.* Oxford, 1967.

Hale, J.R. 'Incitement to Violence? English Divines on the Theme of War, 1578 to 1631.' In *Renaissance War Studies*, 487–517. London, 1983.

Halperin, David M. *One Hundred Years of Homosexuality and Other Essays on Greek Love.* New York, 1990.

Hammond, Gerald. *Fleeting Things: English Poets and Poems 1616–1660.* Cambridge, MA, 1990.

Hannay, Margaret P. *Philip's Phoenix: Mary Sidney, Countess of Pembroke.* New York, 1990.

Hanson, Ellis. 'Sodomy and Kingcraft in *Urania* and *Antony and Cleopatra*.' In *Homosexuality in Renaissance and Enlightenment England: Literary Representations in Historical Context*, ed. Claude J. Summers, 135–51. New York, 1992.

Hardin, Richard F. *Michael Drayton and the Passing of Elizabethan England.* Lawrence, KS, 1973.

Heinemann, Margot. 'Drama and Opinion in the 1620s: Middleton and Massinger.' In *Theatre and Government Under the Early Stuarts*, ed. J.R. Mulryne and Margaret Shewring, 237–65. Cambridge, 1993.

——. *Puritanism and Theatre: Thomas Middleton and Opposition Drama under the Early Stuarts.* Cambridge, 1980.

Herdt, Gilbert (ed.). *Third Sex, Third Gender: Beyond Sexual Dimorphism in Culture and History.* New York, 1994.

Herrup, Cynthia. 'The Patriarch at Home: The Trial of the Second Earl of Castlehaven for Rape and Sodomy.' *History Workshop Journal*, issue 41 (Spring 1996), 1–18.

——. '"To Pluck Bright Honour from the Pale-faced Moon": Gender and Honour in the Castlehaven Story.' *Transactions of the Royal Historical Society*, 6th series, vol. 6 (1996), 137–59.

Hexter, J.H. 'The Apology.' In *For Veronica Wedgwood These: Studies in Seventeenth-Century History*, ed. Richard Ollard and Pamela Tudor-Craig, 13–44. London, 1986.

Hill, Christopher. *Milton and the English Revolution.* Harmondsworth, 1979.

Hirst, Derek. 'Court, Country, and Politics before 1629.' In *Faction and Parliament: Essays on Early Stuart History*, ed. Kevin Sharpe, 105–38. Oxford, 1978.

Hitchcock, Tim. *English Sexualities, 1700–1800.* London, 1997.

Hogrefe, Pearl. *Tudor Women: Commoners and Queens.* Ames, IA, 1975.

Holstun, James. '"God Bless Thee, Little David!": John Felton and his Allies.' *ELH*, 59 (1992), 513–52.

Houston, S.J. *James I.* 2nd edn. London, 1995.

Howard, Jean. 'Crossdressing, The Theatre, and Gender Struggle in Early Modern England.' *Shakespeare Quarterly*, 3, no. 3 (Winter 1988), 418–40.

——. *The Stage and Social Struggle in Early Modern England.* London, 1994.

Hunt, Lynn (ed.). *The Invention of Pornography: Obscenity and the Origins of Modernity, 1500–1800.* New York, 1993.

Hunt, William. 'Spectral Origins of the English Revolution: Legitimation Crisis in Early Stuart England.' In *Reviving the English Revolution: Reflections and*

Elaborations on the Work of Christopher Hill, ed. Geoff Eley and William Hunt, 305–32. London, 1988.

James, Mervyn. *Society, Politics and Culture: Studies in Early Modern England*. Cambridge, 1986.

Jardine, Lisa. 'Boy Actors, Female Roles, and Elizabethan Eroticism.' In *Staging the Renaissance: Reinterpretations of Elizabethan and Jacobean Drama*, ed. David Scott Kastan and Peter Stallybrass, 57–67. New York, 1991.

Jordan, Mark D. *The Invention of Sodomy in Christian Theology*. Chicago, 1997.

Kamps, Ivo. *Historiography and Ideology in Stuart Drama*. Cambridge, 1997.

Kempter, Gerda. *Ganymed: Studien zur Typologie, Ikonographie und Ikonologie*. Cologne, 1980.

Kimmel, Michael S. (ed.). *Love Letters Between a Certain Late Nobleman and the Famous Mr. Wilson*. New York, 1990.

Kunze, Bonnelyn Young and Dwight D. Brautigam (eds). *Court, Country and Culture: Essays on Early Modern British History in Honor of Perez Zagorin*. Rochester, NY, 1992.

Lake, Peter. 'Constitutional Consensus and Puritan Opposition in the 1620s: Thomas Scott and the Spanish Match.' *Historical Journal*, 25, no. 4 (1982), 805–25.

Larner, Christina. 'James VI and I and Witchcraft.' In *The Reign of James VI and I*, ed. Alan G.R. Smith, 74–90. London, 1973.

Lee, Maurice, Jr. 'James I and the Historians: Not a Bad King After All?' *Albion*, 16 (Summer 1984), 157–63.

——. *Government by Pen: Scotland under James VI and I*. London, 1980.

——. *Great Britain's Solomon: James VI and I in His Three Kingdoms*. Urbana, IL, 1990.

——. *James I and Henry IV: An Essay in English Foreign Policy 1603–1610*. Urbana, IL, 1970.

Levack, Brian. *The Formation of the British State: England, Scotland, and the Union 1603–1707*. Oxford, 1987.

Levin, Carole. *The Heart and Stomach of a King: Elizabeth I and the Politics of Sex and Power*. Philadelphia, PA, 1994.

Levine, Laura. 'Men in Women's Clothing: Anti-Theatricality and Effeminization from 1579 to 1642.' *Criticism*, 28, no. 2 (Spring 1986), 121–44.

——. *Men in Women's Clothing: Anti-Theatricality and Effeminization 1579–1642*. Cambridge, 1994.

Lewalski, Barbara Kiefer, 'Anne of Denmark and the Subversions of Masquing.' *Criticism*, 35 (Summer 1993), 341–55.

——. 'Elizabeth, Lady Falkland, and the Authorship of *Edward II*.' In *Writing Women in Jacobean England*, 317–20. Cambridge, MA, 1993.

——. 'Enacting Opposition: Queen Anne and the Subversions of Masquing.' In *Writing Women in Jacobean England*, 15–43. Cambridge, MA, 1993.

——. *Writing Women in Jacobean England*. Cambridge, MA, 1993.

Limon, Jerzy. *Dangerous Matter: English Drama and Politics in 1623/4*. Cambridge, 1986.

Lindley, David. *The Trials of Frances Howard: Fact and Fiction at the Court of King James*. London, 1993.

Lindquist, Eric. 'The Failure of the Great Contract.' *Journal of Modern History*, 57 (December 1985), 617–51.

Lockyer, Roger. *Buckingham: The Life and Political Career of George Villiers, First Duke of Buckingham 1592–1628*. London, 1981.

——. 'An English Valido? Buckingham and James I.' In *For Veronica Wedgwood These: Studies in Seventeenth-Century History*, ed. Richard Ollard and Pamela Tudor-Craig, 45–58. London, 1986.

——. *James VI and I*. Longman, 1998.

Lowe, Ben. 'Religious Wars and the "Common Peace": Anglican Anti-War Sentiment in Elizabethan England.' *Albion*, 28, no. 3 (Fall 1996), 415–35.

Maccubin, Robert Purks (ed.). *'Tis Nature's Fault: Unauthorized Sexuality During the Enlightenment*. Cambridge, 1987.

Macdougall, Norman. *James III: A Political Study*. Edinburgh, 1982.

MacInnes, Allan. *Charles I and the Making of the Covenanting Movement, 1625–1641*. Edinburgh, 1991.

Marcus, Leah S. 'Politics and Pastoral: Writing the Court on the Countryside.' In *Culture and Politics in Early Stuart England*, ed. Kevin Sharpe and Peter Lake, 139–59. Stanford, 1993.

Marwil, Jonathan. *The Trials of Counsel: Francis Bacon in 1621*. Detroit, MI, 1976.

Marx, Steven. 'Shakespeare's Pacifism.' *Renaissance Quarterly*, 45 (Spring 1992), 49–95.

Mathews, Nieves. *Francis Bacon: The History of a Character Assassination*. New Haven, CT, 1996.

Maxwell-Stuart, P.G. 'The Fear of the King is Death: James VI and the Witches of East Lothian.' In *Fear in Early Modern Society*, ed. William G. Naphy and Penny Roberts, 209–25. Manchester, 1997.

McCoy, Richard C. 'Old English Honour in an Evil Time: Aristocratic Principle in the 1620s.' In *The Stuart Court and Europe: Essays in Politics and Culture*, ed. R. Malcolm Smuts, 133–55. Cambridge, 1996.

McCullough, Peter E. *Sermons at Court: Politics and Religion in Elizabethan and Jacobean Preaching*. Cambridge, 1998.

McMullan, Gordon. *The Politics of Unease in the Plays of John Fletcher*. Amherst, MA, 1994.

Miller, Carl. *Stages of Desire: Gay Theatre's Hidden History*. London, 1996.

Mitchison, Rosalind. *Lordship to Patronage: Scotland 1603–1745*. London, 1983.

Moir, Thomas L. *The Addled Parliament of 1614*. Oxford, 1958.

Mosse, George L. *Nationalism and Sexuality: Respectability and Abnormal Sexuality in Modern Europe*. New York, 1985.

Munden, R.C. 'James I and "the growth of mutual distrust": King, Commons, and Reform, 1603–1604.' In *Faction and Parliament: Essays on Early Stuart History*, ed. Kevin Sharpe, 43–72. Oxford, 1978.

Murray, Jacqueline and Konrad Eisenbichler (eds). *Desire and Discipline: Sex and Sexuality in the Premodern West*. Toronto, 1996.

Murray, Stephen O. 'Homosexual Acts and Selves in Early Moden Europe.' In *The Pursuit of Sodomy: Male Homosexuality in Renaissance and Enlightenment Europe*, ed. Kent Gerard and Gert Hekma, 457–78. New York, 1989.

Norton, Rictor. *The Myth of the Modern Homosexual: Queer History and the Search for Cultural Unity*. London, 1997.

Ollard, Richard and Pamela Tudor-Craig (eds). *For Veronica Wedgwood These: Studies in Seventeenth-Century History*. London, 1986.

Orgel, Stephen. 'Nobody's Perfect: Or Why Did the English Stage Take Boys for Women?' In *Displacing Homophobia: Gay Male Perspectives in Literature and Culture*, ed. Ronald R. Butters and others, 7–29. Durham, NC, 1989.

——. *The Illusion of Power: Political Theatre in the English Renaissance*. Berkeley, CA, 1975.

——. *Impersonations: The Performance of Gender in Shakespeare's England*. Cambridge, 1996.

Patterson, Annabel. *Censorship and Interpretation: The Conditions of Writing and Reading in Early Modern England*. Madison, WI, 1984.

Patterson, W.B. *King James VI and I and the Reunion of Christendom*. Cambridge, 1997.

Pearl, V.L. and M.L. Pearl. 'Richard Corbett's "Against the Opposing of the Duke in Parliament, 1628" and the Anonymous Rejoinder, "An Answere to the Same, Lyne for Lyne": The Earliest Dated Manuscript Copies.' *Review of English Studies*, new series 42, no. 165 (February 1991), 32–9.

Peck, Linda Levy. *Court Patronage and Corruption in Early Stuart England*. London, 1990.

——. '"For a King not to be bountiful were a fault": Perspectives on Court Patronage in Early Stuart England.' *Journal of British Studies*, 25 (1986), 31–61.

—— (ed.). *The Mental World of the Jacobean Court*. Cambridge, 1991.

Peltonen, Markku. *Classical Humanism and Republicanism in English Political Thought 1570–1640*. Cambridge, 1995.

Porter, Joseph A. 'Marlowe, Shakespeare, and the Canonization of Heterosexuality.' In *Displacing Homophobia: Gay Male Perspectives in Literature and Culture*, ed. Ronald R. Butters and others, 127–48. Durham, NC, 1989.

Prestwich, Menna. *Cranfield: Politics and Profits under the Early Stuarts: the Career of Lionel Cranfield, Earl of Middlesex*. Oxford, 1966.

Randall, Dale B. *Jonson's Gypsies Unmasked*. Durham, NC, 1975.

Rebholz, Ronald. *The Life of Fulke Greville, First Lord Brooke*. Oxford, 1971.

Reeve, L.J. *Charles I and the Road to Personal Rule*. Cambridge, 1989.

Rocke, Michael. *Forbidden Friendships: Homosexuality and Male Culture in Renaissance Florence*. Oxford, 1996.

Rowse, A.L. *Homosexuals in History: A Study of Ambivalence in Society, Literature and the Arts*. New York, 1977.

Russell, Conrad. 'The British Problem and the English Civil War.' *History*, 72 (1987), 395–415.

——. *The Causes of the English Civil War*. Oxford, 1990.

——. *Unrevolutionary England, 1603–1642*. London, 1990.

——. 'Divine Rights in the Early Seventeenth Century.' In *Public Duty and Private Conscience in Seventeenth-Century England*, ed. John Morrill, Paul Slack and Daniel Woolf, 101–20. Oxford, 1993.

——. 'English Parliaments 1593–1606: One Epoch or Two?' In *The Parliaments of Elizabethan England*, ed. D.M. Dean and N.L. Jones, 191–213. Oxford, 1990.

——. *The Fall of the British Monarchies*. Oxford, 1991.

——. *Parliaments and English Politics 1621–1629*. Oxford, 1979.

Saslow, James M. 'Homosexuality in the Renaissance: Behavior, Identity, and Artistic Expression.' In *Hidden from History: Reclaiming the Gay and Lesbian Past*, ed. Martin Duberman and others, 90–105. New York, 1989.

——. *Ganymede in the Renaissance*. New Haven, 1986.

Salmon, J.H.M. 'Seneca and Tacitus in Jacobean England'. In *The Mental World of the Jacobean Court*, ed. Linda Levy Peck, 169–88. Cambridge, 1991.

Schellhase, Kenneth C. *Tacitus in Renaissance Political Thought*. Chicago, 1976.

Schleiner, Winfried. 'Sciopius' Pen against the English King's Sword: The Political Function of Ambiguity and Anonymity in Early Seventeenth-Century Literature.' *Renaissance and Reformation*, 26 (1990), 271–84.

——. '"That Matter Which Ought Not To Be Heard Of": Homophobic Slurs in Renaissance Cultural Politics.' *Journal of Homosexuality*, 26, no. 4 (1994), 62–5.

Schwarz, Marc L. 'James I and the Historians: Toward a Reconsideration.' *Journal of British Studies*, 13, no. 2 (May 1974), 114–34.

Sedgwick, Eve Kosofsky. *Between Men: English Literature and Male Homosexual Desire*. New York, 1985.

Sharpe, Kevin. *Criticism and Compliment: The Politics of Literature in the England of Charles I*. Cambridge, 1987.

——. 'Crown, Parliament and Locality: Government and Communication in Early Stuart England.' *English Historical Review*, 101 (April 1986), 321–50.

—— (ed.). *Faction and Parliament: Essays on Early Stuart History*. Oxford, 1978; 2nd edn, Oxford, 1985.

——. 'The Image of Virtue: the Court and Household of Charles I, 1625–42.' In *Politics and Ideas in Early Stuart England: Essays and Studies*, 147–73. London, 1989.

——. 'The Personal Rule of Charles I.' In *Politics and Ideas in Early Stuart England: Essays and Studies*, 101–22. London, 1989.

——. *The Personal Rule of Charles I*. New Haven, 1992.

——. *Politics and Ideas in Early Stuart England: Essays and Studies*. London, 1989.

——. 'Private Conscience and Public Duty in the Writings of James VI and I.' In *Public Duty and Private Conscience in Seventeenth-Century England*, ed. John Morrill, Paul Slack, and Daniel Woolf, 77–100. Oxford, 1993.

Shephard, Robert. 'Sexual Rumours in English Politics: The Cases of Elizabeth I and James I.' In *Desire and Discipline: Sex and Sexuality in the Premodern West*, ed. Jacqueline Murray and Konrad Eisenbichler, 101–22. Toronto, 1996.

Shepherd, Simon. *Amazons and Warrior Women: Varieties of Feminism in Seventeenth-Century Drama*. New York, 1981.

——. 'What's So Funny About Ladies' Tailors? A Survey of Some Male (Homo)sexual Types in the Renaissance.' *Textual Practice*, 6 (1992), 17–30.

Sinfield, Alan. *The Wilde Century: Effeminacy, Oscar Wilde and the Queer Moment*. New York, 1994.

Smith, Alan G.R. *The Reign of James VI and I*. London, 1973.

Smith, Bruce R. *Homosexual Desire in Shakespeare's England: A Cultural Poetics*. Chicago, 1991.

Smith, Logan Pearsall (ed.). *The Life and Letters of Sir Henry Wotton*. Oxford, 1966.

Smuts, R. Malcolm. *Court Culture and the Origins of a Royalist Tradition in Early Stuart England*. Philadelphia, 1987.

——. 'Cultural Diversity and Cultural Change at the Court of James I.' In *The Mental World of the Jacobean Court*, ed. Linda Levy Peck, 99–112. Cambridge, 1991.

—— (ed.). *The Stuart Court and Europe: Essays in Politics and Culture*. Cambridge, 1996.

Snow, Vernon F. *Essex the Rebel: The Life of Robert Devereux, the Third Earl of Essex 1591–1646*. Lincoln, NE, 1970.

Sommerville, J. P. 'James I and the Divine Right of Kings.' In *The Mental World of the Jacobean Court*, ed. Linda Levy Peck, 55–70. Cambridge, 1991.

——. *Politics and Ideology in England 1603–1640*. London, 1986.

Starkey, David (ed.). *The English Court from the Wars of the Roses to the Civil War*. London, 1987.

Stein, Edward (ed.). *Forms of Desire: Sexual Orientation and the Social Constructionist Controversy*. New York, 1990.

Stephen, Leslie and Sidney Lee (eds). *The Dictionary of National Biography*. 22 vols. Oxford, 1921–22.

Stone, Lawrence. *The Causes of the English Revolution 1529–1642*. New York, 1972.

——. *The Crisis of the Aristocracy 1558–1641*. Oxford, 1965.

——. *The Family, Sex and Marriage in England 1500–1800*. New York, 1977.

Strong, Roy. 'England and Italy: The Marriage of Henry Prince of Wales.' In *For Veronica Wedgwood These: Studies in Seventeenth-Century History*, ed. Richard Ollard and Pamela Tudor-Craig, 59–88. London, 1986.

——. *Henry, Prince of Wales and England's Lost Renaissance*. London, 1986.

——. *Van Dyck: Charles I on Horseback*. New York, 1972.

Tawney, R.H. *Business and Politics under James I: Lionel Cranfield as Merchant and Minister*. Cambridge, 1958.

Taylor, J.A. 'Two Unpublished Poems on the Duke of Buckingham.' *Review of English Studies*, new series 40, no. 158 (May 1989), 232–40.

Thomson, George Malcolm. *A Kind of Justice: Two Studies in Treason*. London, 1970.

Tite, Colin G.C. *Impeachment and Parliamentary Judicature in Early Stuart England*. London, 1974.

Tomlinson, Howard (ed.). *Before the English Civil War: Essays in Early Stuart Politics and Government*. London, 1983.

Tricomi, Albert H. *Anticourt Drama in England 1603–1642*. Charlottesville, VA, 1989.

Trumbach, Randolph. 'Are Modern Western Lesbian Women and Gay Men a Third Gender?' In *A Queer World: The Center for Lesbian and Gay Studies Reader*, ed. Martin Duberman, pp. 87–99. New York, 1997.

——. 'The Birth of the Queen: Sodomy and the Emergence of Gender Equality in Modern Culture, 1660–1750.' In *Hidden from History: Reclaiming the Gay and Lesbian Past*, ed. Martin Duberman and others, 129–40. New York, 1989.

——. 'Erotic Fantasy and Male Libertinism in Enlightenment England.' In *The Invention of Pornography: Obscenity and the Origins of Modernity, 1500–1800*, ed. Lynn Hunt, 253–82. New York, 1993.

——. 'London's Sapphists: From Three Sexes to Four Genders in the Making of Modern Culture.' In *Third Sex, Third Gender: Beyond Sexual Dimorphism in Culture and History*, ed. Gilbert Herdt, 111–36. New York, 1994.

——. 'London's Sodomites: Homosexual Behavior and Western Culture in the Eighteenth Century.' *Journal of Social History*, 11, no. 1 (Fall 1977), 1–33.

Trumbach, Randolph. *Sex and the Gender Revolution*. Vol. 1, *Heterosexuality and the Third Gender in Enlightenment London*. Chicago, 1998.

———. 'Sodomitical Assaults, Gender Role, and Sexual Development in Eighteenth-Century London.' In *The Pursuit of Sodomy: Male Homosexuality in Renaissance and Enlightenment Europe*, ed. Gilbert Herdt, 407–29. New York, 1989.

———. 'Sodomitical Subcultures, Sodomitical Roles, and the Gender Revolution of the Eighteenth Century: The Recent Historiography.' In *'Tis Nature's Fault: Unauthorized Sexuality During the Enlightenment*, ed. Robert Purks Maccubbin, 109–21. Cambridge, 1987.

———. 'Sodomy Transformed: Aristocratic Libertinage, Public Reputation and the Gender Revolution of the 18th Century.' In *Love Letters Between a Certain Late Nobleman and the Famous Mr. Wilson*, ed. Michael S. Kimmel, 105–24. New York, 1990.

Underdown, David. *A Freeborn People: Politics and the Nation in Seventeenth-Century England*. Oxford, 1996.

Weil, Rachel. 'Sometimes a Scepter is Only a Scepter: Pornography and Politics in Restoration England.' In *The Invention of Pornography: Obscenity and the Origins of Modernity, 1500–1800*, ed. Lynn Hunt, 125–53. New York, 1993.

Williams, Ethel Carleton. *Anne of Denmark: Wife of James VI of Scotland: James I of England*. London, 1970.

Williams, Gordon (ed.). *A Dictionary of Sexual Language and Imagery in Shakespearean and Stuart Literature*. 3 vols. London, 1994.

Williamson, Hugh Ross. *George Villiers, First Duke of Buckingham, Study for a Biography*. London, 1940.

Willson, David H. *King James VI and I*. New York, 1967.

Woodbridge, Linda. *Women and the English Renaissance: Literature and the Nature of Womankind, 1540–1620*. Urbana, IL, 1984.

Woolf, D.R. 'Two Elizabeths: James I and the Late Queen's Famous Memory.' *Canadian Journal of History*, 20 (August 1985), 167–91.

Worden, Blair. 'Milton and Marchamont Nedham.' In *Milton and Republicanism*, ed. David Armitage and others, 156–180. Cambridge, 1995.

———. '"Wit in a Roundhead": the Dilemma of Marchamont Nedham.' In *Political Culture and Cultural Politics in Early Modern England: Essays Presented to David Underdown*, ed. Susan D. Amussen and Mark Kishlansky, 301–37. Manchester, 1995.

Wormald, Jenny. *Court, Kirk, and Community: Scotland 1470–1625*. Toronto, 1981.

———. 'Ecclesiastical Vitriol: the Kirk, the Puritans and the Future King of England.' In *The Reign of Elizabeth I: Court and Culture in the Last Decade*, ed. John Guy, 171–91. Cambridge, 1995.

———. 'Gunpowder, Treason, and Scots.' *Journal of British Studies*, 24, no. 2 (April 1985), 141–68.

———. 'James VI and I, Basilikon Doron and the True Law of Free Monarchies: The Scottish Context and the English Translation.' In *The Mental World of the Jacobean Court*, ed. Linda Levy Peck, 36–54. Cambridge, 1991.

———. 'James VI and I: Two Kings or One?' *History*, 68 (June 1983), 187–209.

———. 'James VI, James I, and the Identity of Britain.' In *The British Problem, c. 1534–1707: State Formation in the Atlantic Archipelago*, ed. Brendan Bradshaw and John Morrill, 148–71. New York, 1996.

——. 'The Union of 1603.' In *Scots and Britons: Scottish Political Thought and the Union of 1603*, ed. Roger A. Mason, 17–40. Cambridge, 1994.

Wright, Louis B. 'Propaganda Against James I's "Appeasement" of Spain.' *The Huntington Library Quarterly*, 6, no. 2 (February 1943), 149–72.

Wynne-Davies, Marion. 'The Queen's Masque: Renaissance Women and the Seventeenth-Century Court Masque.' In *Gloriana's Face: Women, Public and Private, in the English Renaissance*, ed. S.P. Cerasno and Marion Wynne-Davies, 79–104. New York, 1992.

Young, Michael B. 'Buckingham, War, and Parliament: Revisionism Gone Too Far.' *Parliamentary History*, 4 (1985), 45–69.

——. 'Charles I and the Erosion of Trust, 1625–1628.' *Albion*, 22, no. 2 (Summer 1990), 217–35.

——. 'Why Did Prince Charles and the Duke of Buckingham Want War?' In *Selected Papers from the West Virginia Shakespeare and Renaissance Association*, 11 (Spring 1986), 62–71.

Zagorin, Perez. *The Court and the Country: The Beginnings of the English Revolution.* New York, 1971.

——. *Francis Bacon.* Princeton, 1998.

Zaller, Robert. *The Parliament of 1621: A Study in Constitutional Conflict.* Berkeley, CA, 1971.

Index